Managing Risk and Resilience
in the Supply Chain

wk 7.

95-122

123-152

Managing Risk and Resilience in the Supply Chain

David Kaye
FCII, FBCI, FRSA, MIRM

Business
Information

First published in the UK in 2008
by

BSI
389 Chiswick High Road
London W4 4AL

Typeset by Monolith – http://www.monolith.uk.com
Printed in Great Britain by MPG Books, Bodmin, Cornwall

British Library Cataloguing in Publication Data
A catalogue record for this book is available from the British Library

ISBN 978-0-580-60726-4

Contents

Introduction

Risk managers understand that the consequences of damage by an unexpected incident may be measured in more than simply financial terms. There are more ways, and potentially much more destructive ways, of a risk incident harming an organization and its people than the loss of assets, revenues and cash flows, or the financial cost of litigation. The most destructive of impacts from a risk incident can be to render the organization unable to deliver on current contracts and continue to meet its responsibilities to stakeholders. A risk incident can also destroy an organization's ability to manage and retain control, and remain legal and compliant.

The impact may enforce a period of time when the organization cannot remain an effective player in its 'market-place'. It does not take long for that displacement to destroy brand values and other confidences or for competitors to rush in and wreak long-term damage to the organization's customer base and other important stakeholder dependencies. Even when the organization is a monopoly or public service supplier, the way stakeholders and customers react to a real or perceived fall in service levels can turn a hiccup into a disaster.

The risk manager must therefore ensure that all of the operational dependencies and tools necessary for the organization's survival remain accessible quickly enough to be of use. These dependencies are much more than money and assets. They include, crucially, a wide range of intellectual assets, effective business controls, regulatory approvals, legality, regulatory compliance, the confidence of its various stakeholders, its brand values and its reputation. It includes of course whatever assets, tools and skills – wherever they are positioned in the value chain – an organization needs to be able to continue to deliver urgent, contracted products and services, on time and of the expected quality. Extreme financial damage from an unpleasant surprise may indeed be sufficient to divert the financial business model sufficiently to render the organization no longer viable. The non-financial impacts, however, are equally, if not more likely, to bring greater damage or even corporate death.

The cause of that corporate death may be a sudden accident or indeed be a gradually evolving disease. The end result is the same and both are of equal concern to the most senior management, its risk advisers and of course its stakeholders. A gradually developing disease, for example, a supplier's quality problems beginning to affect the brand value, is no less destructive and can be more difficult to manage than a sudden loss. It raises difficult questions of reaction timing, not least the judgement between a hope that the problems can be resolved and a decision that the plug be pulled immediately and the disaster reaction plan, with its own costs and challenges, be triggered.

Within earlier business models, the organization managed most, if not all, aspects of its supply chain from within its own factory, office, warehouse and workforce. It had more than one way of interfacing with its consumers, and maintained stocks of finished goods and raw materials on site to keep it going for days or weeks in the event of a failure or slow down in supply. It employed the workforce directly and thus had day-by-day control over each one of the activities that were part of the final delivery of its product or service. It could also instantly redirect that workforce to meet any new urgencies that had emerged suddenly through an unexpected incident or need.

The model enables inventories (with their expensive capital) management as security demand to be kept to an absolute minimum, often just enough for a few hours' productivity. It also enables the production levels and timing to match precisely with known demand or even pre-booked orders. It therefore dramatically reduces the dependency on accurate statistical forecasting of future demands that can only be based on past experiences and is always subject to variances and external risk influences. In this way, therefore, it can be used as a risk management value, not a risk management threat.

The modern business model, with its just-in-time supply chain, tight compression of margins, direct communication via the web simultaneously to millions of customers at home and abroad, is, however, much more brittle and has never been more susceptible to one single point of catastrophic failure. Furthermore, much of its workforce is now employed by a third party to deliver both intellect and activity, and only and precisely as agreed in a contract that had been negotiated at a time when the incident may not have been anticipated.

Outsourcing is no longer bolt-on for business, but an everyday way of life, at the local, regional, national and global levels. It is a way for businesses to focus on their core strengths and utilize the expertise of others to carry out the functions that the business is not as well equipped to perform. It is well named as a value chain: a name that illustrates that anything that happens in the chain of activities, from raw ingredient to final customer delivery, is designed to add value to that final product or service. If anything does not add value or enables further value to be added, the activity is simply a cost drain and will surely be removed sooner or later.

Customers can move away so much faster – perhaps with just a click of the mouse – as indeed can competitors, upscaling quickly to steal customers. No longer do aggressive competitors, with the same business models available to them, need to raise capital, design and construct factories or office blocks and then recruit staff before they can upscale and attack a weakened organization. They simply sign a few new outsourcing contracts, maybe even with the damaged organization's erstwhile suppliers.

Vodafone reports that it does not actually manufacture anything. In 2006/07, it spent more than £20 billion on purchasing products and services from third-party manufacturers which themselves source components and assembled products from other suppliers.

These models enable the organization itself to upscale and downsize much easier and more quickly than before and thus offers opportunities to spread risk and manage a crisis. A diverse supply chain can therefore be a useful risk-spreading tool as well as, when not effectively risk managed, a way of concentrating risk into single, potentially catastrophic, failure points.

The increasing importance of this wider potential for damage now lies at the very core of business models. It takes the risk manager and the most senior strategic managers of the organization way beyond the range of their financial risk management comfort zones, where, over many years, they have developed sophisticated financial risk models. It takes them into the much more amorphous and difficult arena of operational risk, particularly into areas of very low-frequency but very high-impact risks. It needs them to understand and respond to the fact that they are simultaneously shedding the ability to micro-control, shedding the very tools that they need, whilst exposing themselves to second-hand risks, impacts and frequencies much more difficult to evaluate, communicate and manage.

Throughout this book, the expression 'risk manager' does not just extend to those professionals who may carry this title. Generally speaking it will apply to those persons who have the responsibility to accept risk and/or give advice to senior managers that will place them in a position where they can make more informed, and therefore better, decisions about risk, impact, risk tolerances and risk management. This risk viewpoint can be from any director or manager who needs to address risks, and may come from a wide range of quite different risk-related titles across the organization.

Risk management has moved on from being simply the purchase of insurance products. Business continuity management is emerging from its own historical silo of technology and workstation replacement. Regulators are increasingly pulling operational risk concerns into compliance management, and even credit risk management should not fail to consider operational risks that could take away a debtor's ability to pay, nor indeed the single points of infrastructure failure that could affect separate debtors simultaneously. The realities of modern business models and their risks therefore cut right across these and the other silos of risk management that were, on the whole, previously able to deliver their values in isolation.

Risk exposures now have common roots and causes right across the whole spectrum of risk and strategic management frameworks. Of course risk management is as always as much about risk taking, and thus about opportunity, as it is about damage. Effective management of today's organizations therefore is not just about taking time out occasionally to consider risks, nor to search out ways that they can tick regulators' boxes. It is, quite simply, about good management, and, increasingly, survival. It enables the investment in activities and resources to be measured properly, and not only by the management itself but also by the organization's own stakeholders. Clearly a high return on a risky investment is just not the same value as a high return on a less risky one, a fundamental principle of business from time immemorial. The investor clearly wants a higher return if a higher risk is being carried, and above all, the investors of money, time, resources or reputation, need to be able to understand and measure the risks they are carrying.

Risk management is no less an enabler, when otherwise profitable opportunities are avoided because of an anecdotal fear of the risks that they may carry.

The outsourced value chain is clearly at the very heart of the resilience of modern day organizations, whether they are profit-making, public service or indeed charity. It brings real challenges in gaining an understanding of what those risks are, and indeed it brings a whole new range of risks and potential impact. The outsourced value chain also reduces or removes the manager's ability to micro-manage. It cannot hand over the responsibility for risk to third parties, but conversely it must delegate the management of some important risks to people whose relationship is only as defined within a precisely worded legal document.

These people must always put the interests of their own organization first as they are charged to do so by their own employers and stakeholders. The risks placed in their hands can be potentially lethal and include, not least, the day-to-day ownership and management of crucial dependencies such as intellectual assets, the ability to deliver, legality, reputation, quality, compliance, the availability of workforces and their skills and experience.

This book sees the 'supplier' as a potentially crucial and urgent dependency. It sees the receiver as a dependency too of the 'supplier', which can be damaged or destroyed by the failure of the recipient's ability to receive the goods or services as contracted, or to retain the supplier's confidence that they are going to get paid for them. It sees the organizations further up the value chain delivering the organization's products and services equally as 'suppliers' of these distribution services to the organization. The book sets out to explore the ways that supply chains can go wrong, either suddenly or gradually, and to discuss the strategic risk understanding and management of supply chains that are at the very heart of the effectiveness of modern day management.

This book therefore will explore these business models and in particular the dependency management that has become such a crucial management need, embracing not only infrastructures but also the other equally important corporate life support systems that we have listed.

Above all the book recognizes that outsourcing is so much more than sub-contracting an individual task or the manufacture of items for the production line. It is about the strategic positioning of core elements of the organization and its dependencies into the hands of third parties.

Some outsourcing contracts are huge: in 2005 there were 11 deals valued at over US$1 billion. In a FM Global survey in 2006, 'supply chain' topped the list of risks causing major disruption. A survey by AON lists 'loss of reputation' and 'business interruption' as key concerns, both of which are supply chain dependencies. An interesting case study to set the scene is The Association of Clearing Houses.

The Association has three main constituent companies: Cheque and Credit Clearing Company Limited (bulk paper clearances); CHAPS Clearing Company Limited (same day electronic clearing); and BACS Ltd (bulk electronic clearing).

CHAPS provides core services to 29 banks and financial institutions clearing on average £200 billion a day. This is just part of the picture. BACS, the automated clearing house, handles 14 million electronic debits and credits a day, averaging £9 billion. A high peak day would see 57 million transactions and 80 per cent of UK adults are paid through the BACS system. In addition, the company handles cheque and credit clearing, debit and credit card transactions and processing, and ATM and cash transactions.

Moves to real time settlement have increased single points of risk to exposure that would simultaneously damage or delay these millions of financial transactions and perhaps even the country's economy. Just one of the lessons addressed after the September 2001 debrief was that, whilst there is diversity of backup data, there may not always be diversity of control systems and indeed it is likely that some routings previously perceived to be diverse, actually converge.

The widespread and simultaneous impact of damage by such a service supplier organization could destroy its customers' own continuity plans. Whilst risk activity can be delegated, the responsibility for risk cannot. Dependence on such organizations therefore demands that the recipient organization itself ensures that those exposures are controlled and can illustrate that risk control to its customers and regulators.

In summary, the responsibilities and demands of the strategic management of an organization do not change when a part of the core activity is repositioned with a third party. Understanding and retaining control over the risks of those activities, and retaining at the same time the freedom to fully exploit their commercial value, does however bring very different problems, balancing acts and challenges.

David Kaye
FCII FBCI FRSA MIRM

Davidjkaye@aol.com

1

Risk management and modern day business models

Impact vs risk

A risk manager will routinely consider not only the risk of something happening that could divert the organization from its objectives and responsibilities, but also the likelihood and/or possible frequency of such an incident. Equally important to the risk manager is precisely how the likely impact of that incident could damage the individual sensitivities of the organization and its people. Understanding that impact entails a strategic understanding of the commercial activities of an organization, its role within its market-place, its differentiated positioning from whatever competitors it has, and its sensitivities to holding that positioning.

It also entails understanding what makes the organization tick and the wide range of hard and intellectual dependencies that are keeping that organization in its position. Each organization will have its own individual sensitivities, just two of which will be the ability to remain legal, and to continue to deliver to its own range of stakeholders all of the expectations that have emerged 'in the good times'.

As part of the risk policy statement, the risk manager will have defined graded levels of impact for 'risk-taking colleagues', i.e. all those responsible for a division or support function. This will not only include financial cost; indeed one challenge is to grade financial and non-financial risk in a consistent way. It will include the impact of the organization's inability to deliver on its promises to stakeholders and becoming weaker within its market-place. This will naturally embrace those things that are crucial to that ability to deliver as promised. As a consequence, the element of 'maximum possible time out' is one of the crucial assessment criteria and this will vary from organization to organization and by type of business.

The risk manager will base advice to the board or chief executive on these dimensions of risk and impact who will need to decide whether the organization has the strength and resources to accept such risk and/or impact, or whether one or more of the risk, likelihood or impact needs to be managed down to acceptable levels.

Once the risks are identified and evaluated, the risk management toolbox, in headline form, embraces the options of:

- accept the risk and impact;
- reduce the risk down to tolerable levels;
- reduce the potential impact down to tolerable levels;
- transfer the risk to a third party;
- prepare financial plans to enable the monetary cost to be funded;
- prepare carefully so that the strengths and resources of the organization can be used to manage an incident through and thus contain the impact within acceptable levels.

The organization may decide that the worst-case scenario is one that it could manage through without unacceptable damage. It may decide to remove itself from an activity or responsibility because the risks from that activity are unacceptable, or the cost of risk managing them is too high. It may alternatively look at the potential impact on it of a risk incident and then take steps to control that impact. An obvious example is to back up electronic data frequently and store that backup data well away from the primary risk site.

It could transfer the risk to a third party, say by contract with a supplier, customer or other counterparty, or transfer financial risk by way of insurance. (We will explore residual risks in doing so later in the book.) The organization may decide that the most effective option is to use the strengths and skills available to it by preparing and pre-resourcing business continuity plans.

We will explore these headlines in more detail as the book unfolds. At this time it is sufficient to say that these tools are not exclusive and the advice is likely to be to use a combination that best and most economically meets the risk challenge.

We will also explore and develop the point that risk management is not just an operational management issue. It is equally a strategic management issue and begins at the very first stage of 'should we outsource and, if so, for what reasons and objectives?' We will explore the concept of the cost–benefit analysis that does not only measure immediate financial cost and gain, but which also measures risk. This book's definition of 'cost and benefit' includes the more indistinct, but crucially important, costs and benefits of quality controls, reliability, reputation, management information, flexibility, and both the value and cost of risks being carried.

Hollow organizations

What are now described as modern day outsourced business models have not in any way changed the objectives or the responsibilities of any organization. Rather, it is just the way that they work towards those objectives and how they deliver their products and responsibilities that has changed. Organizations are taking the opportunities of instantaneous database mining, international communications bandwidth, macro and micro technological delivery and communication tools and also the removal of trade barriers that have opened up opportunities to cross physical and political boundaries with ease. With a global, rather than national market-place, this has enabled the true global organization that can sell and deliver worldwide and also resource its value chain from that same worldwide playing field.

One by-product has been the sheer scale of these organizations, which, through inherent growth, mergers, acquisitions and multinationalism, now stride the globe with relative ease. Another by-product of the ability to micro-mine huge databases is the ability to communicate with each client individually and also differentiate the product, customer by each individual customer.

As has been said, outsourcing is so much more than subcontracting, and certainly has moved on significantly from just a way to reduce costs.

BMW manufactures the Mini in the UK, using parts supplied from, and selling this product around, the world. The production line process is computer driven and enables the customer to decide on the individual car from a choice of 250 detail 'packages' of engines, models, trim, wheels and other accessories and parts.

The ingredients of that individual motor car – matched at the beginning of the production line to its own customer – are fed right throughout the supply chain and then, at the precise moment and sequence, into the final production line.

Another opportunity for some businesses puts information, rather than bespoke machinery or a particular workforce, at the very heart of customer delivery and indeed now as its driver. Information, especially electronically stored and accessed information, is of course much more portable than either machinery or people and, as long as it meets local laws, can travel and be accessed around the world instantly and without any constraint.

WS Atkins and other similar organizations provide call centre services to a wide variety of very different clients and types of business. The same WS Atkins call centre operative can, during the working day, provide a customer telephone response to a whole range of industries and organizations.

The telephone number that the caller has used tells the software which organization that customer expects to contact. The software and database then provide the call centre operative with the answers to most questions without the need to be experienced in the intricacies of the individual client organization's business. Electronic communications then immediately set in motion the actual services agreed: either directly with the principal or, again, by instructing another outsourced service supplier.

These and similar call centre services suppliers are of course in the front line of sales and other customer relationships and can, with the increasing bandwidth of international communications, be in any country in the world, not only the currently popular countries of Ireland, India and the Philippines.

Another value of the flexibility possible by outsourcing to a third-party specialist is the ability to turn the old business model on its head in another way. The old model means that the manufacturer or service deliverer produces the product and then sets out to find a customer for it – a supply-led value model. The flexibility and speed now possible enables the product to be sold and then created – a demand-led value model and one that transforms the stock risks and cost implications.

The ultimate outsourcing contract is to enable customers, via the internet, to gain direct access to the software and databases and to then deliver the organization's service promises to themselves. This is now common in many industries, not least the financial services industry and in airline, theatre and hotel bookings.

This means that all of these opportunities move to the heart of the organization's existence and thus become massive dependencies too. As said, this is the strategic positioning of entire sectors of the organization into third-party hands. The relationship makes them a partner and, even with effective risk management, makes each dependent on the other for the survival of that partnership and the ability of these new strategic business shapes to survive.

'There are many innovations in the new Boeing 787 but perhaps one of the most innovative aspects could be the way in which it is being built. For previous models, Boeing played the traditional role of main manufacturer, contracting with an army of suppliers for individual parts and systems, and then laboriously assembling them into the finished product. This time around, major suppliers will design and build entire sections of the plane, shipping them to Boeing for final assembly and testing at Everett, WA. Various components might travel around the world, passing through multiple contractors, before ending up at their final destination. In this way, the majority of each aircraft will actually be built by Boeing's global partners.

The plan will lessen the need for Boeing's own resources while speeding up construction. Each aircraft will be assembled over a three-day period. To make that possible, Boeing had to achieve a whole new level of collaboration with key suppliers around the world.

"Instead of multi-tiered suppliers, we truly have partners," says Tim Opitz, Director of production and support systems for Boeing Commercial Aeroplanes. In all, the company is relying on 135 locations around the world for manufacturing and fabrication. With responsibilities spread so thinly, the slightest delay at any point in the supply chain could paralyse production.'

(Robert Bowman, *Global Logistics & Supply Chain Strategies*, 1 March 2007)

Many a 21st century organization can now therefore be described as a 'hollow company': a corporate life form that consists only of its entrepreneurialism, stakeholders, a small control team, legality, brands and other intellectual assets. The entire supply chain and delivery chain is then supplied by third parties under contract.

There is a risk implication also that the modern, outsourced business model is much leaner and with much less margin for error. Its ability to absorb surprises is much reduced; the potentially catastrophic risks are more focused into one single failure point, and thus the understanding of its risks and managing them has never been more critical.

All this has dramatically shifted the dependencies and indeed the weak points of modern day organizations, but equally it has raised expectations way beyond previously recognizable levels. Customers now expect simultaneous access to their personal information, immediate answers to their questions and instantaneous delivery of the product or service required.

The modern data risk manager has these very few but each potentially catastrophic dependencies as the focus of risk understanding and risk management work. In these models, there are: new relationships, new dependencies and above all new expectations to manage.

As stated at the beginning of this book, an organization's objectives and responsibilities in concept remain just the same but there is little common ground between the playing fields of the earlier generation of risk managers and those of today.

The stakeholder

No discussion on organizational risk is complete without looking at the organization's responsibilities through the eyes of the various stakeholders. It is indeed the stakeholders of the organization who are the 'customers' of the risk management processes as it sets out to deliver on its promises and not expose the stakeholders' interest unduly to unexpected loss.

Even if we can now summarize an organization more simplistically, the list of stakeholders remains almost unaffected. Also, the underlying responsibilities of the organization to those stakeholders remain just the same.

We can usefully split the stakeholders into two categories: those who are stakeholders throughout the good times and those who become stakeholders when they react to an organization in distress. Some stakeholders cross this boundary of course but it is useful to keep this split in mind, even if only to ensure that we do not forget the latter category in our risk and response management.

We will also need to remember that individual stakeholder expectations and demands can be in conflict with each other, turning some decision making into a challenging balancing act. This is especially so whilst an organization is trying to manage a fast-changing, potentially disastrous incident with reduced people, resources and communications, and in the media spotlight.

Types of stakeholder

Stakeholders can be divided into two main categories: those who are continuing stakeholders during the 'good times', and those who become stakeholders by their reaction to an incident (the 'bad times') and, in so doing, can also be categorized by their ability to influence the outcomes of that incident (see Table 1.1).

Table 1.1 Stakeholder categories

In good times	*In bad times*
Employees	The natural environment
Customers	The legal environment
Distribution channels and intermediaries	Regulators
Suppliers	The media
The stock market	The market environment
Other financiers	Potential customers
Partners	Competitors
Trade and trading standards	Potential competitors
	Third parties

'Good times' stakeholders

Employees

Most employees need a job to sustain personal and family life and also self-esteem. The organization's responsibility to employees is of course to continue to provide them with gainful employment.

The relationship however goes beyond this. To gain the best out of an employee workforce, the employer needs to ensure that the workplace is as safe as is reasonably practical. This is also essential to maintain the workforce's morale, trust and pride in the organization for whom it is working.

Those employees who have invested their careers, lifestyles, time and self-esteem in the particular employer have unarguably become stakeholders, and will remain as long as they still have trust and pride in the organization. Their response to an incident can become second category 'bad time' stakeholders too. If the employer cannot maintain their trust as they struggle to handle a risk incident, then employees will worsen the situation significantly by walking away. It is always the best employees who will move on the quickest, by the fact that they are the ones with the greatest choices, and certainly headhunters will target an organization in distress and only be interested in the better employees.

This makes communication and employee relationships very important priorities in business recovery management, not least when the employer, facing unusual and stressful circumstances, needs employees to work beyond the employment contract to keep the organization alive.

Outsourced employees will always of course remain subject to their own employer's directions and priorities. Any workforce flexibility can only be expected within the framework that was set in the detail of the contracts drawn up in the 'good times' with their own employer, the outsourcing company. One of the first risks and impacts therefore of an outsourcing model is the loss of the ability to micro-manage the 'workforce' at all times. This is a subject for a separate section later in the book.

Customers

Customers will remain only whilst the organization can continue to deliver the contracted services or products on time and to the expected quality. An unexpected and unmanaged risk incident can damage this ability. There is, though, more than that. Customers will remain as long as *the expectation* is that they can continue to receive the expected services or products on time and to the expected quality. Customers therefore can be lost long before there is an actual reduction in service levels and once again this makes customer confidence a power to be actively managed in the 'bad times'.

If a customer loses confidence, perhaps by hearing of a risk incident in the organization, the customer (equally whether an end consumer or another business in a value chain) has almost always the choice of moving away to a competitor. Often the debate – once confidence is lost – is only around just how quickly, legally and operationally that change can be made. With modern distribution channels such as e-commerce, customers can move away much quicker than before. Indeed, entire distribution channels can move away in seconds by the touch of a keyboard mouse.

In 2007, Northern Rock found itself in a position where it needed to go to the Bank of England for what are sometimes known as 'emergency funds'. This was caused by inter bank loans and financing drying up quite suddenly due to money market concerns about where precisely the final damage emerging from sub-prime loans was located. This request for support became known and depositors became concerned about the safety of their own deposits with Northern Rock. This concern heightened dramatically when the website capacity became overpowered by unplanned for levels of simultaneous enquiry. Customers could not gain routine access to their accounts and information and therefore became even more concerned.

They then did the only thing still available to them and that was to go to a Northern Rock branch to withdraw their money – a classic 'run on the bank'. Branches could not cope with the levels of simultaneous demand and long queues formed. These long queues caught the attention of the media – pictures and film were broadcast widely raising the temperature of these and other depositors even more.

This increased Northern Rock's existing liquidity problems dramatically with massive additional reputational risks and cash flow damage.

Even public service organizations and monopolies need to retain customer confidence as part of risk management work. In the event of a failure in trust, or a risk incident that removes the ability to gain access by normal channels, customers will feel the need to search for reassurances or take steps to manage that feared impact by themselves. That search may be wholesale, exceeding normal workflow expectations and affecting parts of the organization that are not resourced to cope with such a large flow of enquiries.

This can cause an impossible strain on resources, bringing an already struggling organization to the point of total collapse.

Special cases

Some business models depend entirely on a relationship between supplier and customer remaining orderly and confident. A bank and an insurer need above all to be trusted and they assume responsibilities by contracts that involve billions of pounds. To enable them to gain value out of those premium and investment deposits, they place them in investments that are longer in term than the contracts with their own customers. This assumes that the demand for the return of these funds follows predicted patterns. A run on a bank, as in the Northern Rock example, due to loss of confidence could mean that they need to realize assets quickly from a long-term investment portfolio. Very large volumes of shares placed together onto a stock market can, in themselves, cause a change in the demand and supply balance and cause the price of those shares to fall. Again, existing problems are greatly exacerbated.

There may be special requirements in some contracts that are a core need. Contracts to supply the military or police, for example, will have special demands on information security. Even a small risk incident, if it destroys such special needs, can bring the whole contract to a close.

The impact, urgencies and sensitivities when supplying another organization within a value chain are of course much higher than those of individual customers. A failure to deliver can have an immediate impact on the others' own time-critical processes. Consequentially, a failure to deliver a tiny, and perhaps thought to be inconsequential, ingredient, can have massive impact further up the supply line.

It is likely that the receiving organization has contingency plans in place in case of such failure. It is likely to have other contingency suppliers ready to step in immediately, thus instantly taking the damaged supplier organization out of that chain, probably permanently. This could turn a temporary failure into a total disaster for the supplying organization. This is especially damaging where the supplier contract is such a significant part of the organization's revenue that its loss destroys its own economic viability. One example could be where the produce a farmer supplies to a supermarket is such a large proportion of the supplier's business that, in the event that the one contract is lost, the business cannot then meet its other fixed charges and costs.

We will frequently stress that the risks around supplier/customer relationship dependencies are two-way. There is a mutual dependency and, either way, that dependency can be organization critical.

In 2007, Gloucestershire in the UK took its turn to have devastating floods affecting tens of thousands of homes, infrastructure services and businesses. Farmers' produce was widely ruined but they found themselves in fixed-price contracts with supermarkets with no relevant escape clause.

Even though a normal demand/supply equation would enable prices to rise (and thus enable farmers to cover costs and survive on less output), the contracts meant that they could only charge the prices that had already been contracted into the relationship prior to the floods).

Just like employee relationship management, confidence in the ability to supply into the future is a crucial ingredient of just-in-time logistics management. The receiving organization can – and will – move away quickly and totally should that confidence alone be damaged by a risk-based incident. Any financial or other penalties, and the brand-damaging publicity associated with them, that are built into the wording of a contract, can be devastating to an organization that is already reeling from an unexpected operational incident; yet the risk incident may only have damaged confidences.

Distributors

The responsibilities to distributors are indistinguishable from those to individual customers, except by the volumes involved and perhaps by contract wording that will set in law the ownerships and responsibilities at each step of that relationship.

This is no less so when the recipient of the goods or services 'white labels' them by building them into its own brand name and marketing.

Where the customer 'white labels' the product, i.e. sells it on under its own brand name and packaging, there may be a different reputational issue to be managed than when the product retains the supplier's own name and packaging.

A drug store chain such as Superdrug or a supermarket such as Tesco may choose to retail something under its own brand name – this could be anything from shampoo to breakfast cereal. This is a commercial balancing act between wholesale/retail critical mass, packaging costs and any necessary investment in awareness of the lesser known of the two brand names.

Where the 'customer' chooses to 'white label' the product with its own name then it carries additionally the brand and reputation risks of failure, quality problems and even, if necessary, product recall.

Suppliers

The challenges with suppliers, the primary subject of this book, are two fold. The business models discussed mean that organizations, however large, find themselves totally dependent on the timely delivery of another organization's ingredient, service or intellectual asset. Sometimes 'timely' is measured in hours rather than days, or even, in some e-commerce models, simultaneous with the need.

Loss of life and injury apart, many of the greatest problems facing large organizations after the 11 September 2001 terrorist attack was that, whilst they themselves had a global reach and alternatives, they found that they depended on small but critical suppliers who, without the alternative resources of a multinational, were destroyed.

One example was a small software house in the same building that had been contracted to design, deliver and maintain software that was integral to the large organization's own delivery chain. The failure of that software house in the terrorist attack meant that the large organization did not have the software codes that would enable other technicians to continue to maintain the software.

The second supplier-based challenge could be that the supplier, hearing that the customer is weakened by a risk incident, may need reassurances about its continuing ability to pay. It may be difficult to give reassurances that are satisfactory to that supplier. There may then be a demand to pay before the service is received, which creates new cash flow challenges that can in themselves be difficult to satisfy. The perceived higher credit risk of the now damaged customer could create a demand for more expensive or shorter credit terms that, in themselves, could undermine the organization's financial models and pricing.

The stock market

It can be said that the stock market operates to its own valuation rules, often with little bearing on the underlying value of the organization. Whilst it has indeed a range of influences such as political risk, the competition for capital, and takeover activity, this would be a dangerous simplification.

Public investors and their advisers, stock analysts and credit agencies look not so much at whether the company is making profits, but whether it is about to declare values and dividends in keeping with current expectations. The market does not like surprises at all and will downgrade a share if there are reasons to be concerned that it may be unable to meet its earlier promises. 'Profit warning' statements to the market that downgrade current expectations are very likely to cause a fall in stock value, whether that is as a result of a trading downturn or equally following a risk incident that has removed the company's ability to deliver as promised at the year end.

There are statutory and market regulations that demand that quoted companies keep the market advised of risks being carried and we will discuss these later in the book. Furthermore, a significant reduction in stock value will reduce the relationship between that value and the amount of current borrowing, i.e. the company's 'gearing'. The higher the gearing, the greater the perception of less strength, thus the company's cost of current and further capital borrowing may increase. Organizations equally need positive cash flows as well as capital and revenues. This may turn a short-term crisis into a long-term cost of finance problem that may destroy the financial models on which the company is founded.

Other financiers

Whilst possibly less regulated, the principles above apply equally to other financiers of an organization. It could be a government that is financing a project or non-governmental organization, a charity raising funds from donations or indeed a subsidiary looking to its parent to finance development.

Private financiers and partners too will be looking for confirmation that the organization is setting out to understand its risks, communicating them and managing them effectively. They may stop future funding or even be able, under the contracted relationship, to demand the return of funds already supplied.

Partners

'Partners' may come in all shapes and sizes, from individuals to large organizations. The relationship may be informal, defined by contract or be a significant shareholding and working relationship in a quoted or other legal entity.

Partners invest more than time and money. They invest their reputation – formal brand values and other confidences – and also the opportunity cost of choosing this particular activity over others. They are therefore important stakeholders, relying on each partner to manage the risks that could destroy the other.

The partnership agreement may well define legal liabilities and ownerships between partners but the rights in law defined by these agreements are of value only when the organization or person being sued has the means to meet any agreed liability for their failure. If they are 'of straw' (or become 'of straw' because of the incident) the legal rights are worthless as they are uncollectable. They are most certainly no substitute for effective, two-way, risk and impact management.

Trade standards

A risk creating a damaging incident may have the effect of removing quality control and bringing the organization to the attention of its fellow market players and, more formally, trading standards regulators. The brand value is damaged, as is the wider confidence of current and prospective customers and other stakeholders.

Stakeholders emerging in 'bad times'

Whilst some stakeholders can fit in both the categories described on page 6, the following stakeholders are usefully considered primarily for their ability, indeed propensity, to cause further damage just as the organization is already struggling to respond effectively to an unpleasant surprise.

The natural environment

Organizations are increasingly facing expectations that they respect the natural environment and the safety of the environment within which they operate. This not only means a demand that they do not actually harm that environment, but also, increasingly, they are expected to proactively protect or improve the environment around them.

They need to respect their neighbours' access and ability to operate and thus not allow a risk incident to damage them too. They may find that their ability to respond to a damaging incident is constrained by these responsibilities.

They may even find that the pubic services are not able to assist as fully as expected. A fire and rescue service may, for example, not be able to pour water and chemicals on a fire if the run off from the building's contents will contaminate the natural watercourses nearby. The fire and rescue service and the organization's own recovery teams may be held back from the site by police controllers who consider the site as yet unsafe for human entry, or indeed as a scene of crime.

Therefore, we have two challenges for the risk manager. One is to ensure that the organization will protect, i.e. risk manage, the ability to meet these responsibilities. The second is to understand the constraints that may dramatically increase the maximum probable loss of an incident.

Customers (again)

An occurrence of damage or potential damage to customers is not just about keeping them as customers thereafter. There may be indemnities to pay for damage caused and also, perhaps even more difficult, huge numbers of products may have to be recalled, should they be considered unsafe or not of 'merchantable quality'.

The process of recalling products is a hugely difficult one, especially as it is always conducted in the eye of the public and the media. It is a greater challenge when the cause of the lack of safety lies deep in a supply chain and the distributions lie deep within a delivery chain. Those difficulties are operational, intellectual, legal and often technological, and are discussed later in this book.

The legal environment

It is an obvious point that the organization must always remain legal within each legal jurisdiction within which it operates. This embraces civil law, criminal law and the host of regulatory requirements that are demanded around its activities, people and products.

The risk manager needs therefore to be aware of these requirements and when developing the risk management envelope around the organization ensure that these needs are being met and will continue to be met, whatever happens.

Regulators not only expect organizations to be compliant but expect them to be able to demonstrate that they have been compliant and continue to be compliant. If the compliance audit trail therefore is not secured against any risk incident, that loss could be the very first cause of organizational death.

The power of a regulator is not just to impose financial penalties. The publicity can destroy brands and confidences, and the regulator can demand compensation be paid to third parties, alter credit ratings and, above all, instruct a cessation of trading.

The regulator may bring its own unique demands and requirements. During the UK financial services scandal of the 1990s when organizations were accused of misselling pension contracts, the Financial Services Authority demanded that the companies write to each of their pension fund customers. They were required, in effect, to ask customers to let them know whether they felt that they had products missold to them. They were then required to respond to each reply individually.

Professional indemnity insurers' policy wording precluded the insured financial services companies from 'soliciting claims'. Caught between them both, many pension fund providers had to take in a huge administration burden and reimburse customers without the benefit of professional indemnity insurance recoveries.

The media

We have already mentioned the importance of brand and reputation – one of the small number, but crucially important, headline dependencies of a modern organization.

The media is, of course, a wholesale purveyor of brand values and indeed, conversely, destroyers of brands and confidence.

An attack by the media, whether justifiable or not, can be destructive to the entire organization and its positioning. The attack may not be directed specifically at the risk manager's organization but may be an attack on the work environment within which the organization operates or, relevant to this book, on one of the suppliers with whom the organization is identified.

Again, a strategic risk issue is to operate the business ethically and well so that it reduces the risk of attack. The media risk can be managed too by ensuring that media management resources and skills are ready in place for use during an attack or as a risk incident unfolds.

Doing nothing may not be an option. Any failure to communicate too often creates gaps that are soon filled with rumour, whispers, vested interests or just simply malice.

Potential customers

We are in this chapter considering the potential impact of stakeholders which become so by their reaction to a risk incident. We have already mentioned brand and confidence with regards to the media, above, and also with regard to existing customers and other stakeholders.

The risk management of an incident will also affect the confidence of the wider public and especially those who may become future customers. Reputational damage that destroys the sales team's ability to produce new orders going forward can not only be damaging but can also be destructive.

Conversely, it is possible, by effective risk management and communications, to use a damage situation to good benefit by illustrating clearly how seriously the management takes its responsibilities, even during the diversion of unexpected damage.

Competitors

Competitors read newspapers too and a weakened competitor may be seen simply as a business opportunity. They can, using the macro- and micro-communication tools that are now available, set out to target customers with offers and marketing. The damaged organization may wish to secure as best it can its market position by fighting back with discounts and offers of its own. The cost of those offers are no less a cost of the incident itself.

With the opportunities of outsourcing and offshoring, these competitors do not need to raise capital, obtain planning permission, go out to tender and then build factories before they begin to compete. They do not even need to recruit and train a workforce. They simply need to set up a new range of outsourcing contracts, perhaps even with the erstwhile suppliers to the damaged competitor.

These are real impact assessment factors for risk managers and their boards and management to consider. Public service organizations and charities also have competitors for the purses that supply them. A public service organization losing the trust of its masters or stakeholders for any reason may cause a shift in responsibility to another department or even an approach by a private finance initiative.

> 'Directors of Heart of England Tourist Board have decided not to continue trading beyond the end of this financial year.
>
> Tourist Board chief executive, David Moyser, said, "Advantage West Midlands, the regional development agency, had decided not to renew its contract with Heart of England to deliver a range of regional tourism marketing and support activities"'.
>
> (http://www.thisisgloucestershire.co.uk, June 2007)

Potential competitors

The removal or weakening of one player in the market-place may reduce competition to the point that a third party sees the new demand/supply imbalance as a worthwhile opportunity emerging for it in that particular market-place.

The opportunities now to enter a new market without huge initial investment are the same ones, and just as quick and easy as an existing competitor setting out to upsize.

Third parties

An organization and its people remain subject to the civil law of their playing fields and if they harm other people with their activities or products then they must expect those people to litigate against them.

The level of damages awarded may far exceed the free assets of the organization, especially in some jurisdictions, such as the USA and Canada, where the awards may include huge punitive damages as well as indemnities. These and other jurisdictions may demand that one defendant is jointly and severally liable for the whole claim, even if it only contributed to the cause of the loss.

Most, but by no means all, such liabilities are insurable and arranging insurance and indemnity levels across a diverse organization and against incidents that can only be guessed at is one of risk management's minefields. We will explore this in more detail in a later chapter.

Bringing stakeholders and risks together

We have now begun to look at some of the potential ways that a risk incident can damage an organization and its wide array of different stakeholders. We can now begin to build a matrix of these responsibilities against the operational dependencies that, if lost or damaged, can cause unacceptable damage to them.

Before we do so, there is value here in a reminder that all activity is risky to a greater or lesser extent. All commercial activity is a fine balancing act between risk and reward and the risk manager's responsibility is not to remove all risk. Rather, it is to ensure that boards and managers make better-informed, and thus better-quality, decisions around this balancing act of risk and reward. We will proceed therefore to deal with risks where the full and wide-ranging consequences have been evaluated and found unacceptable.

We also need to make another assumption, and that is that the risk levels thought acceptable to the management have been communicated clearly to the stakeholders and have been accepted by them too.

> The board of a multinational insurance company accepted that its balance sheet, cash flow and revenue strengths allowed a risk tolerance level of £1 million per incident. The board agreed to accept that potential loss for its net account and reduced its insurance covers accordingly, saving a substantial amount of insurance premiums.
>
> Its subsidiary in South Africa had a minority local shareholder and operational partner owning 40 per cent of the shares in that subsidiary. That decision in effect imposed on that shareholder a potential unprotected loss of £400,000, a level well beyond that shareholder's tolerance levels.
>
> Clearly, there is a massive responsibility to advise that shareholder and perhaps join in arranging internal insurance or other protections.

Stakeholders: a summary

The management of an organization has many different stakeholders to which it has quite different and sometimes conflicting responsibilities. Furthermore, suppliers' own reactions to risk can in themselves create or add to potentially disastrous scenarios that need to be anticipated, protected against and perhaps even managed through as they happen.

The supply chain participants, as stakeholders in the organization too, fit into the organization's risk profiles both as a dependency and a responsibility. The damage that can emerge from supply chain participants is potentially catastrophic and as soon as any one of them in the (sometimes long) chain fails, the organization next in line is affected. A supplier that perceives weaknesses in its customer, the next receiver organization in the line, may withhold supply. That change leads to far-reaching damage to many relationships. A different cause of loss, perhaps, but, sadly, the same damage to the final customer delivery.

This is not the most comfortable of messages when the decision to outsource has removed core elements of resources, information, customer relationships, workforce control, legality, brand and other dependencies out to that third-party organization. Getting them back again has many operational, legal and practical problems to overcome that can remove the organization from its fast-moving market-place.

Back to basics

The risk manager can be involved at all levels of risk within the organization. The total monetary cost of low-level, high-frequency losses within one accounting period can be risk managed out by effective investment in risk measures. An example would be the shoplifting risk across a chain of supermarkets. Risk measure investment could see increased security around warehouses, redesign of the shop floor, increased CCTV and other security, increased vigilance at staff exits and more security floor walkers around the stores and at exits. Additional measures include supporting the local police and using radio/telephone warning systems between retailers when known shoplifters are recognized.

These risk management activities have relatively routine cost–benefit balancing acts to evaluate and implement. The subject here, however, is the resilience of the supply chain, so we will go on mainly to discuss the more difficult risk challenges of managing potential loss or damage that can threaten the very viability of the business model, and indeed the very survival of the organization. The just-in-time, business-critical supply chain dependencies bring these kinds of challenge. These exposures are critical to the crucial dependencies that have already been defined as:

- enabling continuing entrepreneurialism;
- a wide range of stakeholders;
- the small control team;
- legality and compliance;
- brands and wider confidence;
- other intellectual assets; and
- the (mostly outsourced) supply chain and delivery chain.

This book will stay with supply chain risks but must, to be meaningful, embrace these other exposures insofar as the supply chain brings risks to these dependencies.

2

Risk management, supply chain management and bringing the two together as supply chain risk management

Risk management and its role

Before we enter into detail on the subject of risk management of any organization, not least a heavily outsourced one, it is crucial to state an underlying principle which will remain relevant throughout the whole of this book.

Risk management is never at its best when it is bolted on as a separate function to the overall management of the organization.

To be fully successful, it is crucial that the risk tools, processes, decision making and reporting are just one part of the wide-field cultures, objectives, sensitivities, existing control processes and, not least, the strategies of both the organization and its range of stakeholders.

This applies equally to operational management needs and to the strategic management insofar as they are separate and insofar as they themselves come together to form one management value.

There would be gain therefore in discussing these wider culture and management issues before we delve further into how risk management and continuity management can add important further value. We will then take these wider management issues through the discipline of risk management into the dependency management of the value chain.

> The objective of this or any section of the book is not, however, to encourage or recommend one management style or culture, but simply to understand that each organization will have its own, forming the backdrop for all risk work.

The many dimensions of management

The culture of the organization

The culture of an organization, not least its propensity for risk taking, reflects not only the personalities at the top of the organization but also the responsibilities that are defined by the organization's various stakeholder expectations. These stakeholders include of course both existing, and potential, customers and the fact that each individual wider market-place will have its own atmospheres and expectations. Bolted onto this blend will be further external drivers such as industry and product demands, the legal, regulatory and economic environments and the cultures and expectations of the regions and countries within which the organization is trading.

An oil company will invest billions of pounds or dollars in researching potential new oilfields, knowing that a percentage of those investments will produce no commercially viable oil. A financial services company such as a bank or insurance company, living on its reputation for permanence, will clearly need not only to be permanent, but also to be able to illustrate that permanence within its brands and within its visible risk and continuity strategies.

> Sir Stelios Haji-Ioannou, in a presentation to the Institute of Risk Management, explained his comfort with putting very large sums at risk when investing his own money into a new 'easy' venture.
>
> He went on to explain that, once the business is off the ground and starts taking on responsibilities to others, he knows that his own personal risk tolerance level is far too high for these new stakeholders. It is therefore his firm strategy then to pass the company's day-to-day management fully to professional managers.

Organizations are of course made up of human beings, all of whom will have their own personal attitude to risk; and this applies at all levels of seniority in the organization. In some cases, their attitude to their own safety and career risk may not coincide with the risk approaches of their employers and colleagues. This is in itself a risk to be managed with control and governance mechanisms.

> 'The art of management consists of issuing orders based on inaccurate, incomplete and archaic data, to meet a challenge which is dimly understood and which frequently is misinterpreted; to accomplish a purpose about which many of the personnel are not enthusiastic.'
>
> (Anon)

Perhaps the view of management penned above is a little overly cynical but there are important issues raised about accuracy, completeness and currency of information on which decisions are made. He raises the possibly of miscommunication and mismatching of agendas. These are important issues and are worthy of thought and respect when making assumptions about orders that are passed down through a chain of managers.

Managers are notorious for resisting the thought that things could possibly go wrong under their expert and stunning leadership, and equally for struggling to drag their concentration away from things that are already happening to those things that only may happen at some undefined time in the future.

An employee or director comfortable with putting the employer at long-term risk to satisfy personal short-term career development is a great danger, and control processes and remuneration policies are designed as best as possible to keep the two 'cultures' in line. An employer or director may have other agendas, maybe personal gain, career planning or a political agenda, that may be clouding otherwise clear risk issues.

If a project is not going well, the owner of the original idea may not be the best person to decide the next steps forward. Personal risk and corporate risk may have become too close to ensure a detached view of the latter.

> A director of a motor vehicle insurance company convinced the board that the best way forward in managing vehicle damage claims would be to invest millions of pounds to build and run its own chain of subsidiary motor vehicle workshops.
>
> The workshops found that as manufacturers of the vehicles retained control over pricing of replacement parts, and insurers were reluctant to accept other parts, savings over using vehicle main dealers for repair work were not as much as had been promised.

> The discussion then focused on whether or not many more workshops should be built to create a stronger power base in negotiating the purchase of parts, or in fact to simply accept that the idea had not worked as planned. There is no 'right' answer to offer within this book and the point being made is simply that this new decision needs a wider viewpoint than that of the original director who has perhaps vested interests in expanding but thus raising the risk profile even further.

The risk tolerances of the organization

Impact tolerance

Once we have reasonable assurances that the corporate and individual risk tolerances have come together we can begin to consider what tolerance there is to accepting risk.

An underlying principle of this book worth repeating here is that risk is integral to all activity and that risk managers cannot, indeed should not, set out to remove all risk. It is destructive to try to do so and stifles initiative – and furthermore is not actually achievable. Too often, even doing nothing is not a valid risk option as risk and reward are the two sides of the same coin.

Even in 'health and safety', considered to be the most risk averse of arenas, there is an increasingly balanced approach to risk. Judith Hackitt, chair of the UK Health and Safety Commission (HSC), has spoken out against the growing risk aversion in UK society. In an HSC press release in November 2007, Ms Hackitt stated that:

'Sensible risk management IS NOT about:

- Creating a totally risk free society;
- Generating useless paperwork mountains;
- Scaring people by exaggerating or publicising trivial risks;
- Stopping important recreational and learning activities for individuals where the risks are managed; and
- Reducing protection of people from risks that cause real harm and suffering.

Sensible risk management IS about:

- Ensuring that workers and the public are properly protected;
- Providing overall benefit to society by balancing benefits and risks, with a focus on reducing real risks – both those which arise more often and those with serious consequences;
- Ensuring that those who create risks manage them responsibly and understand that failure to manage real risks responsibly is likely to lead to robust action; and
- Enabling individuals to understand that as well as the right to protection, they also have to exercise responsibility.'

One tolerance level may be a financial one; in other words, the organization could ride the strengths of its balance sheet, its cash flows and revenues to soak up quite substantial amounts of financial loss before the effect on objectives and responsibilities is noticeable. That financial loss tolerance level is not just as a result of one incident. There may be a number of identical incidents and related losses within the same accountancy period.

There are many more ways, however, that a risk incident can damage an organization and it is the impact side of the risk and impact matrix that decides 'risk tolerance', more than the cause of the loss or damage.

Similar fires in two different factories can bring widely different levels of damage to an organization. The impact will be decided, not so much by the cost of the buildings and contents, but by the activities that had been undertaken in that factory and the relative importance and urgency of those functions in the value chain. For example, the damage in the case of a central computer suite, an urgent, critical supply chain dependency, may be felt by the organization way beyond the walls of the building itself.

If there are alternative sources of supply of the ingredients delivered by that one factory, a multimillion asset fire may not damage 'the operations' at all. This is especially true if the burned asset losses are insured and thus will leave the risk manager only concerned about how quickly the products or services can be obtained to complete once again the value chain.

Perhaps, therefore, the more common expression 'risk tolerance' should be more suitably called 'impact tolerance'.

The business resilience promise

What exactly is the business resilience promise? The expression 'business continuity management' is commonly used but it has many different definitions coined by its various specialists. The words, however, are quite free-standing and self-explanatory in the English language. They state simply and obviously that the business will continue. The implication, and therefore the promise made by the very existence of a risk manager or business continuity manager, is that whatever happens the 'organization' will survive.

The reality of course is that that is a desperately wild promise to make, not least because we are dealing with so many internal and external unknowns. Risk managers' own stakeholders, that is, their own managers and boards, and of course these stakeholders' own wider range of stakeholders, could not care less about the detail. The intricacies of lots of different continuity and crisis response plans, call out technology, computer plans, lead time recoveries, business impact analyses and risk assessments are lost on them. They are 'bottom line' people – they simply want to know that the person branded with the name of 'business recovery manager' or 'risk manager' has removed the exposure in order that the organization cannot possibly be damaged by events to the point that it no longer exists. An impossible task, certainly.

There is, therefore, in addition to the day job of managing risks, an important communication task to manage expectations and to ensure that they remain realistic ones. Indeed, many would say that this is the very heart of the day job.

That communication task is two directional. One direction is that the board and its wider stakeholders need to be told clearly and realistically what the current wide-risk resilience picture is. The other communication challenge is in the opposite direction. Risk managers do not carry the ultimate responsibility for the risks carried around the organization. They do, though, have the important responsibility to offer advice to the board, offer understandings on risk and consequences, and thus place the board in a position where it can make better-informed, and thus better-quality, decisions about risk tolerances and risk management.

To properly support this important role, the whole organization itself must take the primary ownership of risks and go on to offer to the risk manager the time and energy to contribute information fully and openly to the resilience challenge.

This takes us neatly back to the difficult additional challenge where crucial parts of the business have become owned and managed by third-party organizations whose risk strategies could easily be inwards looking and inwardly focused, and without the same levels of risk tolerances as the customer organization.

Risk management and its tools

The risk manager's toolboxes vary organization by organization, objective by objective, but there are some principles that are common to all. One way to summarize this is in Figure 2.1.

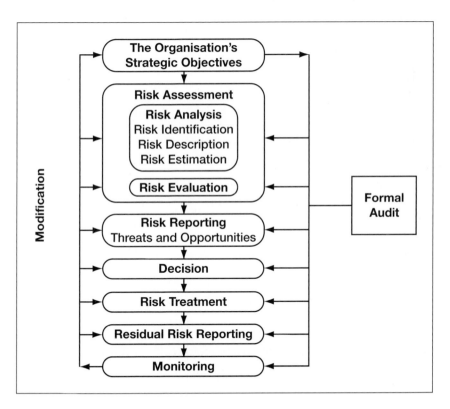

(Source: *A Risk Management Standard*, published by IRM, ALARM, AIRMIC: 2002)

Figure 2.1 The risk management process

Stage 1: the organization's strategic objectives

We have stated that no commercially realistic and effective risk management can be trusted without the project first of all setting out to understand the objectives and responsibilities of the organization and focusing on those objectives and responsibilities. It is against the sensitivities to those objectives, and thus the responsibilities, that any assessment of risk or impact can be measured.

The overall objectives and deliverables of risk management therefore need to begin with a consistent, clear and organization-wide understanding of those corporate objectives and responsibilities. The risk management objectives themselves may then be documented in a widely publicized mission statement. An example of such a mission statement can be seen below.

Risk mission statement

The strategy is to identify and control factors that are perceived as threatening the health and safety, the security and the stability of the organization and its ability to deliver on its promises. The responsibility lies with each operating manager to manage risks to his or her area of operations. This will embrace risks to his or her operations directly and also where operations depend on others to supply crucial services to themselves.

The organization will, as a matter of ongoing good management, set out to understand those exposures and quantify them. These exposures will then be measured against levels of each risk that are deemed formally to be acceptable. Those that are thereby found to be unacceptable will be managed to the point that, wherever realistically possible, the exposure will be reduced down to within this agreed and acceptable level.

Where significant risks remain, the company will put in place and exercise a recovery plan designed to meet urgent responsibilities and accelerate recovery back to normal working and, by doing so, minimize the impact on Company operations and control.

The Group Risk Manager will fulfil an advisory role to these Managers and report quarterly on risk exposures to the Board. Operational managers have the responsibility to ensure that the Risk Manager is kept aware of risk and changes in risk.

The statement may go on into detail about methods, definitions, detailed expectations and the actual levels of risk acceptance. More often this is left for a separate risk manual type document or booklet.

Stage 2: risk assessment

With that clear focus on objectives, risks and potential impacts can be evaluated and captured within a risk register. That register will then set the priorities, ask for recommendations, and set the decisions that are needed. It is also an audit trail against which future changes and risk profiles can be measured.

A typical risk assessment format may look something like the one shown in Table 2.1.

Table 2.1 Risk/impact analysis format

Risk Reference Number: _____   Date _____

Scenario

Caused by:	Nature of impact and parties affected	Severity rating	Probability rating	Opportunity to manage severity or likelihood	Other issues raised and actions needed	Overall priority

To get to this stage, however, needs the risk manager to be able to make assumptions about the severity of an incident as far as it will affect the organization itself, namely its objectives, responsibilities, stakeholders and people. That assumption can only be based on consistency of information from right across the organization. This needs the whole organization to feed back into the risk department an understanding and feel for risk, frequency and impact, but stated within the same defined and thus pre-set criteria.

The board will agree and define beforehand a set of impact definitions. They may, for example, be defined as negligible, marginal, critical or catastrophic. Those definitions will then be used throughout as the background to any agreement to accept, or not, individual risks and potential impacts. The definitions will enable the risks to be prioritized and will also help to quantify the level of risk management resources to be applied at each level.

Remembering that potentially catastrophic impact is much more likely to be loss or damage other than the loss of money and assets, a typical catastrophic risk definition may be as follows.

- Inability to deliver contracted services for x hours/minutes/days.
- Loss of regulatory approval.
- Loss of confidence in the brand name by the general public/media attack.
- Loss of confidence in the brand name by shareholders.
- Loss of confidence within the client base.
- Loss of confidence within the workforce.
- Financial losses within one accountancy period measured in a) capital, b) revenue, and c) working cash flows.
- Credit rating fall of one full level.
- Unacceptable risk of life or injury.
- Loss of business or financial control.

At the other end of the scale would be the decision that a certain level of risk and impact would be acceptable. This would fall within the definitions of negligible or even marginal risk. This would be defined at a level of impact that would not divert the organization from its stated objectives, or that it would have the strengths to work its way through the incident without such a diversion.

The definition of impact levels within a subsidiary or to a business unit may need to be driven by the group strategy in supporting a subsidiary under stress, and whether any minority shareholder is comfortable with its own share of retained loss. Equally, an impact measure will be around whether that subsidiary is itself in a supply chain that supplies ingredients critical to the ability of the parent group to deliver its products or services.

The concept of risk tolerance has regulator approval and, for example, the UK Financial Services Authority's *Risk-Assessment Framework* dated August 2006 makes the following statement:

> '2.8 We have, therefore, made a conscious decision to be a risk-based regulator. We regularly review the amount of risk we are prepared to accept and focus our resources on the risks that matter most. By doing so, we believe we can make the greatest overall difference in the UK financial services market, without stifling competitiveness. And from the point of view of those we regulate, our interventions in the marketplace can be justified in terms of the level of risk to our statutory objectives and consequent harm that would otherwise be present.'

Basel II (see later chapter for detail) regulator controls on banks and others is all about being able to measure retained risk and then understand the level of retained capital that is needed to support that level of risk.

Stage 3: risk reporting

The next stage is about risk reporting and is intended to embrace not only internal reporting but also the regulatory and good practice needs to report risk levels to all stakeholders. We need to begin, however, with the importance of the clear reporting of risks internally to enable effective and informed decision making about the risks that have been identified and evaluated.

With the risk definitions in place and the risk assessments completed, the risk manager can then begin to absorb risk information and present the risk picture and the recommendations to the board or chief executive for decisions.

Each business unit manager also needs to be made aware of the risks that he or she carries and the potential damage to the wider organization should his or her particular unit fail due to a risk incident. For example, computer services managers may be aware of the technicalities of the unit, but they may not be aware precisely how a particular failure or length of 'time out' period could damage the wider organization's sensitivities. This is especially so where the technology supports widely different operations across a diverse group.

Therefore the continuity planning of a central computer suite is not safely left to the technicians alone. It needs to be built up from a risk and impact understanding, developed in a clear information-sharing partnership between operational managers and technical managers that will enable cost-effective, but above all, workable resilience planning.

Preparing to very quickly replace damaged technology and the workstations around them is very expensive indeed – especially if the speed requirement is so fast that it needs them to be pre-positioned or contracted to a specialist contingency supplier. The nearer the replacement is needed to the incident time, the higher the cost curve. If the technology continuity planning delivers too much replacement equipment than is needed to feed the emergency business requirements, or provides it too quickly, there is clearly a huge waste of money. If the technology replacement plans do not provide enough resources, or not quickly enough to feed the urgent survival requirements, then the organization dies anyway. In the latter case, the spend had in any event been a waste of time.

The risk and impact matrix

There are choices of ways risk information can be presented for decision making. One way may be with the use of a matrix format, as shown in Table 2.2.

Table 2.2 Risk and probability matrix

			1 *Negligible*	2 *Marginal*	3 *Critical*	4 *Catastrophic*
Probability	5	>5 times per year				
	4	Annually	Risk 10	Risk 3		Risk 7, 8
	3	1 to 5 years			Risk 1, 2, 5	
	2	5 to 10 years	Risk 11	Risk 4	Risk 6, 9, 12	
	1	<10 years				
			Severity			

The shaded portion of the matrix could be for the risks that fall within the agreed definitions of accepted risks. Clearly, therefore, risks allocated numbers 7 and 8 in the risk register demand priority attention in that they are expected to happen annually, and can damage to a catastrophic extent.

Risks 1, 2 and 5 are of concern, too, as they can cause critical damage within a 1-year to 5-year period of time. Risks 6, 9 and 12 also demand attention.

The danger of this format is that frequency and impact can be given equal importance whereas impact is much more crucial. Some risk managers simply multiply the impact score by the probability score to create a priority order by highest resultant number.

An organization, or one of its key suppliers, may be in a hurricane zone. The mathematical likelihood of a hurricane hitting in the current year is of much less interest to a risk manager than the fact that a hurricane could possibly hit this year, and that the consequences would be devastating to the business objectives. The relative importance of severity over probability needs to be built into the strategies and presentations.

Stage 4: risk decisions

Once the risks are known and evaluated, the board or chief executive has a choice of response. Now risk aware, the option of making no decision is no longer available. This is not only a legal or regulatory issue, it is basic good stakeholder relationship management.

We have, however, stated that different organizations – and even personalities within an organization – can take very different views on acceptability and unacceptability of risk exposures. They will make these decisions within their different backgrounds and cultures, also recognizing the quite different pressures upon them.

A bank, servicing credit cards and cash machines 24 hours, seven days a week, will take an entirely different view on acceptable gaps in service to an organization where customers could reasonably wait a few days for a response. Some organizations, especially those using e-commerce distribution, may have competitors that can upsize and respond incredibly quickly to any difficulties seen in another player in their market-place. It is for this reason that the amount of time lost or 'time out' from the market-place is another vital consequence for the risk manager considering the decisions to be made around continuity exposures.

Equally, an organization cannot allow any circumstances at all whereby damage could possibly destroy its financial and other business controls over itself. An insurance company may, for example, be dealing at any one time with current claims valued at many billions of pounds and will have reserved and reinsured accordingly. To lose records and thus intellectual control over such a claims portfolio could totally destroy that organization.

As always, the responsibility for risk understanding and management rests firmly with the board or the most senior management. It may delegate the processes for achieving risk understanding and risk management but it cannot delegate the responsibility itself. This is not just a regulatory issue, it is quite simply and obviously good management.

The decision could be that the exposure is an acceptable one. This might be a reasonable decision if the potential worst-case consequences are clearly understood and the board considers that they could not possibly have an unacceptable impact on its objectives and responsibilities. This impact could be not least to their own people, on its stakeholders, balance sheets, ability to control, legality, market presence, brand values, revenue accounts nor cash flows.

Care needs to be taken with the expression 'MPL'. It is used often but it can mean two entirely different things. It can mean 'maximum probable loss' or it can mean 'maximum possible loss'. It is used often in the insurance industry where an insurer can make an assessment of a probable loss outcome, e.g. that windstorm damage to a £100 million shopping arcade would not cost more than say, £20 million, to repair. The insurer will be happy with such an estimate of worst-case scenario in its books, based partly on considerable experience but not least that it can purchase reinsurance against a failure in setting an adequate 'MPL'.

An organization making its own assessment of maximum probable loss does not have either that experience or the luxury of reinsurance against getting it wrong. This leads to the wider question of whether the main drivers to risk decision making should be around the anticipated cause of loss, 'scenario setting', or the anticipated damage that can emerge.

The problem with scenario setting is that the scenario is very likely to be very different than expected. There are countless examples where science, nature or indeed the human race has shown the ability to surprise risk managers massively and unpleasantly.

Just a few of these failed scenarios are:

- Gloucestershire floods 2007;
- St Mary Axe Bomb 1993;
- Hurricane Katrina, New Orleans 2005;
- UK House prices early 1990s;
- Stock market falls early 2000;
- Asian Tsunami 2004;
- World Trade Center 2001;
- Buncefield Oil Storage Depot 2005;
- Chernobyl 1986;
- Piper Alpha oil platform fire 1988;
- Auckland power failure 1998;
- Iraq war.

The risk reporting therefore needs to be clear in its messages about how the worst-case scenarios have been assessed and the risk of getting that wrong. This need is of course equally important whether cause or impact is being discussed.

Within the context of this section, we should restate the decision-making choices available. If the exposure is deemed to be unacceptable then the organization has further choices to make, as follows.

- The board can invest resources to manage down the exposure to the incident to what is considered to be the acceptable level.
- The board can invest resources to manage down the potential consequences to what is considered to be the acceptable level.
- It could of course decide to avoid the particular activity or environment altogether.
- It can enter into a contract to transfer the risk into an insurance product or to another counterparty.
- It can prepare beforehand for the consequences of a risk incident, knowing that such preparation leads to safeguarding business-critical dependencies and the ability to manage through the consequences without unacceptable damage.

The risk manager could recommend one of the tools listed above, but in practice is more likely to advise the most cost-effective and commercially realistic combination. In addition, the risk manager should always consider the risk that the risk management processes themselves may fail. The following is just one example.

An organization's lawyers could transfer, by contract wording, the potential cost of risk to suppliers, distributors or other counterparties. There is no real value, however, when a risk incident destroys a just-in-time and critical supplier or a distributor leading to the risk manager's own organization being damaged or destroyed. The lawyer's promises need backing up with the additional and important dimension of business continuity, i.e. the ability to resource alternative supplies fast enough, and indeed credit risk assessments on that counterparty.

The point also begs the question whether the consequential management of the potentially destructive risks to one's own organization should safely be left to that third party. Furthermore, the positioning of risk and impact is likely to be part of the initial contract negotiations.

The organization may use a relatively strong negotiating position to drive the passing of risk to the third party. The organization retaining the risk is then likely to require compensation for that retention within the pricing of the relationship. Its counterparty may then be left with the position that it is paying for that risk transfer in the agreed contract pricing and additionally that it has lost effective control over the risk management of that important exposure. Furthermore, the cost of the risk's management may be made more expensive by the counterparty's lower tolerance to risk.

It is useful to remember here that the most destructive of risks highlighted in the definition of catastrophic risk are not insurable ones in the conventional insurance market. 'We didn't need risk management because we had insurance' is too often a cry from the corporate grave. We will explore these two issues more deeply in a later chapter.

Stage 5: risk treatment

This section is worthy of a book in itself and it is possible here only to touch on the subject. Some of the options available will be explored in later chapters. Needless to say, any risk treatment must be commercially realistic, and thus be cost effective, when measured against the potential impact. Remember that the objective of the risk treatment is not to remove all risk, but to bring the risk and consequences down to within the comfort zone of the agreed tolerances to risk.

Investment in risk treatment is not just about bolting on such things as sprinkler systems and security alarms. Risk treatment is indivisible from the very strategy of the organization and its objectives. It can be at a cost of an otherwise profitable opportunity that is considered, on reflection, to bring uncomfortable levels of risk to the wider organization. That risk expenditure can be an 'opportunity cost' where the risk encourages a decision to avoid an activity, product or market-place altogether. It is particularly relevant to be risk aware within decisions to narrow the supply chain and use the resultant powers to bully a single or small number of suppliers on costs and terms.

Labour costs in developing countries may be attractive to finance directors but is the lack of infrastructure and safety a worthy risk-balancing act? Making economies by putting all the workforce and equipment into one building is not just a financial decision, it is no less a risk decision too.

A company had a sales car fleet of thousands of vehicles. There was a very poor accident record, putting lives at risk, and causing loss of employee time and very high insurance premiums.

The company decided on a range of risk treatment measures. It cancelled damage insurance for the fleet's cars and advised all sales managers that damage costs would be deducted from their business unit's profitability statements, on which part of their bonuses were calculated. It restricted the driving of the cars to the sales persons themselves and to any family member over 25 years old. High-powered cars were removed from the sales force's options.

Accidents and costs reduced dramatically as unit managers were incentivized to take ownership of the losses and deal with their frequent bad drivers. The 'risk treatment' therefore was no less a human resources issue and a sales force recruitment and management challenge.

A difficult decision is where the risk considered is an infrequent but potentially catastrophic exposure. Should you insure and prepare contingency resources in case of an earthquake in the UK that would be so damaging as to close down a factory or a supplier? Or perhaps this is an acceptable risk?

Severe hurricanes in the Southern Caribbean are very rare indeed but as Ivan reminded us in Grenada in 2004, they are always possible. These are very difficult decisions to make.

Stage 6: residual risk reporting

Commercially realistic decisions about treating the risks down to 'acceptable levels' implies that risks will remain. The fact that the board has taken views on commercial realism and acceptability levels does not in any way imply that there are no risks left to be reported. That reporting process is often a formal one as directed by regulators.

It is also a crucial internal management one so that all business unit managers are aware of the risk they retain as they go about their business and the expectancy that they include risk management as a key task objective.

Stage 7: monitoring

Introducing risk treatment does not suggest that the task is complete. The risk manager will wish to monitor whether the action has been successful and fine tune as is necessary.

Probably the only guarantee an organization can offer to its risk manager is that it will change in one way or another. That change may be widespread or be one of fine detail. So often in risk management, the danger lies in the detail, and it is from such an item of small detail that important exposures can evolve and magnify as they work their way through the chain of consequence throughout the organization's supply chain. A sales manager's decision to supply a new customer, an American aircraft manufacturer, with nuts and bolts changes the liability risk profile dramatically if it had erstwhile only supplied, say, the furniture industry.

There may be changes in the legal and market backgrounds within which risk decisions were made. They could include new regulatory controls, a new legal environment, new political risks, new scientific knowledge on health concerns, a new compensation culture for defective products and other liabilities, different security needs for people, assets and information, and competitor behaviours. There can be new dependencies on distributors, shipping and other service suppliers, new customer behaviour patterns, and changing counterparty and contract risks, currency exchange rate risks and currency conversion risks.

Terrorism risk assessments change constantly as do terrorists' preferred methods of attack. Bombs are not new in Western culture, but the suicide bomber is a relatively new phenomenon in these areas, requiring entirely new types of security and responses.

The risk manager will need to be aware of those changes, and have pre-prepared responses. In the UK, the Security Service (MI5) and the Joint

Terrorism Analysis Centre work together to constantly review the terrorism risk and set at any one time one of the following assessments:

- critical – an attack is expected imminently;
- severe – an attack is highly likely;
- substantial – an attack is a strong possibility;
- moderate – an attack is possible but not likely;
- low – an attack is unlikely.

This list is by no means complete and the changes may not only apply to the organization's risk to its direct supply chain, but the suppliers themselves will certainly be facing changes that will outdate the due diligence and capability studies completed at the time of contract.

It is difficult enough keeping up to date and understanding the wide view of the consequences of change in the organization's own activities. It is many times more difficult staying on top of the changes deep within a supplier organization and across each of the critical and urgent suppliers in the chains feeding the capability to deliver.

It is for this reason that change management is clearly an ongoing and never-ending task for the risk department. We will develop this theme, including audits, in another chapter.

Risk managing an external supply chain

We will now move on to consider the task of risk managing the supply chain in more than one dimension.

It is rare that an organization, if it is to take full advantage of all of the opportunities available with outsourcing, simply takes a part of its organization and moves it into a third-party organization. It is very likely to make major structural changes within its own organization at the same time. There is therefore a significant project risk management task that is required right through the change process from concept to delivery.

Once positioned and running, risk managing the risks of failure within that chain is an ongoing need. That failure may not be just an external event such as fire or terrorism, but can be a gradually evolving failure such as quality or reputational issues that could at any moment in time be moving into the realm of unacceptable risk. Sobering thoughts emerged from a Gartner survey that said that the failure rate of outsourcing contracts is over 50 per cent.

Furthermore, there is almost certainly going to be more than one supply chain, indeed there may be hundreds.

British Aerospace spends approximately £4 billion a year on 15 suppliers. Coca-Cola allegedly has 48,000 suppliers.

Gartner reported that in 2005 there were 11 known outsourcing contracts worth over £1 billion each.

The need for risk management disciplines starts right at the very beginning with the discussions on objectives and deliverables, and continues right through the various project stages to implementation.

Before the organization even thinks about signing a contract, there are strategic decisions that cannot be easily altered afterwards. There are sensitivities to be managed such as existing workforce concerns and reactions, in addition to the more obvious challenges of making the right decisions regarding the choice of supplier and how that relationship will actually work intellectually, operationally and legally.

Above all, the organization needs to be clear within that strategy whether it is simply subcontracting some activity, interfacing some of its activities with a third-party organization or fully integrating its own organization with one or more others. They are three very different relationships in the processes transferred and in the risk consequences that need to be managed.

This philosophy will dictate how the supplier is selected and how the relationship then works. Do the relative power bases of the negotiators drive the contract negotiations? Will the ongoing relationship be confrontational and again based around the relative power of one party over the other? Will the deliveries be seen as transactional or will they be part of a much wider partnership collaboration? Will the policing be around inspections and penalties, or in co-operating towards ensuring continuity of quality? Above all, will the detail of the relationships as contracted always retain an equality of purpose and value? Those 'purposes' no less include risks as they include the costs and the rewards.

A life assurance company in Malaysia in effect outsourced its sales process by exclusively using independent financial advisers and sales teams. It quickly established a market position by paying generous introductory commissions spread over the first three years of the policy's life. It also used the independent financial advisers to collect annual and quarterly renewal premiums.

After three years, the company found that it had a massive and potentially business destructive lapse rate on the first-year policy renewals. The independent contractors had simply less interest in applying resources to the collection of the renewal premiums of three-year plus policies. The problem evolved year by year with devastating consequences to its renewal retention rate.

These questions may indeed be cultural and relationship management questions but are no less risk management questions too. If the initial relationship is flawed, problems will almost inevitably follow.

Therefore, the risk challenges start with getting the strategies right in the first place and then measuring all later decisions, risk management and continuity management constantly against those agreed strategies and measurable deliverables. It is far too late for an executive in a hurry to secretly negotiate outsourcing ('because of price sensitivity, commercial sensitivity or staff sensitivity') and its consequential process re-engineering, and then bring in the risk professionals to do 'risk management' or 'continuity management' thereafter. Risk management starts with getting the strategy right and then integrating the understanding of risk and its management into the very first strategic and cost–benefit discussions.

Therefore, we will return to the subject of risk management of the project and around the ongoing outsourced supply chain once we have discussed what those strategies are likely to be.

'Launching products and services that best fit customer requirements is clearly the top objective for new product development. Lower introduction costs and first-to-market strategies are not considered key strategies for new product development, in comparison to bringing to market innovative products that meet customer wants and needs.'

(IBM survey, *Scoring High on the Supply Chain Maturity Model – A European perspective*, 2005)

Outsourcing has moved on a long way from reducing costs alone as, alongside the other opportunities of technology, communications bandwidth and removal of national trading barriers, there are now opportunities to create entirely new business models that maximize all of these tools and opportunities together.

To be risk aware, we need to look at the very reason why outsourcing is being considered and the organization-wide 'benefits' that the project ambassadors are selling to the board.

Organizations need supply chains that not only cut cost and management time, but are adaptable, agile and aligned precisely with the perceived customer requirements. The agility, variability and speed that are enabled by an effective supply chain enable the very relationship between supply and demand to be reversed. The driver for the creation of each and every product or service can now be the demand for that item, rather than the need to find a buyer for an availability of supplies. Thus, the value chain from ingredient to customer is a lean one, is demand led and is so much shorter and single-customer focused.

Organizations use the supply chain to enable them to differentiate themselves and their products from competitors. The agility requirement is to enable them to bring products to market so much more quickly, communicate directly and respond immediately to changes in market demands and opportunities. The other side of the coin, of course, is that this customer by customer differentiation, direct communication and instantaneous responses have changed forever the expectations of customers and even entire market-places.

It is the risks that lie in wait around those expectations that we need to manage and they are very different to the risk management challenges of erstwhile business models.

> A bank stated that if the period of time for a new product to get from concept to critical mass exceeds three months it is considered a failure.

The risk manager who does not take the risk of losing these new-age dependencies into the risk assessments is missing the very core dependability. Promises and customer relationship management are now integral, not peripheral, to the very business model and failure to deliver is in effect failure of the whole organization. They form a complex web of risks that lie around the relationships with third-party suppliers right through to the legalities of bringing third parties into the value chain. The 'baggage' that comes with outsourcing may be the communications and process technology that feeds the relationship, the ownership of intellectual assets, and the risks that come with internationalism.

> 'The dramatic rise in supply dependencies with Asia, and in particular China, creates significant and diverse risk exposures, several of which are unique to the region in terms of their nature or severity. Intellectual property, counterfeiting and ethical risks are often just as important as the more traditional infrastructure, financial and natural disaster considerations and should be given equal weighting on a company's risk agenda.'
>
> (Matthew Elkington, Vice-President, Marsh Risk Consulting Practice, quoted in a news article at www.continuitycentral.com/news02756.htm)

In the next chapter, we will consider the risks that come alongside the decisions and the processes of outsourcing key elements of the business. We will also discuss the risks that will continue throughout the outsourcing relationships.

3

The special risk features of the supply chain project

Generic outsourcing risk issues

There are two dimensions to outsourcing risk and, whilst they are related, they are worthy of separation for the purposes of bringing out the key issues of each. The two fundamental concerns are a) the initial risks around the business changes that come with outsourcing and then b) the risks associated with those changed organizational structures once they are in place. We will begin this chapter by looking at concerns and opportunities related to generic outsourcing risk.

Once completed, the generic risk assessments will have made more clear the understanding around the organization's crucial objectives and sensitivities. The risk picture will have identified which dependencies lie deep within the intellectual assets, the legalities, the physical resources, stakeholder support, the ability to maintain business control and the people skills that are needed to stay 'in business'. This will apply equally whether that 'business' is profit making, public service or charity.

Part of the strategic understanding that emerges will be clarity about what precise values the organization expects from its internal and outsourced supply chains. As stated, a move towards outsourcing those values may be simply to reduce costs and management time and/or to enable more competitive product pricing. The objectives may, however, be much deeper, with a strategic placing of part of the wider business model that will enable flexibility, customer product differentiation, differentiation from competitors and/or to enable entirely new product lines.

It is only from a clear understanding of these objectives and perceived deliverables that the risk manager can then begin to fully understand the outsourced supply chain and consider what additional risks it brings, and indeed how it can itself be used as a risk management opportunity.

Criticality

We have already stated that the criticality of risk and potential impacts inherent within the decision to outsource must be considered before contracts are signed. They are, essentially, to be integrated within the very strategies to be adopted.

To reinforce the point, an organization can create the cheapest supply chain by focusing all supply needs on one supplier, perhaps in a low-cost, low-currency value, developing country. That exclusivity could enable the receiving organization to use critical mass with that supplier to force the prices down even further. The organization may, however, decide that this brings unacceptable risk and will wish to diversify supply amongst suppliers and countries. The second choice comes at increased cost. The organization may decide that the additional costs of the multiple-source supply chain are an acceptable and valuable risk management 'expense'.

To understand and communicate these exposures effectively, a supply chain needs first to be mapped so that each link can be risk assessed. One important piece of risk information is whether the organization will have a supply chain that is itself dependent on a further, long supply chain or whether the link is more self-contained. Clearly, the further the end organization is from key ingredient providers way down the line, the more difficulty there is in risk managing those ingredients, not least when risk understanding and management is necessarily third hand, fourth hand or more. A single self-contained link, however, again brings its own single point of potentially catastrophic failure.

The business-critical needs may be operational, a physical ingredient or intellectual. The organization will need to consider where these needs fit into Table 3.1 of urgency and the availability of alternatives.

The three levels of urgency may be defined as a measure of time ranging from simultaneous (for some e-commerce businesses, for example) to measures in minutes, days or even weeks. This will vary organization by organization, according to the need to meet the urgent contractual and market needs and to retain stakeholder confidence.

Table 3.1 Urgency and alternatives

Speed required	Alternatives
Immediate dependency	Not available elsewhere in volume, quality and quickly enough
Immediate dependency	Available elsewhere in volume, quality and quickly enough
Mid-term dependency	Not available elsewhere in volume, quality and quickly enough
Mid-term dependency	Available elsewhere in volume, quality and quickly enough
Non-urgent dependency	Not available elsewhere in volume, quality and quickly enough
Non-urgent dependency	Available elsewhere in volume, quality and quickly enough

Dependency is equally about the impact of the loss of that supply chain ingredient on each of the criticalities that has been defined in the risk policy statement as being critical or potentially catastrophic. One approach therefore would be to take the previously agreed definition of potentially catastrophic risk and then measure against that definition the importance of the 'dependency' under review.

For example, if a particular supply chain failure could cause the loss of regulatory compliance, it would be a primary risk consideration. Compliance and legality are clearly 'killer risks'. It is likely also to be in category 1 as there will be an immediate need to be able to illustrate compliance to the regulator. To repeat, that immediate urgency is not only to remain compliant, it is equally important still to be able to illustrate that compliance in the period leading up to the risk incident. The loss of an audit trail that is needed to give those reassurances can be just as destructive as then losing control of the business to the point that new activity fails to meet compliance requirements.

The word 'available' used in the table, however, is not just about the delivery of physical parts for the production line of a motor car or piece of machinery. It is equally about how fast the host organization can regain all of the things that it needs to enable it to provide the value chain items themselves, or arrange supply from another source. There may be vital business-to-business communication software, databases that themselves need skilled staff, and software and hardware to access and use. The software may need the software source code to enable other technicians to service and upgrade it and these are no less crucial dependencies.

The 'availability' also needs to be defined in the ability to source the ingredient to the required specification, volumes and quality, and deliverable to the site or website required. 'Availability' needs to be defined too in terms of the costs of the alternatives that enable the receiving organizations' pricing and financial models to remain valid. The cost levels will again not only cover the actual monetary cost but the credit terms available. If an organization's financial models depend on positive cash flows, then those same credit terms applied equally to the alternative supply are, again, no less a 'dependency'.

Furthermore, dependency is no less related to 'ownership' of the databases, software and other intellectual assets that are also crucial to the delivery. Additional questions raised will be whether these intellectual assets are recoverable at all, and if so, how? Are there legal barriers such as contract terms, and what is the ease and speed of being able legally to transfer the ownership of the very wide range of intellectual assets? Who now owns the brand names? Are there statutory barriers such as the Data Protection Act 1998 (UK)? This Act, and others in other jurisdictions, demands that the name of the 'Data Controller' is registered wherever personal data is used, and specifies how that data can and cannot be used and thus limits the use of that data for the registered purpose and by the registered person. Gaining access fast enough to a personal information database almost certainly will need pre-registration of that alternative data controller.

To reaffirm, these are questions that cannot be usefully raised once the contractual relationships and dependencies between the supplier and the receiver have already been set in stone.

The outsourcing project

We have once again two important inner risk dimensions:

1. the need to understand and take on board the risk implications whilst the strategic decision making is unfolding;
2. the re-engineering risks being carried whilst the outsourcing, in whatever way it is agreed, is being implemented into the existing organization.

1. The need to understand and take on board the risk implications whilst the strategic decision making is unfolding

Perhaps the greatest of all risks that lie within the project is the confidence amongst the project owners that their brilliant and stunning management decisions cannot possibly go wrong. This 'can do' philosophy and, conversely, a fear of a blame culture, vary organization by organization. It may, though, rest no more than in the individual executive's desire to show to those who will be influencing his or her future career, just how brilliant he or she is. The result of this approach can be that crucially dependent relationships are created with no exit strategy at all.

The project deliverables are unsafe if they do not include a 'prenuptial' agreement that defines just how the divorce will unfold and how the widely defined assets of the relationships are to be divided and accessed. Access to those assets, whether they are people, equipment or intellectual, is not just a physical and legal consideration. 'Access' needs to embrace the operational ability to use and gain the required values from those assets, and the wider legality in how the assets can be used.

This is especially important in the light of research by Metrica, a UK research firm, which suggested the following were the greatest worries of risk managers involved in outsourced processes:

- losing control over the process;
- losing control over customer relationships;
- potential loss of quality;
- threats to brand and reputation;
- the operational and financial stability of the supplier.

These may be 'soft' or less well-defined risks to manage but they lie at the very heart of the survivability of the organization.

Clearly the project is just waiting for failure if the objectives are neither clear nor realistic, and these of course include the initial cost of the project to bed the outsourced elements into the existing and wider organization. Items such as the employee cost of redundancy and pension fund shortfalls can alone destroy the viability of a project.

Taking great care in getting this clear and right is a crucial process of risk management.

We can usefully drill down further into the 'soft' but absolutely crucial risk issues surrounding the decision making that precedes a decision whether to outsource or not, and if so, how. The following checklist embraces some more generic project specific issues.

- Are the objectives clear and communicated?
- Is the sponsorship at the correct level?
- Are programme management and communication tools agreed and up to the task?
- Who is measuring and who is accepting any uncertainties and risks? Do they know that they are?
- Are communication and risk-reporting mechanisms clear between the above and the project workers at all levels?
- Whose job is it to stop 'creeping' of the original project objectives?
- Are this and similar responsibilities embedded at the right level and function within the organization?
- Are the time deadlines realistic and the project adequately resourced to deliver without unacceptable stresses?
- Have existing stakeholders been brought in?
- Have potential stakeholders been brought in?
- What is the ability to accurately plan and estimate, and are the margins of error acknowledged?
- Is there ability to control and monitor, and by whom?
- Is 'shop floor' real input and team working in place?
- Is the 'consultation' a genuine effort to listen or just a ritual designed towards getting agreement?
- Can issues that emerge be quickly escalated for business-critical understanding and decision making?
- Can a possible decision not to proceed remain an option as the detail emerges?
- How rigorous is the testing, including volume testing?
- Could the clear strategic rationale be subsumed as the project unfolds?
- Will the re-engineered processes be pushed into the organization or received by an organization that is on board, enthusiastic even, and ready to make the changes?
- Will the control procedures ensure that personal agendas and politics are removed from the decision path? Is it possible to bypass any vested interest?

Probability trees

Decision trees

All business schools and consultants offer models for decision making. They can range from being very valuable to very dangerous. The dangerous ones are where managers find that they are feeding the model and software rather than feeding the business. This happens when, deep in the model or software, the focus on the 'big issues' is well and truly lost.

A simple model, either using software or paper and pencil, is to try to consider what could happen if a particular decision is made. The result of that decision and its range of consequences could probably be described in worst-case and best-case terms. These worst- and best-case terms may be financial, depending on customer and competitor response, or operational, depending on, for example, employee response.

The reality is that the outcome will likely be somewhere between worst-case and best-case scenarios but, with the worst and best understood, a view can then be taken – what could the next decisions be in each of these circumstances? That decision will itself no doubt bring about a set of responses and reactions that will again lead to worst-case and best-case scenarios.

This can proceed further as long as value is perceived in doing so. The value of this tool is that managers can project the likely best-case and worse-case result of a series of decision making. They can take an early view on whether each of these possible scenarios, three or four steps down the line, continues to meet the project objectives and remains within both the objective and the risk tolerances of the organization and its stakeholders.

Fault trees

Fault trees consider what would be an unacceptable adverse event, for example, a supplier failure, and then work backward to possible root causes of such a failure. The project planning can then consider each of these causes and how best they can be designed out.

Dangers in scenario setting

There are great dangers in scenario setting. The reality of the world of risk is that the only guarantee is that it will surprise. There are countless examples of where scenario projections have failed. Examples include the first of the large-scale Provisional IRA bombs in London, the collapse of not only one but two of the World Trade Center Towers, the Buncefield Oil Depot Fire 2005 spreading to other storage tanks, the world spread of the 2004 Tsunami, science that linked asbestos and smoking with cancer, the slow-moving Hurricane Katrina in New Orleans, the sheer repetition of serious tropical hurricanes in 2005, the 2007 Gloucestershire floods and so many more.

The other problem with scenario setting is that we only have past experience to go on in anticipating future events. Not only do we have the surprises suggested above but also changing environments and trends can change the influences emerging from similar incidents. Examples include an increasingly litigious society, global warming, new terrorism strategies, political change, increased life expectancies and new laws and regulatory demands.

Therefore pure risk is constantly changing and scenario setting is much better driven by the possible consequences of the loss of a dependency, rather than burning up energy worrying about what might or might not cause that loss to occur. Clearly 'blue-sky thinking' needs to be as much about the loss of crucial dependencies from any cause, as about possible causes of that loss.

This reminds us of the need for caution around risk matrices. As said earlier, they do have the danger that they can give probability and 'risk impact' equal weight, whereas it is the actual consequences of a loss of an asset or ability on the particular organization's survivability that are the most important drivers for risk understanding and management. This causes particularly dangerous distortions when the concern is about a low probability but potentially catastrophic impact exposure.

2. The re-engineering risks being carried whilst the outsourcing, in whatever way it is agreed, is being implemented into the existing organization

The organization already has crucial dependencies on which the delivery of its values, services, effective controls, financial models and market-place segmentation depends. This 'old' business model relies on these continuing, even whilst the changes are underway, and the new outsourced organizational model can then fully take up the strain.

Not least will these dependencies include the retention and morale of key staff and the teams that are likely to be affected. Another stakeholder issue will be to retain the confidence of creditors, investors, regulators and other stakeholders throughout the change-over period.

The project therefore needs to have a clear communication strategy with all these stakeholders to inform them of the developments in a realistic and timely manner, and may entail some short-term costs in keeping them on board throughout the change over. Key staff may, for example, need to be retained by offering loyalty bonuses until they are no longer needed and these costs will need to be built into the cost–benefit calculations of the decision to proceed.

Richard Granger resigned as the head of the UK Government's agency, Connecting for Health, in 2007. He was the third manager to do so.

> '… But Granger seemed to epitomise the Labour Government's belief that the big decisions were best taken at the start, by those with the power and the mandate. One of the key reasons why the fate of the National Programme for IT still hangs in the balance is that consultation has been treated as a means of securing acceptance, not as a cooperative process aimed at reaching the best solution.
>
> This is not a throw-away criticism, but a central one. Among the organisations that have articulated concerns about the lack of consultation or the imposition of inappropriate solutions are the British Medical Association; The Royal College of Surgeons; the Royal College of Physicians; the British Medical Journal; the Royal College of Nursing; London School of Hygiene and Tropical Medicine; and the Renal Association.
>
> One of the obvious flaws of the Connecting for Health project … is that it more or less mandated the replacement of good, reliable and heavily used "legacy" solutions.'
>
> (Andrew Laurence, *Information Age*, July 2007)

Project risk management

Project risk management is a subject worthy of a book in itself and we only have space here for some headlines and to bring out relevancies to any project to change a supply chain. This section crucially must be read within the context of the generic supply chain risk features discussed above.

Realistically defining the results to be expected is always the bloodstream of any project.

'Top supply chains do have a common trait: the ability to respond quickly and in an integrated way to shifts in demand with innovative products and services. To do this, they employ a variety of business strategies and models, coupled with leading management practices. And they consistently measure their performance based on a handful of key indicators:

- perfect order attainment;
- demand accuracy;
- time to value;
- cash-to-cash cycle time;
- supply chain cost.

These indicators of supply chain performance are the gauges used to monitor the efficiency of the business.'

(From a summary of *Follow the leaders: Scoring high on the supply chain maturity model – A European perspective*, published by IBM at: www-935.ibm.com/services/uk/index.wss/summary/igs/a1022740)

Within a project to change the supply chain, those 'results' include at least:

- what the supplier is obliged to deliver;
- the recipient's obligations;
- the speed and quality of delivery and the delivery location;
- consistency of speed and quality of delivery;
- all potential needs into the future and thus flexibility;
- financial expectations and variances;
- ability to measure service levels, including possible benchmarking;
- reporting requirements;
- risk positioning on each of the parties involved;
- contingency plans and arrangements during exceptional circumstances, including contingency service level agreements;
- legalities and ownership of work in hand, work in transit, tools and equipment, information and other intellectual assets;
- dispute resolution and, if necessary, the pre-agreed exit processes.

If the project entails offshoring of the supply chain, this brings its own additional risks to be considered, not least:

- the reputational risks that lurk within different employment standards and other cultural differences;
- cross-border tax, compliance, fraud, corruption, currency conversion, exchange controls and other financial matters;
- morale and staffing quality risks, including the home country staff who are still needed to manage within new environments;
- different legal regimes and expectations, including regulatory demands;
- cultural issues around product delivery and timeliness;
- the changed risk levels within other country infrastructures including environmental, political, safety, crime and other risks affecting continuity and delivery, and the ability of the country to react to such incidents.

Principles of project management

As we have frequently reinforced, risk management is integral to, not separated from, other management, and this applies no less to project management. It is perhaps useful to mention here some of the aspects that embrace effective project management.

> Project management is the discipline of organizing and managing resources in such a way that the project is completed within the defined scope, quality, time and cost restraint.
>
> A project is a temporary and one time endeavour undertaken to create a unique product or service, which brings about beneficial change or added value.

Clearly the project must deliver against clear expectations and within the stated constraints. These constraints are scope, time, cost and risk, and it is, of course, a four-item balancing act to stay within them or within any acceptable variations.

Acceptable variations may be predefined, such as in the creation of a contingency budget. The 'scope' will be defined precisely, and will include quality definitions and measurable reporting within the scope definitions. On the other hand, some projects will have elements that are not variable at all. The project to complete an Olympic stadium, for example, has a rigid delivery date and a delay of one day, in a six-year project, beyond the date that the Games start is entirely unacceptable.

The initiation and thus scope-setting stage will include the establishment and gaining of approval for the business needs, and this will include risk tolerances. It will need to clearly understand current operations, the essential controls now in place and the relationship between the new and the old – not least in human resources. The new organizational structure needs, of course, to be designed and the resultant needs and financial models made clear.

Stakeholders need to be selected and, in the case of a supply chain project, this will include the suppliers themselves which need to be assessed and judged for their suitability to deliver requirements in quality, consistency and speed, and without unacceptable risk. The delivery of the project will not only cover the establishment of the agreed ingredients but also the transition of the 'old' business system to the new one.

The risks to be identified and managed appear at each stage, not least the transition period. The delivery will also include not just the new system, but assurances that the new system is measurable, benchmarked, legal and delivering services as set in the project scope. No less, risks need to be understood, measured and with a risk level communicated and formally accepted by the most senior management. Clearly, also, the project scope will need to consider the potential for collateral damage to other parts of the organization.

There is a range of tools available to the project manager and they include PERT charts and Gantt charts, and also a range of financial tools. There is a range of professional bodies that are centres of excellence and advice. These include the Association for Project Management (UK) (http://www.apm.org.uk) and The Project Management Institute (http://www.pmi.org). There is also a British Standard *Guide to Project Management* (BS 6079). Finally, there are also other international standards, including ISO 9000 and ISO 10006.

A Gantt chart is a method of bringing together the various project ingredients, their relativity and required delivery dates. A simplified example is shown in Figure 3.1 and in practice the 'tasks' will be broken down into various headings and also with subheadings, potentially of many pages.

PERT (project evaluation review technique) charts contain detailed information relating to the activities necessary to produce the required end delivery of the project itself. A PERT chart evolves from a product flow diagram by considering in turn all the tasks that are needed to reach the project goal. All of the resources that are required to complete each stage are highlighted on the PERT chart, which is continually updated. An example of a simple PERT chart to manage a recruitment project is shown in Figure 3.2.

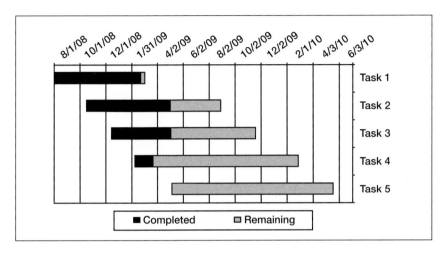

Figure 3.1 Simplified example of a Gantt chart

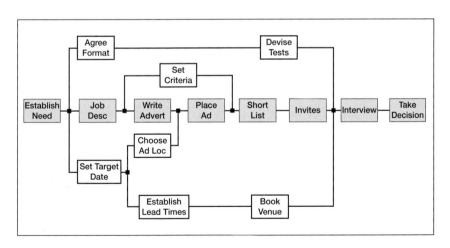

(Source: Chris Everett at http://www.spottydog.u-net.com/guides/faq/faq.html)

Figure 3.2 Example PERT chart for managing a recruitment project

The need to get the project objectives right is worthy of a little deeper consideration in view of its importance. As stated, we can begin with the four underlying objectives of scope, time, cost and risk.

Scope

The project may be a part of a wider business objective and business plan and clearly the project managers need to be aware of the precise role that they are playing in that wider picture and what they are charged to deliver to that wider picture.

That precise role and, indeed, precise scope must be signed off by the board and relevant stakeholders so that there is no miscommunication. For example, are the individual project managers charged to embrace all the transfer costs from the old delivery infrastructure to the new? That could include redundancy payments, handling staff morale issues, existing contract get-out costs and immediate top-up of pension funds for employees transferred to another employer.

Too many times projects are started without that clarity and focus. Not only is it difficult to measure the success of a project against unclear objectives but it also leaves the door open to one of the greatest threats to the successful completion of a project. That threat can best be described as 'project drift', where people have the bright idea that 'whilst we are doing this we might as well change these other things too'. Indeed, it may be a bright idea but too often the vital steps are not taken to take the project back for an entirely new review of its fundamentals of scope, time, cost and risk.

There is a clear 'scope' issue that may or may not be considered part of the project team's brief. Is it part of the scope for that project team to continually keep under review, as its work unfolds, whether the entire project is unworkable? Can it thus be charged with coming back to the board, if necessary, with a view that the objectives have been found not to be achievable in the way originally proposed? Alternatively, is the project team being told that decisions to proceed have been made and that it is simply 'to make it happen' as best it can?

These are two entirely different atmospheres within which the project team will work and will wish to illustrate success. The risk atmospheres between the two are entirely different.

Time

The project may indeed include a delivery date in its 'wish list'. It is, however, a crucial risk issue to understand precisely the level of importance of meeting that delivery date. The first and obvious reason is the way that time and cost are often two aspects of the same threat. Projects failing to meet delivery dates will inevitably incur much greater costs as they work on towards completion.

Those costs may simply be in the operational costs of the project's own infrastructure. It is also likely to create an opportunity cost where the budgeted saving and opportunities of the new sourcing systems are not being delivered when planned. This double whammy of costs and lost opportunities can be sufficient to destroy the organization altogether.

As mentioned above regarding the Olympic Games project, failure to meet some timetables can remove the very heart of the project and threaten the rest of the organization. Other projects will have their own urgencies and time criticalities. It may be that competitors are changing the market-place away from the organization's ability to compete, or there may be precisely timed regulatory or tax regime changes that are one of the reasons for change. Time then becomes a critical risk factor that needs interim progress and risk measures built into the project to ensure that it does not fail.

Those risk measures will of course vary by project and by time urgencies. It may be that the project ingredients themselves may need to be multi-sourced to reduce the risk of failure. As always, risk management needs to remain integral to the entire project scope.

A risk manager of another major sports event expressed the concern that building contractors were deliberately delaying their work with the purpose of putting the authorities into a position where they will be forced, at the eleventh hour, to access the contingency funds and to also reduce quality standards. When delivery time is named as a key risk, getting the building contracts right is no less one of risk management.

Again, when the project has important time drivers, it needs to be embraced into the wider organization's contingency planning. Most contingency planning will identify urgencies within the operational functions of the organization through its business impact analysis (BIA). Often the activities and dependencies covered by the BIA will be customer-facing and otherwise stakeholder-facing. It is a great danger to miss the point that a development project, quietly unfolding in a 'back room' and perhaps even still secret, should no less be included in all of the wider business continuity work. Otherwise, the result will be that the infrastructures reinstated urgently by the continuity plan will exclude a dependency that in itself is now threatening the corporate existence.

Cost

Expenditure controls are clearly important in any organization, especially ones with a competitive business model that has crucial financial models that enable them to stay competitive and, thus, in business at all. Sadly, government and public service projects seem to have less need for financial controls and containment. Nonetheless, in public service, failures to meet budgets can have serious political consequences, such as in the London Dome, the Scottish Parliament Building and so many other such budgetary failures.

Once again, but relevant to this section, the project objectives need to define what budgets are to be met and whether they include just the project's own costs or the budgets of the resultant structure that the project is charged to design and deliver.

Risk

This brings us back to the very subject of this book and the need for risk to be inherent in all conceptual 'blue-sky thinking', process design, the elements of the organizational structures and dependencies going forward. Risks lie in the potential for the project design to miss crucial elements, in the project process and decision making and, of course, in the re-engineering of the organization that will emerge from completion of the project. Throughout all steps, there are people risks that can range from skill inadequacies to a mismatch of personal agendas, to the sudden loss by accident or other departure of key players.

Project deliverables

Whilst we have considered scope, time, cost and risk we should not forget the obvious and equally important driver that the project ends up delivering precisely what it is charged to deliver. As has been stated, this can only be evaluated when it is precisely clear and measurable what was supposed to be delivered in the first place.

In an outsourcing project, the net deliverable is a resilient, trusted, consistent supply of whatever is needed. This supply needs to fit accepted risk tolerances, and within all of the cost, quality, time, specification and consistency essentials to enable, in turn, the receiving organization to fulfil its own additional role in the value chain moving forward.

Due diligence and dependencies

Due diligence is a process of investigation into financial, commercial and operational aspects of a third party prior to the transfer of assets and/or the creation of obligations between counterparties. Such relationships clearly create new risks between them and the due diligence enquiry seeks to understand those risks, mitigate them and perhaps position carefully any post-agreement risks and consequences.

The project will undoubtedly include a due diligence process to assist decision making that decides which suppliers to embrace in the research, which then to choose, and finally how best they can fulfil a role in the wider value chain. The accountants will no doubt have their say, as will the lawyers and the logistics managers. This is clearly not enough and there then needs to be a strategic overview that balances all opportunities, all costs and all risk. The cheapest supplier may not be the most resilient and a risk premium may need to be factored into the debate.

Due diligence is much more than lawyers satisfying themselves about the legality of the arrangement and accountants satisfying themselves that the figures add up. It is as much about becoming satisfied that the third party is 'fit for purpose'. 'Fit for purpose' obviously entails not introducing any unacceptable current or future risks to the counterparty.

It is impossible to overstate the importance of due diligence and that it embraces all aspects of operability, risk and commercialism. This clearly entails understanding precisely what dependencies have been outsourced and, by working alongside the organization's risk register, understanding the importance and urgency of such dependencies. The due diligence enquiry should also assess the achievability of the exit strategy, whether that exit be planned and gradual, or as the result of a sudden emergency.

At the risk of stating the obvious, a due diligence enquiry left to a lawyer will provide legal due diligence. Due diligence left only to an accountant will provide financial due diligence. Both are valuable, but if only it was that simple at the commercial coalface! In a major project that clearly re-engineers risks and opportunities, the organization will structure its due diligence enquiries under different headings, and thus with clear agendas may see that the sections may require different skills to be delivered. These headings will embrace the following:

- financial models and sustainability;
- legality across all jurisdictions and compliance requirements;
- operational ability to deliver in time, volume and cost, and to specification;
- quality assurance, not just of the product itself but of the branding and reputational consequences of how it is produced;
- quality sustainability;
- subjective overviews against continuing objectives.

There may be more than this list for an individual project in hand. An insurance company, for example, may wish to outsource its claims handling processing. It will wish to do all the above. In addition, it will wish to check that future figures delivered will be correct and, to do so, it will wish to take a view on the supplier's claims reserving skills, procedures and controls.

Claims reserving is an actuarial-, legal- and insurance-skilled operation, and considers the average lifecycle of a type of claim that will enable anticipation of future cash flows. It also considers the impact of interest rates, award trends and inflation so that it can deliver an assessment of the current day valuation of a future claim payment. Misstatements in massive current and ongoing claims portfolios can in themselves destroy the viability of insurance businesses. There is always a vital need for confidence that figures offered can be trusted.

The subjective due diligence heading decisions need to be undertaken after all the specialist reports are in, when the project owner stands back and takes a subjective 'helicopter view' of all of the opportunities, threats, risks and costs – and whether they still encourage a decision to proceed. A crucial due diligence decision under such a heading would be to gain an understanding of the proposed supplier's own culture and attitudes. This is not least whether it shares the project manager's own organization's passions within its attitudes to stakeholder importance, its views on urgencies and the acceptability or otherwise of failure.

Things go wrong in the best-regulated circles but what separates organizations is the response to those incidents. This too is very much a cultural matter and defines whether a proposed supplier can comfortably fit within the required mindset.

In 'The Case Against Mergers', *Business Week* magazine in October 1995 stated that many US mergers and acquisitions had failed to deliver on their promises. It identified inadequate due diligence as one of the most important factors. The report stated that on too many occasions managers had failed to identify and evaluate risks primarily because they did not have experience of the complexities involved.

A further subjective due diligence view of risk could be one taken on the organization's own sensitivities to threats. With some dependencies and criticalities the project manager may specifically undertake a security threat analysis that will embrace the potential of being a target and thus the protections built around that potentiality. For example, organizations that have 'America' in their name and are situated where that threat is higher than normal are more likely to be targeted by terrorism.

Due diligence, furthermore, is not just a matter to be put away after the early negotiations to create a 'heads of agreement' letter or any other broad agreement to proceed. The formal due diligence reports are indeed completed at this time but they need to continue right throughout the supply chain project as it assesses the information unfolding, and continually re-address the findings of the initial due diligence report. If the initial 'heads of agreement' letter denies this opportunity then that letter becomes a risk factor in itself.

The due diligence is not just to identify factors that could be 'deal breakers'. The organization is more important than the deal and 'organization breakers' may lie within the risks assumed. If these are not understood and managed they can trigger no less than destruction of the entire organization at a much later date.

Furthermore, the due diligence reports need to illustrate comfort or discomfort with all of the logistics integration plans and their weaknesses and strengths. These weaknesses and strengths may be internal as the two management models are integrated, and examples would be the reaction of important skilled workforces or the capital requirements as a sudden growth surge needs financing.

They may also be as a result of an external reaction to the proposed changes, perhaps by an existing customer base, distributors or a regulator. That 'external' influence may also be legal, environmental or stakeholder support, or take the form of competitor reaction.

> Warranties demanding post-agreement activity are no substitute for effective due diligence when crucial operational and strategic dependencies are passed out to a third party. An organization that has already died because of a critical supply chain failure is not in the strongest position to subsequently demand adherence to warranties!
>
> When the organization needs to reach for its warranties to argue a point with a crucial just-in-time supplier, irretrievable damage almost certainly has already been done.

There can be many reasons why a prospective supplier can fail to meet financial and legal due diligence. It could be inadequacy of capital or cash flow, the potential for litigation, views about credit risks or compliance with regulations. The third party may be comfortable with clear and measurable concerns, as they can be priced and/or managed. The third party is, however, much more likely to be uncomfortable with uncertainty, whereby the likelihood or depth of any exposure is unclear and can be neither quantified nor priced.

It was just this uncertainty that ratcheted up the credit crisis amongst banks in 2007. It was not so much that there was a problem, but because of the habit of buying and selling loan portfolios, the lending institutions just did not know where the exposures had finally landed amongst banks and other financial institutions.

It is not good practice for a chief executive to delegate difficult decision making to consultants. Consultants are suppliers of advice on the specific aspect of a proposal that has been delegated to them. The advice they can offer is no more or no less than was described within their own terms of reference and brief. They cannot be held responsible for aspects or outcomes beyond that brief.

Consultants, for example, may be charged with finding ways of reducing staffing levels by the deadline of 1 January of the following year. This may be to meet short-term stock market expectation to report administrative savings following a merger. It is unreasonable to blame the consultants if their recommendations cause a need to recruit new, more expensive and inexperienced staff the following year because the year one staff redundancies were found to create crucial workplace needs that had been glossed over in the drive to meet the objective. The consultants had done only what they were told to do and the organization's managers will always retain the need for their own wider vision and responsibilities.

A crucial and formal step is for the board to consider all the advice given. Then it needs to balance that advice within its own cultures, objectives, risk tolerances, long-term views and 'gut feel' for future market developments. Only then can it make an informed decision whether or not to proceed. In other words, the subjective due diligence decision mentioned above.

If the board members feel uncomfortable that they do not have the skills amongst themselves to independently evaluate advice and come to their own decision, then this begs the question whether they should re-skill, or just decide it would be too risky for them to proceed with such weaknesses.

Project checklists

Project managers will have checklists and prompts against which they will assess the initial project setting, the various stages of the project and then as a sign-off assurance. These checklists and prompts can be detailed and extensive and can often be used to communicate the project objectives and risks to the wider organization and its stakeholders.

One prompt list may be a constant reminder of the potential changes to risks around the wider organization that may, without further thought, be considered to be unaffected. Many projects devise and then put into effect business strategies in which these wider area impacts cannot be ignored. This is especially when the strategic project is around crucial supply chains and where existing infrastructures may already be stretched. A headline checklist may embrace the following with numerous subheadings related to the specific project or business:

Prompt list 1

Existing operational risks

    Currently managed by operational management

    Risk recognized as exposing the project itself to failure to meet objectives

Business strategic risks

> To be managed by the project until proposals agreed?

> When and how risks are formally transferred back in to the mainstream business

> The monitoring process by named project sponsors

Project risks

> The identification, measuring and communicating of the risks when identified

New operational risks

> How the project ensures that they are identified and reported

> Whether the project manager or another takes the responsibility of managing these until handover

> The monitoring process by named project sponsors

The situation appraisal checklist will assist those who need to retain a vision of the developing project. These will include the project sponsors, internal and external auditors, those carrying specific responsibilities such as compliance, finance, brand management, human resources, technology delivery and legality, and also other colleagues around the organization whose area of responsibility may be affected in any way.

The concepts that these checklists feed are to ensure that there is no loss of focus on the project, that the risk registers and quantification tools are consistent across the organization and that the ownership of controls and risk activity is clear and accepted by the owner of those responsibilities. Furthermore, they will ensure structured and regular reviews and visibility.

Overview: situation appraisal checklists

The checklists may cover four types of situation:

1. project-generated situations;
2. environmental influences;
3. inherent, operational business issues;
4. business initiatives in parallel.

Plus ongoing measurement of project progress against the project drivers of scope, time and cost, and, of course, risk.

The project-generated risk checklist can be subdivided to reflect many different types of issues, including:

- strategic;
- business;
- project size and scope;
- project organization;
- project planning;
- user implications;
- technical;
- implementation;
- operations' ongoing support.

The environment checklist, for example, may be subdivided to reflect:

- economics;
- legal and regulatory;
- political;
- security;
- business continuity threats.

Managing risks within contracts

Clearly the organization needs to have its pre-agreed governance standards and requirements for any contracts to be agreed with third parties. The value of this is that there are no unexpected responsibilities or risk surprises from managers' individually negotiated contracts. Therefore, the project team should not start out without these standards being clear, and especially without understanding the organization's 'no-go' areas of contracted responsibilities. It does need to remember that often corporate risks lie in the detail, not only in the 'big picture' issues.

Furthermore, one common law principle is that a contract is formed with an offer being made and a perception of acceptance of that offer. It does not, other than in certain exceptions, need to be in writing. A clash of two counterparties' different standard conditions needs not only the lawyer to arbitrate but also the board's view on the operational and risk consequences of accepting a variance from its 'norm'.

There is another common law principle in the UK and elsewhere worthy of note within the context of this section. This principle is that two parties cannot contract to remove the current rights of a third party, for example, an existing stakeholder. A contract that sets out to do so is illegal and so any current legal rights of counterparties and third parties need to be understood and accommodated in the changes proposed.

The ability to claim damages within a contract's wording for contractual failure is not always as straightforward as it sounds. Normally, it is possible to recover only what can be seen to be a reasonably foreseeable loss and that may not include, for example, damage to reputation or management time in resolving a difficulty. Certainly a failure to supply one ingredient may indeed bring down the entire organization that was expecting it. That total collapse will not automatically be seen as a reasonably foreseeable loss of that failure.

The contract may include a penalty clause but in critical supply chain dependencies this financial amount is unlikely to be able to keep the principal organization in business. This is because the non-financial impacts are the ones more likely to remove it from its market-place.

Risk can be excluded or limited under the contract wording but is unenforceable if it is regarded under the terms of the Unfair Contract Terms Act 1977 (UK) as 'unfair' on one party. This could be where the relative negotiating powers of the two parties are significantly imbalanced. This Act creates legal restrictions on liability exclusions, and was extended in 1994 by the Unfair Terms in Consumer Contracts Regulations.

There are other legislative constraints such as the sale of goods and services legislation and the General Product Safety Directive that apply a test of reasonableness. Any 'force majeure' clause may have to pass the standards required in this legislation.

The contract wording may need to embrace the risks around the counterparty itself and embrace guarantees, performance standards and bonds, ownership and access to intellectual and other assets. There are the risks around the future partnership's standards and specifications, limitations and exclusions, financial risks and credit, legalities and, of course, the risks around the jointly produced products themselves.

Finally, in most jurisdictions, should a contract's wording be unclear, it is normally interpreted against the writer of that contract wording.

A major challenge is agreeing contract wording written in peaceful times that is ready to face all sorts of unexpected scenarios.

Farmers who had significant crop damage and then shortages in the 2007 Gloucestershire floods found that they were committed by contract to supply supermarkets at prices fixed when crops were plentiful and sales volumes gave them a living.

Security around sensitive projects

There are two issues to address here. The project may be sensitive in that the impact of the changes may have important implications for others, not least the existing key employees, existing counterparties and customers. In such a case, the information flow needs to be carefully managed and controlled. The project may indeed be 'price sensitive' in that the stock market may react to the proposed changes. Therefore, the project will have important information security and control requirements as it is unfolding.

Following the first major terrorist bomb incident in the City of London, papers were blown from people's desks and distributed around the streets of the city. Some companies did not have at the time, or did not implement, a 'clear desk' policy for the end of the working day as part of their risk management regime.

Much of this information was sensitive to share price, competitor positioning, contract negotiations and relationships with employees and third parties. Much sensitive information had been entrusted to these companies by others, for which they had the important responsibility of secrecy.

The damage to an organization by the uncontrolled release of any of this information could be the most damaging impact of the terrorist incident. This damage could be in cost, in project failure and in reputation.

In later incidents the police took the arbitrary decision to shred all papers found on the streets, as part of incident management and prior to the opening of the site cordons.

Information security is more suited for a book by itself and here we just cover some principles. Security ensures staff knowledge is restricted to a 'need to know' basis as the project unfolds and information standards controls need to be in place throughout. Employees involved need to specifically understand the secrecy requirements and controls. File storage and use, systems' access controls, code names, secure work areas, private telephone lines, emails, document audit trails, stand-alone PCs and networking facilities, and segregated backups are bread and butter secrecy controls, ranging even to regular 'debugging' if the sensitivity assessment requires this. Furthermore, the sensitivity assessment may require screening of the employees and advisers to be involved.

It is the responsibility of the project manager to ensure that the project, if considered urgent and critical to the organization, is included in the wide area continuity planning or has its own. Later in this book there is a separate section on continuity planning and its needs.

Detailed decision making

We have discussed the headlines of ensuring that the project processes and controls do encourage, ultimately, the right decision.

This is not to say that, within one individual project, there will be a host of detail opportunities to consider. The headline issues, however, are there within each individual decision, not least, of course, the tolerances to risk and organization-wide impact.

One example would be whether to brand the product or service delivery in the name of the supplier or the distributor. Should Corn Flakes be branded 'Kellogg's' or 'Tesco'? Should a shampoo be branded in the name of the original manufacturer or as a 'Superdrug' store's own label product?

The balancing act will no doubt embrace the relative strengths and brand awareness of each name, and the cost of the investment that later may or may not then be necessary in creating brand awareness. There will be cost differences between buying in complete packages and in buying wholesale and then packaging internally.

There are also quite different crucial brand, liability and product recall impacts if, for any reason, there is a loss of public confidence in the product. In many businesses the brand value is by far and wide the greatest asset many organizations possess, and risks to that brand value should no less be on the table for careful inclusion at decision time.

Case study

A very topical place for the study of supply chain risks is China, from where an ever increasing number of suppliers and manufacturers source their products and materials.

Mattel, the manufacturer of a wide range of toys, suffered massive financial and reputational loses in 2007 when it was discovered that its products, sourced in China, were unsafe. The reputational damage for Mattel was particularly hard because of the emotions and sensitivities of parents, regulators and also the media around child safety. It needed to recall 380,000 Galaxy Warriors, 43,000 Halloween plastic teeth and 16,000 toy military vehicles allegedly because of the amount of lead paint used in their manufacture. Further recalls included 18 million toys containing small magnets that could become a choking risk.

Many of these toys were sourced from one factory in China and it appeared that Mattel had relaxed its sourcing quality controls with this supplier, with whom it had had a relationship for over 15 years. Other manufacturers and importers from China have watched this unfold in horror and have urgently readdressed their source quality controls, in respect of both individual factories and regions and countries where they cannot rely on sophisticated, quality legislation and the implementation of that legislation, or indeed where local factors such as corruption can dilute the impact of those controls.

China itself, especially the region involved, Guangdong, has recognized this challenge and has urgently set out, with an inspection force said to be 200,000 strong, on an inspection campaign beginning with 1,700 factories. 764 had their licences revoked or suspended and 690 were ordered to make improvements. This is, of course, a classic, 'after the horse has bolted' measure and is still no substitute for any company retaining full vigilance over suppliers' qualities just as it would any internal process. The Chief Officer of the factory, whose main problem seemed to be the paint and other materials used, again sourced from an external supplier, committed suicide.

The direct financial damage to Mattel is, of course, huge but this could pale against the longer-term loss of confidence in its branded products and the ability of competitors to move in and fill the gaps left behind, creating their own replacement, long-term relationships in the process. The reputational damage has a spin-off also to all other industries which source from China, and not only the pet foods, lorry tyres, batteries and toothpaste industries that are safety sensitive and have also suffered recent product recalls. Even China itself may suffer in the long term as manufacturers, nervous of trust issues, litigation and/or recurrences begin to look elsewhere, such as to Vietnam, to supply their materials and products.

4

Risk managing a supply chain dependency or dependencies

The process

This chapter will begin to address the challenges and opportunities of risk managing the supply chain once it is in place. The chapter will continue to assume the underlying principle that risk management is as much about enabling opportunities as it is about worrying about nasty things going bang in the night. Specifically, outsourcing of a supply chain may bring risk management opportunities as well as threats. This is when multi-sourcing through external supply chains can in fact reduce the dependency on one single point of failure.

The chapter will also continue to assume that no truly effective risk management is achievable when it is bolted onto management structures, control procedures and cultures. It cannot work when designed only to enable ticks in a regulator's checkboxes. Understanding risks and dealing with them is simply effective management, and integral within good and measurable management.

Other underlying principles about risk management are repeated here as a specific setting for the chapter:

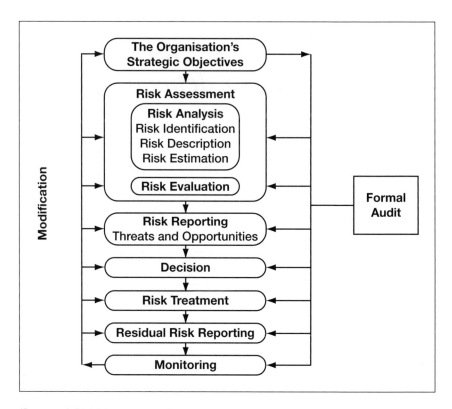

(Source: *A Risk Management Standard*, published by IRM, ALARM, AIRMIC: 2002)

Figure 4.1 The risk management process

Strategic objectives

Those charged with understanding and managing risk of supply chain failure have a few different, but related challenges. We will discuss these challenges and then consider how the supply chain aids them or creates additional problems to be resolved.

The risk management foundation stone will always be a risk management policy that is formally agreed and documented by the board or chief executive.

It is then communicated to the organization's managers and built into the wider governance controls that are in place.

This policy will embrace at least:

- aims and scope of the policy;
- definitions and approaches;
- the organization's appetite for risk;
- the management and governance framework;
- roles and responsibilities;
- assessment, reporting and performance processes;
- the expected management commitment and currency.

The challenges are as given below.

1. Clearly managers need to understand, in a way that is commercially realistic, the risks and the potential impact of risks on their areas of responsibility.

This could not be achieved without risk professionals' own investigations and also without their work being supported by other managers right across the organization. These other managers carry the risks within their operating units, and nobody knows the risks and potential impact of diversions better than they do.

This entails an embedded, consistent risk culture, risk awareness and risk ownership that are consistent throughout all levels of the organization.

2. A formal agreement on the organization's tolerances to risk – that is, the ability to absorb levels of financial and non-financial damage without putting the organization and its stakeholders into unacceptable losses.

This agreement clearly needs to be consistent right across the organization and its value chain if it is going to enable risk activity that is commercially realistic and cost balanced.

3. The ability throughout the value chain also to take and implement the decisions about acceptable and unacceptable risks and impacts.

4. To prepare contingency plans that will work. Such plans bring together pre-prepared resources and people fast enough to enable the organization to manage its way through all the aspects of a potentially destructive crisis.

Contingency plans have many demands on them. One demand that is almost always needed is that the planned response to a potential disaster engineers a common purpose and co-operation right across the whole of the affected enterprise.

This chapter will therefore first discuss the day-to-day elements of implementing effective risk management within an organization and then discuss these elements where they have additional challenges because the supply chain has been outsourced.

Also in this chapter, as indeed elsewhere in this book, the expression 'risk manager' does not just extend to those professionals who may carry this particular title. Generally speaking, it will apply to those persons who have the responsibility to advise the board on risk matters and to place that board in a position where it can make more informed, and therefore better, decisions about risk, impact, risk tolerances and risk management. This source of risk guidance can be from any director or manager who feels that he or she should be addressing risks, and may come from a wide range of quite different risk-related titles or external advisers across the organization. These titles could include any one or more of the following: business continuity managers, internal and external auditors, compliance managers, risk managers, business security managers, insurance managers, facilities managers, purchasing managers, finance directors, regulators, stock market analysts, credit managers, bankers, counterparty relationship managers and credit agencies. Individual stakeholders and potential stakeholders may demand risk understanding.

1. The need to understand, in a way that is commercially realistic, the risks and the potential impact of risks on their areas of responsibility

There can be no effective evaluation of the performance of any business or other organizational unit without knowing the risk levels that that unit is bringing to itself and also to the entire organization. Only then can the perceived rewards from the existence of that unit be measured effectively. High risks, high rewards can be a chosen business strategy, as long as those risks are measured and all stakeholders are comfortable with that formula.

With that understanding, however, the decision may be that the rewards from that division are just not enough to balance the level of risk that it may be bringing to the entire organization. That activity may then close and any remaining activity that is still needed should be handled in a different way.

Some reminders relevant to this chapter

With real risk management, the need is so much more than doing the minimum 'because we have to', e.g. writing a business continuity plan because the regulator or a client requires a tick in a box. To be really effective and worth the paper that it is written on, the risk professional needs to get the message over that risk management is simply one, rather essential, integral part of good management. It is never a bolt-on, nor, especially, a minimum cost centre activity to get a client or regulator off one's back.

Most risk managers will say that embedding a consistent risk culture across the organization is a first-level challenge and one where some of the greatest difficulties lie. It is difficult enough to engineer consistent, owned, ongoing responsibility and activity right across a diverse, multicultural organization. Where crucial and urgent elements of that organization are outsourced, and thus beyond even the board's ability to micro-manage, that difficulty is multiplied many times. Furthermore, when those crucial and urgent elements are overseas, there is a further range of difficulties placed before this first task.

The importance of this uniformity and organization-wide commitment is undoubted. The first reason is that ownership and commitment are crucial if information on risks and potential impacts it to be collected and presented in a consistent format for decision making and then presented on to stakeholder interests. Uniformity of risk and impact definitions and risk tolerances enables the board to prioritize between the many risks presented to it for attention and resources.

Secondly, once the risk strategies and controls are in place, then it is straight back into the organization itself to implement those risk controls and activities (or lack of activities).

Corporate governance procedure documents are not in themselves enough. Risk professionals need to be able to gain the hearts as well as the minds of all other managers within the group. Managers' diaries are totally full of what is already happening. The risk manager's task is to convince them to put aside these urgent and existing problems and divert time and resources into something that may never happen.

Whilst the 'art of management' quote given on page 25 may be extreme, it does make valid points about the challenges of day-to-day management that are not often raised in management textbooks, and brings out, too, the additional challenge for the professionals who need to manage not only current issues, but also more ill-defined risk events that may never happen anyway.

The balancing act is to ensure that the risk professionals, by their very existence, do not give the impression that operational managers or suppliers no longer need to worry about risk – 'because we have someone doing it for us'. The role of the risk professional is a very straightforward one. It is to guide and thus enable the real risk carriers, from the chairman through to everyone responsible for an activity or asset, to make better-informed decisions about risk, risk tolerance and risk management.

It is worth repeating within the context of this section that the risk procedures themselves, and all the risk issues, are best embedded within the existing corporate governance cultures and procedures, rather than trying to develop additional ones. There will be a much greater chance of success if the whole weight of corporate governance, procedures and audits simply take on board the individual risk objectives as set by the risk and continuity manager.

There is the additional hurdle to overcome. Aggressive, forward-thinking, corporate-speak, sound bite driven, career-building, bonus-seeking, competitive and self-assessed 'brilliant managers' find it a struggle to admit to themselves and their besotted admirers that things could actually go wrong on their patch or with their product! Risk managing these people is both a science and an art.

It is crucial, as said earlier, that every single activity is built around one approved, commercially realistic, definition of risk and impact criticalities that bring together, within that one definition, both financial impact and non-financial impacts.

These concepts need to apply not only to risk assessing new situations. The concepts apply equally to the need to keep it all up to date. One certainty for almost all organizations of the 21st century is that risk will change. That change may be an internal one or may be changes in an external threat or environment. Out-of-date risk management is probably no more useful than no risk management at all.

The point we need to keep in mind throughout this book is that these needs apply to every crucial link in the supply chain, whether that link is internal, and subject to the organization's governance controls, or external and thus defined only by the original contract.

Getting risk and the need for business continuity onto agendas and into priorities

The chapter will now move on to examine how someone charged with the matrix responsibility for risk across the organization can engineer the consistent activity that is so crucial to getting the initial risk understood and the resultant risk management activity taking place.

The chapter moves forward this way, looking first at internal infrastructures, and will then bring out some real control problems when we address the additional challenges of creating consistent activity across a supply chain that may be in part internal and in part external, or even overseas.

By the use of 'external', of course, we mean that the outsourced suppliers which, being different legal entities, necessarily have different agendas, different stakeholders, different cultures, different politics and different legality and compliance demands. Furthermore, the control mechanism that ties them and their employees to the recipient organization's needs is no more than a piece of paper drawn up by lawyers in times when it was not known what would go wrong, nor when!

1. Risk tsar

The risk professional needs to impose his or her requirements across the organization and demand time, energy and sometimes money from managers over whom he or she has no reporting responsibility. In effect the risk professional is saying, 'I know your mind and diary are full of what is already happening and your own measured performance objectives. However, I want you to divert your time and resources on something that may or may not happen and, even if it did, may not happen on your watch'.

This is a real challenge to do and especially to get the priorities built into measurable work plans consistently right across the organization. A 'risk tsar' is often appointed from within the existing board with (possibly part-time but certainly) matrix responsibility for ensuring that risk remains on the board agenda, and that there is risk measurement and management activity suitably prioritized right down the layers of responsibility.

Larger business units or subsidiaries need an equivalent role on each subsidiary board or management committee. Risk managers then have an additional reporting line and responsibility to advise and enable each and every one of these directors in turn to engineer consistency and meet the risk responsibilities.

Such a role does not need to be a risk professional, but simply someone with the interest, responsibility and, above all, influence to ensure that timely activity is generated and suitably empowered and prioritized right across the group.

2. Use of audit

The audit committee is a very powerful corporate management control tool. Often made up of executives, non-executive directors, external auditors and others, it has independent powers that are often embedded within regulatory or stock market regulations to demand answers from every level of management and report on them.

Risk management is a clear audit committee responsibility and the risk professional or 'tsar' can usefully be charged to deliver periodic risk presentations, reporting directly into the audit committee. This will advise the members of risk activity, risks accepted, risks managed, risks retained and outstanding risk issues. All departments and responsible individuals that have outstanding and ongoing tasks will be named in this reporting so that the existing audit committee control measures will work naturally to encourage completion of those tasks.

There is another 'soft' but important side benefit. The risk professional can contact any overdue department a couple of weeks before the audit committee meeting to put them on alert that they will need to be mentioned by name. The long-awaited activity and responses may just appear miraculously before the date!

The risk professional can also usefully work with compliance and internal audit teams. These auditors can advise the risk professional of scheduled visits and request a risk comfort level statement. Outstanding matters will then be listed and defined by levels of criticality and urgency. Auditors can schedule these matters into their audit programme, embrace them in the risk report and also report responses and any actions agreed to be completed by timed deadlines.

Again, risk management is thus embedded within existing organizational controls. Such audit teams and their ability to co-operate with suppliers' audit teams and committees will depend entirely on any rights to audit and the extent to which such audit rights are embodied in the original outsourcing contract.

3. Objective setting and performance assessments

Human resources management is able to include risk awareness and activity within employee performance assessment criteria. The routine performance assessments can embrace generic risk issues, as can any project management task setting.

Reviewing managers can then be required to include the risk department in their research prior to undertaking key management performance interviews, feeding the views into the performance assessment discussions. If generic risk appreciation is able, in a measurable way, to be included in key task objectives, there is then a clear incentive to ensure that risk concerns are not bypassed in the single-minded focus on delivering other measurable and bonus-earning objectives.

Once again, any performance assessment of suppliers – in this case, corporation to corporation rather than corporation to individual – can emerge only from any risk measurement criteria and the way that a criterion is measured being built into the contract-based relationships.

4. Corporate governance

Corporate governance sets the levels of both decision making and activity authorities from the board downwards, and they are thus formally stated as part of governance procedures.

Some delegated authorities can be measured simply on monetary 'spending' limits. The potential consequences of a misjudged risk can bear no relationship whatsoever to the original contract value or the cost of an individual piece of work or project. This is especially so with any liabilities that may emerge and damage such crucial issues as legality, supply chain failures, insurability, brand values and workforces.

Therefore, to be risk effective, the delegated authorities need to embrace additional, non-monetary limitations.

5. Board decision making

This need for responsibility control applies no less to the board itself or the chief executive. The limits of the board's own powers will be defined and may, for example, demand an approach to shareholders for certain decisions.

Corporate governance procedures will publicize the structure required for all papers to be presented to the board and/or shareholders for a decision. One demand may be for a mandatory risk section that sets out risks within the proposal, the criticality level suggested, and how the risks or risk tolerances have been measured against group risk management standards. The demand may also be to set out how risks are costed within the proposal. The board may demand that every proposal has potential risks measured within the pre-agreed criticality definitions, and is to include the risk professional's opinion.

6. Constraints on delegated responsibilities

Both the delegated responsibilities to employees and the requirements for inclusions into papers to the board may include at least the following constraints.

Corporate governance

Group directors' and managers' authorities

A. Monetary limits (as a percentage of turnover or budgets – both divisional and group) as decided by the audit committee and the board.

B. Non-monetary controls could exclude authority to make decisions that:

1. could have an impact or change any group brand and reputation;
2. will need changes in group-wide arrangements and services such as the governance, insurance, continuity, health and safety programmes;
3. enter a new country or territory;
4. deliver a new product or service;
5. could impact the market, workforce or product of another division;
6. could affect the legal or regulatory requirements on the group;
7. could affect the confidence of employees and other stakeholders;
8. are likely to attract significant or negative media interest;
9. significantly change the financial gearing of the division; and
10. (a catch all) could change the risk profile of the group or have a bearing on the stated corporate objectives.

C. Any proposals to a divisional board, and to the group board, should always require a statement of risk issues, changes to be made by the proposal to existing risk profiles and how these changes will be managed.

D. No contract will be signed with any third party for *supply or delivery* of goods or services without a documented statement of risk and continuity risks involved and how these risks are factored and priced into the relationship.

7. Getting feedback on risk information

There are many ways of obtaining information consistently across a wide organization. Each of them has its own place and conversely each has its weaknesses and indeed exposure to critical failure. Questionnaires can be sent for completion and be returned. People may be interviewed individually, or workshops and brainstorms can bring teams together to discuss and decide on risk issues. The risk professional can then assess these responses and measure them against his or her wider risk understanding and research, and the group-wide objectives, tolerances and philosophies.

Often one single division or supplier may not fully understand the criticality or urgency of its product as it becomes an ingredient further up the value chain. Risk information is therefore a two-way process. If an ingredient is sourced elsewhere and is crucial to a unit's own delivery, then that unit carries the responsibility to trace that source back and assess and manage the risk of failure. The supplier cannot always be expected to understand the criticality and urgency of, nor the lack of alternatives for, the ingredient further up the supply chain.

The consistent foundation of risk policy, risk definitions, criticality definitions and a clear and authorized placing of responsibilities is the enabler to ensure this process adds real value.

We have already mentioned the need to ensure all other managers share the risk manager's view on the importance and timeliness of considering risks. The 'risk tsar' sat at the top level of management is, of course, a powerful ally in setting measurable work priorities. A challenge for workshops and brainstorms is delegates' apologies, often on the day, sent in 'as something more urgent has cropped up'. The invitation to the workshop needs to be from the 'risk tsar' or chief executive with the clear objectives and deliverables stated.

A workshop can be designed to reduce this risk of absenteeism. If it commences at the beginning of the day there is less chance of a manager being diverted beforehand by a phone call or something in the inbox. The location of the exercise can best be away from the normal work environment to avoid people 'popping back to their desks' at a break to see what is happening. Also, mobiles and other hand-held devices should be turned off with a message desk (notified beforehand) available for real crises.

A halfway house between a surprise exercise and a planned one is for the chief executive to have a routine board meeting or to call a meeting to discuss some other aspect of strategy. With that executive's prior and secret approval, that meeting is then interrupted by a surprise exercise on continuity or other risk threat. This has the people in place but also brings in the valuable element of surprise into the crisis exercise, just like the real thing.

There are challenges to get the best out of risk research, difficult enough within parts of the organization that share the same reporting line, cultures and management control mechanisms. The difficulties multiply tremendously without these drivers towards conformity. Furthermore, if these risk assessments can be demanded prior to the signing of the contract; they are no less needed to ensure that future changes in the internal and external risk profiles are understood and managed.

Once again, the only formal relationship driver between the outsourced supplier and the organization's own ultimate delivery responsibilities is a pre-relationship understanding embodied within the words of a contract. That understanding will even then be sensitive to change, differing agendas, stakeholders and risk tolerances.

Gaining respect

There are 'softer' issues that will enable activity or conversely create a barrier to risk achievements. They go as far as the choice of skill and personality when recruiting the risk manager. It is in part a technical job indeed but it is overwhelmingly a job that requires people skills and leadership skills.

The person must be able to talk to directors and managers in their own language and with an ability to join in their focus on 'the bottom line' organizational objectives. Risk retention and risk management are business opportunities just as much as business controls and the audience will be lost if the risk professional considers only the latter.

Ownership of risk: a postscript

A real danger lies in the response that 'I agree, and what we need is a quick hit!' This 'quick hit' is likely to be the first and also the 'last hit' that will appear as other more immediate pressures take hold. Similarly dangerous is the superficially encouraging response that the importance is understood and the manager 'will get round to it as soon as they have a free afternoon'. Free afternoons just do not exist in the modern business world.

> Dr Henry Kissinger (whilst US Secretary of State) is quoted as saying, 'Next week there cannot be any crisis. My schedule is already full'.

As stated above, there will be benefit in specifically ensuring that risk managers do not imply that they have the responsibility for the risks being carried. That responsibility remains with the most senior executive and, whilst activity can be delegated, responsibility cannot. This applies no less when there are critical and urgent dependables within an external supply chain.

Boards may usefully be reminded that knowledge of a risk is not only a useful decision-making tool. That knowledge, once gained, carries with it an unavoidable need to respond to that knowledge with, first, decisions about the acceptability of that risk and, if unacceptable, what the board is now going to do about it.

There is no option available to make no decision about a known risk. That knowledge also carries another vital responsibility, and that is to advise justifiably interested stakeholders of that risk. These responsibilities may not only be a matter of good stakeholder relationships, they are likely also to be matters of corporate law or regulation.

The risk management environment

As stated at the beginning of the chapter, the real and most difficult challenge of a risk manager is to ensure that the entire organization takes responsibility for the measuring and managing of the risks that come with each activity and asset.

Only then can the most senior executive realistically be confident that there will be fewer unpleasant surprises. However, it goes much further than that. Only then, too, can there be a real understanding of the real performance of divisions across the group, and an ability to report on risk levels to regulators and all the other external stakeholders who have a right to know. These measures include the cost levels of risk and the returns to the stakeholder being made on accepting risk.

Supply chain risks

Ever more so, an important and urgent section of the organization is in the legal and physical hands, not of the board and employees, but an entirely different organization. It becomes immediately obvious that many of the tools and resources available to the risk professional to create activity and consistency are no longer available or are at least much more difficult to implement.

As said, the role and responsibility in understanding the recipient organization's risks are only and specifically as defined in the contract, and no more. The wording, considered in more peaceful times, may not have envisaged the current crisis at all – sadly it may not even have anticipated any failure.

The supplier, responsible to its own stakeholders, may offer sympathy but, where there is a conflict of objective, will always need to respond to those stakeholders' own objectives. A bank, for example, may reconsider its own credit risk assessment, and may consequently demand repayment of a loan for working capital, just as the borrower needs that money to give itself half a chance of recovering from a risk incident. The supplier of call centre services, a crucial customer interface, may be unable to divert staff to the crisis situation because of contracted responsibilities to other clients.

Both of these are critical suppliers to the organization: one supplying credit and the other supplying customer interface. Both 'supplies', if very different, are equally crucial to organizational survival.

All suppliers may simply regard the principal that has been damaged by a risk incident as becoming a high-risk client for their products or services. Suppliers may simply become concerned that they may not get paid and wish to renegotiate the contracts in a way that could destroy the principal's business or financial models. They may have wider concerns that their product is now being included in a final sale further up the value chain that has quality compromises. In many ways, the receiving principal may, as a result of its damage, become in breach itself of the contract between itself and the supplier.

The ability to manage supplier relationships during the principal's own crisis is no less a significant risk matter for risk understanding and management.

This chapter will therefore consider in more depth the contractual issues between suppliers and principals, and, specifically, the need to build in an exit strategy.

Contracting suppliers

It needs to be said right at the beginning that all supply chains need very clear statements of the obligations and expectations around any link between supplier and receiver. That applies no less to relationships between divisions within one corporation as it does between third parties, i.e. different legal entities.

If the supply chain is in part internal, it is likely that a legally drawn contract is not considered necessary and the different parties share the same overall controls, cultures and objectives. It is still crucial, however, that there is a service level agreement that makes those obligations clear.

One example would be for an information services department to agree a service level agreement with any of the other divisions of the organization that depends on its technology infrastructure and services. Such an agreement would define the service levels, and would probably include acceptable levels of outage periods and, of course, budgets. A common omission, however, is that such a service level agreement defines only the service delivery 'in good times'. It does not define in that same contract what contingency services the organization could expect from information services in exceptional circumstances, e.g. in the event of flooding or fire of the primary computer farms.

The service level agreement should also define what is, in effect, promised within the information services contingency planning in matters of lost data, software reinstatement, maximum time outage of the central processing, communication technologies and reinstatement of end user workstations and equipment.

There are important values of such a contingency service level inclusion in the service level agreement. The first is that the expected contingency service levels are communicated clearly to the 'customer', which then becomes charged with assessing whether that planned service level will enable it to meet its own crucial and urgent continuity services to its own customers.

This will lead to negotiation, if levels are thought to be unacceptable, towards a contingency service level that the 'customer' feels able to accept, and agreement on the inevitable cost implications.

Another value is that the decision making around acceptable levels of spend and resources applied to contingency planning is moved into, or approved by, the departments that best understand the sensitivities about their own delivery responsibilities. Should the user reject the speed or quality of disaster response as inadequate for urgent and critical business needs, then it is a straightforward matter for the information services manager to produce a budget for the upgrade of contingency planning.

The operational managers then have the choice of agreeing the investment or perhaps reconsidering what they had previously considered essential.

The user of such services therefore takes ownership of the contingency service levels and has sole responsibility in making the cost–benefit decisions about levels and speed of recovery.

All this is relatively straightforward where there is a consistent approach to engineering this relationship, understanding and agreement. There are always opportunities, too, for the board or chief executive to arbitrate between divisions. Where some of those players, however, are third parties with no arbitration tool other than the agreement established in the contract wording, the challenges rise exponentially.

The outsourcing contract document

The very first challenge may be that the contract is worded by lawyers, and may then be additionally subject to interpretation in the minefields of law courts. Any lack of clarity in that contract wording is construed against the writer and, in a supply/delivery counterparty relationship, that writer is often the receiver of the goods or services, perhaps the one most at risk of supply chain failure.

Above all, the principal needs to be reassured within the wording that the supplier's own contingency planning suitably prioritizes the principal's own risk and recovery concerns. The supplier, not unnaturally, will have prioritized its own survival needs and this may only include the needs of those large customers that are sufficiently important to it that their needs are in themselves survival issues for the supplier itself.

We have already stated that any corporate bullying by a powerful buyer over a less powerful supplier is likely to be thrown out by the courts under the terms of the Unfair Contract Terms Act 1997 (UK) removing, at a stroke, any risk protections the organization thought that it had demanded.

Finally, a lawyer is a lawyer, not a manager. The temptation is to leave the wording to the lawyer, relaxed in the assurance that either: a) the wording transfers the risk to the supplier; or b) that if the supplier fails we can within the contract wording successfully sue it for financial compensation. Should that supplier fail its principal in the delivery of a critical ingredient of some urgency, and in turn the principal is removed too long from its own market-place, no amount of monetary compensation will replace the principal's ultimate and complete corporate failure. Furthermore, suing a weakened supplier is likely to push it over the brink and cause the collapse of any chances of supply being reinstated.

Indeed, legally drawn up contracts between counterparties are vital tools in law and to define service expectations in good times and in bad, but their purpose can only be to reflect, not create, the sharing of agreed principles and common objectives around the relationship. Planned only as a weapon, it can fire in two opposing directions where critical and urgent supplies are the reason for its existence.

Where the negotiations are in themselves a one-sided battle between a powerful organization and a much weaker supplier, the temptation to use that power to squeeze the supplier can rebound appallingly. The contract itself can become the risk.

Risk management strategies

Once a risk assessment identifies a link in the supply chain to be critical and possibly urgent, clearly that risk needs to be managed. The risk can, as in all risk management, be designed out. The decision may, for example, be that suppliers in certain insecure countries be excluded from the selection process. The impact can be reduced down to acceptable levels, by, for example, having a twin and totally independent parallel source of the ingredient. The risk management choice could be the decision to use the suppliers so that the loss of one would only slow productivity for a time and ensuring that emergency supplies remain within an acceptable level.

The risk can be transferred to a third party; but we have already said that a consequence of a critical and urgent supply chain failure is quite hard to fully transfer out. It may indeed be possible to impose penalty clauses within the contract, or to sue a failing supplier under the contract terms. These values are, however, peripheral and a sideshow to the real damage being caused to the receiving organization. The subject of insurability, its promises and minefields, is covered in another chapter.

The remaining risk management strategy is to prepare for the loss, and position resources and information that will enable the loss to be effectively managed without unacceptable damage. Normally described as continuity management or resilience management, this needs all the resources, responses and reaction tools of the organization's wider continuity planning that can interface comfortably with whatever emergency exit strategies are built into the outsourcing relationships.

There are many additional challenges to the risk professional's ability to continually understand and embed risk, even within his or her own organization:

- supply chain failure can come from distant links of the chain;
- the insurance market may well be unable to provide real survival assistance;
- there are different agendas, ownerships of critical assets and stakeholder responsibilities likely to conflict as organizations strive to create a consistent response to a disaster;
- legal processes may well be unable to provide real assistance;
- risk attitudes, cultures, controls and tolerances will vary throughout the chain.

The risk management challenges and opportunities amongst external suppliers are almost certainly more than in any other type of risk, and are primarily in the relationship management that is planned well before the risk strategies and the contracts are concluded. We have at this point come to a reinforcement of a point made earlier in the book. It is just not achievable for a secret project team to negotiate and conclude outsourcing arrangements and then to subsequently approach risk and continuity managers to develop risk strategies.

'There is no magical number that you can call to extricate yourself from such predicaments. You are in a fix; you get yourself out of it. It is that simple. There is no way to run a sausage machine backwards and get pigs out of the other end. After all, if a solution was that simple, it would not be a crisis.'

(Norman Augustine, *Harvard Business Review on Crisis Management*, 1995)

The exit strategies need to be built into the relationships, equally whether that 'exit' is a planned moving on or a sudden failure that brings about a surprise and immediate exit. They are two quite different circumstances but they share many common denominators. We will develop the discussion on those differences and similarities in a later chapter. Before we do so, it will be of value to establish some ground rules by taking a critical look at the precise dependencies that may have been handed over to one or more third parties.

5

Dependencies outsourced

The crown jewels

This chapter will take a look at some individual abilities and dependencies that have been passed over into the hands of third-party individuals and corporates. We will consider how the access to, and ability to control, these dependencies may then not be possible, and the fact that contract wording with counterparties is now the only roadmap to future operability. The needs for access and use may change within the contract period and, of course, there may be the need to recover them back again in the event that the relationship, for any reason, is failing the corporate objectives. That need, of course, may be crucial to survival and is one to be secured before, and not after, changes or problems emerge.

For the purposes of this chapter, we are assuming that the assets and abilities discussed have already been identified in the risk register as ones that are crucial to service delivery and possibly that urgency itself is a crucial dependency. 'Crucial' may be defined in many ways and each organization will have its own pressure points and sensitivities. It is possible in a book such as this only to cover headlines and even then there can be different, equally credible, cuts on these headlines. However, it is important above all to look beyond the obvious and touchable needs and see the softer ones as at least as destructive and possibly more so. We have in an earlier chapter set out to define what crucial dependencies are.

The crown jewels may be an individual dependency in another single organization or it can be the dependency in an entire industry, country or culture. Following the Mattel toy safety crisis and other quality scandals, the provincial authorities in Guangdong undertook a survey of manufacturers' quality and safety standards. Guangdong is where 60 per cent of the world's toys are manufactured and the 200,000 surveyors visited 1,726 factories. A total of 85 per cent of the factories inspected had their licences revoked or were ordered to renovate their facilities. This is at a time when China is beginning to lose out to its rival Vietnam for the location of some of its labour intensive industries.

Another and more detailed cut in establishing the key elements that make up a modern organization is as below.

The organization's stated objectives

Cultures

- Stakeholder relationship management
- Intellectual assets and their importance
- Market and contractual expectations
- Current projects
- Tolerance to uncertainty

Market positioning

- The agreed strategic direction
- Growth and competitive strategies
- Sensitivities to holding market positioning
- Brand management and wider confidence

Overall organizational structure

- Maintaining capital, revenues and cash flow models
- Logistics control processes
- People skills and employee relationships
- Intellectual assets and knowledge transfer
- Risk and control environment
- Audit trails
- Legality
- Compliance
- Technology
- Web-enabled processes and assets

- Workstations, engineering materials and machinery
- Environmental management
- Communication tools throughout the value chain and between all other stakeholders
- Information, asset and people security

Delivery logistics from raw materials to finished goods

- People skills
- Transportation and storage – inwards and outwards
- Packaging
- Material handling logistics and inventory controls
- Order processing
- Electricity and possibly gas
- Industrial water and drinking water
- Technology support and maintenance
- Demand forecasting and responses
- Procurement processes and contracting
- Receiving and processing returned goods
- Customer and service support, including advice and parts
- Environmentally achievable waste disposal

It is of course possible that an organization can successfully transfer the administration of some risks to a third party, but what is not possible is the transfer of responsibility for that risk in so far as it affects the stakeholders of the organization itself. As that responsibility for risk therefore remains unable to be delegated, it follows that the organization has the unavoidable responsibility to ensure that the administration of those risks are to a standard acceptable to the organization's own governance control processes and stakeholder needs.

Furthermore, if in the contract wording there is an enthusiastic transfer of risk itself from the purchaser to the supplier, the latter will no doubt be pricing that risk into the negotiations on price and terms, thus costing the principal a risk premium within the price agreements eventually reached. The mismatch may be that the supplier's tolerance for risk may be different to that of the principal, with the result that the principal may be paying the wrong cost for uncertainty management.

The ability to deliver in volumes, in quality and in time

The obvious place to start is the fact that the organization has most likely removed its own ability to supply some elements that are necessary ingredients of the final product to be delivered on. This could be a vehicle manufacturer transferring the chassis creation to another. It could be vital technology and information services, or it could be that the only ability to interface with customers has been transferred to a third-party call centre service or webmaster.

We have raised the concern that some risk assessments or business impact assessments spend a great deal of energy trying to assess what misfortune could come along and cause harm. The concern is that such a concentration loses the focus on the dependability itself yet the key issue is not the cause of failure, but precisely how that loss of service or access will hurt the organization. Whilst different causes can create damage, the cause is (almost) irrelevant, during the crisis itself. An organization struggling with the loss of a client database is not really concerned whether the cause was flooding, fire or technological. It does not really matter to the organization's immediate problems if the delivery failure was a shipping disaster, civil disorder, customs restraints or a local petrol strike. What does matter is that delivery has stopped and the particular financial, operational and market-place implications of such a stoppage.

Should we need to reinforce the point about weaknesses in only looking at potential causes of loss rather than impact, we need only to look back at the scenarios listed in Chapter 3, at the causes of some recent disasters that had not figured at all in scenario planners' 'blue-sky thinking'. Sadly, disasters continually have the capacity to surprise and set unperceived levels of difficulty.

Each of the ingredients identified as critical, those that are either touchable and/or intellectual, needs to be assessed. That need may be one not only of urgency but also of immediacy. If the risk level is not acceptable then decisions, activity and/or investment is needed to risk manage each and every one of those things needed to enable delivery to the point that the risk of failure reduces down to acceptable levels.

A dependency on electricity supplies may be such that risk expenditure considered may be to provide backup generators with adequate fuel supplies. A risk measure could be that the legal ownership and accessibility of an always current client database be established within a contract to outsource to a call centre, as well as the software that makes that database useable. It would need continuous and live backups into software within the organization's own physical and legal environment.

Case study

The Gloucestershire floods 2007

In July 2007 there were serious floods in Gloucestershire. There had been a dependency on Central Networks to provide risk management around a power distribution site that is a major infrastructure dependency for hundreds and thousands of homes, businesses, hospitals, farms, care homes and other crucial dependencies. It was the massive infrastructure dependencies created by the inability to provide supplies around these plants to the community that should have been the risk management driver.

That risk protection could have taken the position of either careful protection of the assets, and/or the ability to divert power and water from national grids into the areas affected by the failure of the one site.

Both plants were in a well-known flood plain. Flood protection around the site would have been relatively inexpensive to do, complemented by investment in the ability to bypass the plants.

Even as custodians of such major infrastructure dependencies, and even with the reporting of eye-watering profits, sadly, neither of these risk measures was in place. It needed hundreds of fire and rescue personnel, supported by many hundreds more military personnel, funded by the taxpayer, to work over 15 hours non-stop to construct a sandbag wall kilometres long around the power site to save the large community from power failures. These personnel were diverted from helping thousands of Gloucestershire residents whose lives, homes and livelihoods were at risk.

Sadly, Severn Trent Water, a company again announcing record profits of over £300 million, similarly failed at this most basic level. Despite the heroic work of yet more emergency services personnel, 150,000 residents were without water for as much as two weeks and were without safe drinking water for much longer. Major infrastructure services such as hospitals had to cancel thousands of operations and, for example, patients requiring kidney dialysis treatment had to make daily 100-mile round trip journeys to Birmingham.

This failure to meet simple good management standards is an example of where customers rely on service suppliers, and without a critical assessment of risk and consequences on their behalf, they are failed. Had the suppliers done so, no 'recovery plan' would have been necessary for these two major dependencies.

The Gloucestershire power and water failures are also an example of the importance of risk managers taking care to understand how risks constantly change around them. A major organization in Gloucestershire, with just one of its buildings housing 1,000 people, had considered the risk of power failure. Based on past experience, it was thought that the maximum likely period of failure could be 12 hours. This was based on experience of previous 'time-outs' and the ability of the power distribution company to quickly reinstate supplies. The view was also based on an assumption that in the event of a catastrophic failure of one switching plant, that power could be diverted around that plant to customers. That assumption is now known to be seriously flawed, changing the risk profile of any organization depending on Central Networks for its power.

Therefore, an erstwhile risk management decision to install ports into the building to enable a mobile generator to be sourced and connected may not now be the correct risk management response, especially now that it is understood that this failure could affect an entire county and 600,000 people simultaneously. The risk manager may now decide, in the light of this new risk information and with a mind, as always, to the criticality and urgency of the building's role, to invest much more in installing the building's own stand-by generator.

Delivery and its components

Acceptable supplier delivery includes the necessary volumes and expected quality and consistency, as well as being in time for the crucial need. The contract may demand that the supplier has a 'contingency plan' to ensure deliveries are maintained. We have cautioned about the dangers in ensuring that the plan is workable and embraces the receiving organization's own critical risks. Such a plan is of no value whatsoever to the receiving organization if it embraces only the supplier's own survival risks. The subject of continuity planning is addressed in a different chapter.

Clearly, and before any contracts are in place, the risk managing organization needs to have its own survival plan B in place with all the control issues, the hard and the soft ingredients, re-accessible and in time. This plan B is a bringing together of the exit plan perhaps already set within the project, with an additional layer of planning that can respond to a sudden and unexpected loss of the supply. Both embrace the logistics of replacing the service asset or product in time to meet obligations and to retain one's position in the market-place but the pressures of a sudden and unexpected loss are far more dramatic and critical.

Therefore, risk managing delivery uncertainties combines process engineering that is able to react to the loss effectively and adequately, with taking care that the entire counterparty relationship reduces as best as possible the risk of failure. Clearly, the most effective continuity management is that which ensures that there is no 'disaster' to manage.

However carefully that relationship is managed there always remains the risk of change or disaster that will close down completely that supplier's ability to deliver. That plan B therefore will need to assume, in the worst-case scenario, that the supplier has totally failed as an organization and the receiving organization will need to source its ingredients from somewhere entirely different. Keeping such contingency supply options open or retaining dual supply sources is a risk management matter and potentially a risk management investment.

A customer may demand that the supplier maintains a supply of completed stock at all times ready for delivery. One example could be a health service demanding that a supplier keeps an emergency supply of drugs always available in case of an epidemic or pandemic. This brings two challenges: one is the capital, storage and security cost of that standing stock. The other is the fact that the stock must always be current and within its sell-by date.

The cost is, of course, to be priced within the contract price and the currency can be managed by the supplier feeding all new stock through that same warehouse, replacing stock when sold and ensuring that the stock levels never fall below the minimum demanded. This process can be used in a wide variety of circumstances to manage the impact of delivery disruptions.

A further way that ingredient disruption can be minimized is to ensure, wherever achievable, that as many ingredients as possible conform to the same specification. A motor car manufacturing group will have many common ingredients, e.g. switches, cabling, engines and chassis. Variances will only be in the areas that are necessary to differentiate the models and brands across the group. This again will raise opportunities for cross supply of parts in the event of failure.

The converse, however, is that if there is only one source of supply of an ingredient that is needed across a wide range of models and subsidiaries, then that failure will provide extensive additional failures simultaneously right across the group. It could not only close the product down but also the entire organization.

Brand and confidence

Reputation is coming more and more to the forefront of an organization's risk agenda. There is, seemingly, increasing publicity about corporate failures giving the impression that total failures are increasing. This indeed may be so as modern business models create more focus on single risks that are each potentially enterprise-destructive. Whether as a consequence or as a cause, corporate governance and regulatory requirements are becoming tougher to satisfy and regulators are becoming more sophisticated in their implementation. Stakeholders are more aware and active, especially with the web and email as communication tools, and as the media takes more and more interest in perceived abuses of corporate power and influence.

We can relate this back to the comments early in this book that the modern business model, that entails much of its operations and its value chain being outsourced, can fairly be described as a hollow business. This means that, however multinational, and however many billions worth of value, there are few human beings 'at home' and it consists in the operational sense of very few, but each vitally important, ingredients. One of these ingredients was stated to be its brand values and its wider confidence amongst its range of stakeholders.

Brand and reputation therefore have become ever-increasing parts of the perceived total value of organizations. The value also embraces the value of future profits and therefore corporate valuers need to be sure that the organization will remain to deliver on those promises too. In Coca-Cola, for example, about 4 per cent of combined share value is measurable in 'hard' assets. The rest is presumably in the intellectual assets, most of which can be described as 'brand value'.

Therefore the modern business model is much leaner and with much less margin for error. Its ability to absorb surprise has reduced significantly, and thus understanding its risks and managing them has never been more critical. The ever-increasing interest in its reputation and in the resilience of the organization is a natural development of these concerns.

The brand can be measured in monetary terms and is often priced into the amount of money that changes hands during mergers and acquisitions. It can, however, be much more than monetary value, even the very thing on which an organization survives or does not survive, in its public service or commercial market-place.

A total of 160 million bottles of Perrier, the French mineral water, had to be withdrawn from sale worldwide after traces of benzene, a solvent which has been linked with cancer, was discovered.

The decision to dispose of the distinctively shaped bottles cost an estimated £40 million and was taken despite Perrier's insistence that the 'infinitesimal' traces of the toxic substance discovered in supplies did not pose the slightest threat to consumers' health.

This financial cost, however, was a fraction of the reputational damage and the opportunity it gave for competitors to seize elements of their market that had until then almost been Perrier monopolies.

The management of the risks to brand must be consistent with the organization's strategic objectives and day-to-day activities. As in risk management, brand management cannot be fully successful if it is seen to be distant from the way the organization runs its mainstream activities and even distant from other risk management activity. Therefore, with reputation we retain again the challenges of managing risk when crucial and urgent activities and assets, in this case, reputation, are under the control of third parties. These challenges are made much more difficult by the combination of loss of control and the much more indistinct nature of reputation and brand value.

Brand management will eventually fail if left, in isolation, to a department of 'spin doctors' who are skilled in uttering corporate speak that bears little or no relation to the qualities delivered by other parts of the organization's value chain. Brand value protection comes in various parts:

- delivering products that match expectation, i.e. as described in 'the packaging';
- doing that consistently;
- ensuring that the target audience is aware of the qualities on offer;
- managing problems and failures in such a way that the brand can be maintained or even enhanced.

'Products' to customers can be anything from machinery parts to complete aeroplanes and also services from financial promises for the future to safely repairing motor cars. 'Products' to other stakeholders is a much wider concept and can range from trust for employees to value for investors, visibility for regulators and a wide variety of other stakeholder expectations. Above all, it can mean that the organization conducts itself in such a way that it will not encourage aggressive media attention and the enthusiastic searching out for villains to portray and complete the balance in its storylines.

To protect and retain this value, the organization does not only need to deliver on its promises of service, product quality and time, but also needs the wider world to always feel that it will do so into the future. Brand management, therefore, is not only about delivering, it is also about managing expectations. The need is for the public to be able to have confidence that it has, and will have, what it is that they had expected it to have, no more, no less. If that expectation was unreasonable and incorrectly focused, then that 'no less' is a brand management issue.

Sometimes doing nothing where brand is under threat is not an option. One of our bullet points above is not only about meeting those expectations 'in good times' but also facing up to the spotlight when the organization is expected to respond to difficult circumstances. An effective and concerned crisis response can illustrate, from right within the spotlight, how serious an organization is about its qualities and its stakeholders. Handled well at that time, it is an opportunity for brand building that could bring the equivalent value of countless pounds of publicity and marketing investment. Handled badly at that time, again in such a spotlight, it can just as easily turn a problem into a reputational, and thus an organization-wide, disaster.

Indubitably, therefore, the counterparties that form an outsourced supply chain are truly integral to all of these crucial responsibilities, and to the survival and recovery opportunities and threats.

There are countless examples of where brand damage has destroyed an organization or reduced it into something that did not enjoy its earlier positioning and value. Just a few are:

- ENRON (criminality and fraud at the very top);
- Anderson Consulting (association with such fraud and criminality leading to other organizations fearing lack of trust to be seen to be advised or audited by them);
- Perrier Water (inclusion of pollutants);
- Barings Bank (lack of basic elementary internal control);
- Next and Nike (child labour);
- British Airways (employment conditions within a supplier).

It needs to be said that brand and reputation is not just a concern for commercial, competitive organizations. It can no less be a concern for public service companies and charities too. The concern here is that the clients or customers of such services will react in a different way in the event that that trust is lost, as in the case study of the British Passport Office failure, below.

'From early in 1999, the Passport Agency had increasing difficulties in meeting the demand for passports.

They had a target of issuing a passport in 10 working days but delays occurred and were creeping up to 25 days, 50 days and by June 1999 there were 600,000 applications awaiting processing.

How could this be when passports had been successfully issued for the best part of a century? The problems occurred because the Passport Agency had embarked on a number of changes simultaneously and had not assessed the risks attached to each one and certainly not to the coincidence of problems occurring together. The Agency were simultaneously seeking to do three things. They were implementing a new policy of issuing child passports, introducing a new IT system and also relocating a lot of staff to new offices.

All this was going on without any pilot tests to see if it could be achieved and without any training of the staff in the new IT system. They were doing this against a timetable that had been set for political reasons because the Secretary of State said that this was all going to happen by a specific date without consideration as to how long it would take to achieve.

So, a failure to assess the risks and the coincidence of risks eventuating together caused the enormous backlog, with a great deal of worry for the public and business trips held up, etc. What they also did not allow for was a 'run on the bank' because when people found that their passports were taking a day or longer to arrive they all pitched in and created even greater delays.'

(Speech by Sir John Bourn, Comptroller and Auditor General, National Audit Office, UK for the Institute of Risk Management in June 2001)

The essence of the Passport Agency problem was that it was riding not just three significant risks but that there was a fourth and perhaps most difficult risk: the ambition to do these all at the same time.

Perhaps the protection of the brand value is the most important thing that an organization will find itself outsourcing with the new arrangements. It certainly has the capacity to cause the most immediate and destructive of organizational damage. It is indeed indistinct and difficult to keep under control. The two dimensions, the importance of ongoing protection and also being able to respond quickly when under threat, are both absolutely vital.

Clearly both ongoing management and response are much more difficult to do when the brand and reputation has come under the immediate care of a third party.

It is also possible for the risk manager's own organization to fall foul of a counterparty's own branding damage. Perhaps the most famous of all is the damage to Arthur Andersen which had a massive backlash to its own reputation as the auditors of Enron. Many organizations felt uncomfortable with their own image portrayal had they continued to have an Arthur Andersen approval of their published accounts and statements.

Moody's also suffered reputational damage when Northern Rock Building Society had a well-publicized reputational failure and customer 'run on the bank' shortly after it had confirmed a good credit rating.

Lambeth Housing Association, The UK Education Authority and the UK Criminal Records Bureau suffered in 2007 as well as Capita itself when the media reported on a letter bomb campaign that targeted the latter company.

The Times included in its report:

- 'hundreds complained' when they ran the Lambeth housing benefit system;
- Education Minister 'deeply dissatisfied' when they failed to check all school staff by start of 2002 school year;
- alleged misuse of individual learning accounts spend of £265 million;
- whilst valued at £2.9 billion dubbed by opponents as 'Crapita';
- accused of 'bidding deliberately low' to secure contracts then going over budget;
- UK Criminal Records Bureau delayed 'badly' by Capita'.

The Times February 6, 2007

Protecting the brand is, of course, the ongoing art of conducting oneself as an organization in a way that media and other commentators cannot find criticisms to broadcast. It is also about security envelopes around information and activities that may be damaging or misunderstood.

This now needs to bring in suppliers too and others whose name may be closely identified with the risk manager's own organization. It is in particular about suppliers maintaining relationships with all their customers and other stakeholders in such a way that they feel that they are receiving no less than expected. As in Andersen's relationship with Enron, the other organizations audited by Andersen suffered brand and confidence issues because of their association with that firm, yet had no part to play in the Enron/Andersen relationship per se. Many felt that they needed to move auditors quickly to reinstate that trust in their published accounts and governance.

Branding and reputation are more than the perception that drives a customer to remain or a prospective customer to buy. It goes to the very heart of the financial models of the organization, as the perceived value of its hard assets and intellectual assets, such as brand, will dictate the cost of capital and terms on which third-party organizations will contract for services and products. Reputation and confidence can be a reason why employees join the organization, remain or leave.

It is remarkably difficult to continually manage the reputation of a large and diverse organization, especially a multinational that may spread over many different cultures, legalities, values that are attached to safety and environment and also child and adult employment practices.

Life is thankfully not as simple as it was in the 19th century:

'We must find new lands from which we can easily obtain raw materials and at the same time exploit the cheap slave labour that is available from the natives of the colonies. The colonies would also provide a dumping ground for the surplus goods produced in our factories.'

(Cecil Rhodes, the 19th-century colonialist, quoted in *Reputational Risk; A question of trust*, Derek Atkins, Ian Bates, Lynn Drennan, 2006)

The media

The media of course is a wholesale purveyor of reputations, both good reputations and bad. Mostly it enjoys the bad ones as the news media pursues its own ratings wars by being in the business of entertainment as well as informing the public. The journalist Kate Adie coined the phrase 'info-tainment' to describe the approach taken by many news editors with 24-hour, 7-day week news programmes to fill. The implication is that every story must have a human victim and a villain in order to capture and retain the viewer's interest. With a victim in place, corporates so easily fill the public's vision of villainy.

> 'News is something someone doesn't want to see in print. All the rest is advertising.'
>
> (Randolph Hearst)

In summary, the difficulty of brand risk management and threat response is increased multifold where key elements of the value chain do not even come under direct control of the organization's own most senior managers. There are no easy answers but it does reinforce very strongly the importance of pre-contract operational and reputational due diligence. It also reinforces the importance of an ongoing partnership between suppliers and principals that work closely together to maintain the ethics of each. If a compromise between standards and cultures must be made then that compromise must be clearly understood as a risk, evaluated and then formally accepted and/or otherwise managed.

Technology

There are so very few businesses in the 21st century that do not have crucial dependencies on technological processes and/or technologically stored information.

Before considering the risks in technology and, in particular, the technological logistics that have been outsourced, it may be useful to begin this section with a sideways and risk-related look at what technological logistics have brought to the modern day organization.

- Computerization has over the years replaced very large numbers of trained and experienced staff who are no longer on the payroll and thus accessible to give support. Some skills have become extinct, as some processes are now almost all done by technological software. Some product development, for example, large product design engineering, is so technological that it can only be developed and maintained technologically.
- The opportunities brought by computerization have enabled – and changed forever – the ability to have live-time and simultaneous relationships with a massive number of individual customers. Layers of wholesalers and intermediaries have been removed from the supply chain and customer relationship management. Such intermediaries could have been vital resources in a crisis for both suppliers and customers.

- Huge databases can be mined instantaneously and segmented from entirely different angles, from different perspectives and for different needs, to supply the baseline product and client information and for other targeted communications.
- Computers retain an audit trail for the satisfaction of financial recording, for internal and external controls, compliance and other legal reasons.
- Management, quality control, marketing, product and other information is instantly accessible from within the information databases held.
- There is strong credibility in the completeness and accuracy of computerized outputs.
- Corporate process standards, controls and formulae are built into the software.
- Other interested departments and authorized third parties and partners can gain access to an up-to-date, common database.
- Sensitive information (whether corporate, client, employee, counterparty or third party) is secured.

These values in the way computerization is used have of course become, conversely, crucial dependencies on which the entire organization depends.

There are underlying risk issues, which are endemic to both values and dependencies, to consider when thinking about technological frameworks.

One is the safety and accessibility of the intellectual assets, the software and the data, over which the technology is custodian. Are they all safe whatever happens? And can they be accessed and useable, fast enough, and trusted, should the primary storage facility be damaged? Accessibility is not just technological – the access must enable use for the purpose needed. 'Use for the purpose intended' will embrace legality, compliance, ownership, contract constraints and other needs, as well as the operational ability to process and communicate that information, fast enough to meet commercial and stakeholder needs.

'Accessibility' embraces all of the hardware, communications, interfaces with staff and equipment, end user equipment in sufficient numbers and bandwidth for the organization to get back 'in business' fast enough to be able to survive.

Should anyone consider that they can continue the business after a technology supplier failure by using people and paper whilst waiting for a computer system to be reinstated, they need to carefully consider each and every one of the dependencies listed above. They will also need to consider any others that are organization specific.

Therefore, we must consider not just the need for the information stored and the need to reinstate the service delivery, but just how fast that service delivery is needed if the organization is to remain alive, keep its stakeholders on board and remain in its market-place. In differing businesses that need for speed could be measured in seconds, minutes, hours, days or even weeks. Business continuity managers sometimes refer to this need as 'maximum time out' or 'MTO'.

The crucial dependencies that may have been outsourced therefore include access to the hardware needed, the data and, also, all of the software that make it useable. That software may have been developed by, or for, the supplier or it is likely to be licensed specifically to that supplier. Software manufacturers protect their licensing boundaries and their wider product security by the use of code words that may or may not be advised to the purchasers. These code words are crucial to the ability to undertake any technological maintenance and may even make the use of the software date limited. The software may be licensed, and thus technologically limited, to one (supplier's) building.

Should any such software – internal or elsewhere in the supply chain – be identified as crucial, these code words need to be risk managed too and emergency access agreed by contract. This contract may not only be with the service supplier, but also with the supplier of the software services. This will include, of course, the recognition, in the primary risk assessment, of the software designer as a primary dependency.

Access, for example, may be by storage with a third party (lawyer or bank?) with the circumstances enabling access pre-determined by contract that is also filed safely with the storage facility.

It is too easy, of course, to overlook the software developer and maintenance team as a crucial link in any supply chain. A difficult learning point during the terrorist attack on the World Trade Center was that the multinational financial services companies could transfer dealings to staff in Zurich, London, Tokyo and elsewhere but found they had critical dependencies on small software developers that were damaged in the same set of buildings.

Any organization-critical data is, of course, another key dependency, whether that be current client information or the formulae and other data around which that operating data is processed. In most businesses, that data will need to be right up to date for the organization to illustrate to itself, its regulators and its stakeholders that it remains in control of the business.

The definition of 'up to date' will have different meanings and criticalities in different organizations: some will see this can only be live-time accuracy. Clear legalities and downloading live-time data to file servers under the control of the risk managers' own organization will in some circumstances be the only acceptable risk management of that data. Others may be happy with a worst-case loss of one week's data, confident that they can reinstate the lost data and throughout be able to illustrate that effective control remains in place.

These risk challenges are difficult enough when the computerization and its own dependencies of communications and end user equipment are in-house. The challenge, above all, is to ensure that the levels and speeds of computer recovery planning meet all business-critical needs. This decision is, of course, an operational decision and not a technological one. Conversely, any technological recovery planning that delivers more than the critical and urgent needs is a waste of money and resources. Getting this focus right across an external supply chain, with two or indeed many more organizations' pressure points and individual Achilles' heels, is a much greater challenge.

Contingency planning of computerization

This book will consider contingency planning as a separate subject but it is important here to remember also that many computer failure response plans do, in effect, outsource that response to specialist contingency suppliers. They are no less a part of a critical supply chain even if their need is hopefully infrequent or even, never. This particular outsourcing contract will only be needed under a dire emergency that is already threatening the survival of the entire organization.

Due diligence enquiries therefore are absolutely vital to ensure that this contingency service will not only deliver as promised, but that the promise is in the first place carefully defined and understood. Exercising is valuable but no exercising, however carefully worked through, can replace an actual incident and its fresh surprises.

The concept is that the contracted contingency supplier will agree to maintain hardware, workstations and communications equipment to enable processing to continue from its own contingency site or by bringing in replacement equipment to the customer's own site, if still useable. The package of needs will include the facilities, of course, but also confidence, security, 24/7 accessibility and the supplier's own technological support staff.

Preparedness

111

One important risk feature is the fact that, to be commercially realistic, the supplier will maintain equipment less than what is needed if all its customers invoked their contract simultaneously. The gap between it keeping 100 per cent of all equipment ready for each and every client and commercially realistic reality is within its own risk management processes, whereby the supplier will assess the numbers of clients likely to invoke at the same time and then resource accordingly. This assessment may be on geographical areas or some other boundaries and it will restrict the number of clients within those boundaries to its ability to deliver contingency services. However, as risk continues to bring surprises, this can never be a guarantee.

This necessarily will retain the risk of the failure of that risk management process, e.g. if the scale of the incident is unprecedented and unexpected. There are sadly many examples where incidents have brought new boundaries of impact, not least the terrorist attack on the World Trade Center in New York in 2001, the Asian Tsunami, UK floods in 2007, the 1993 terrorist attack on London and Hurricane Katrina.

Some organizations, sensitive to their own risk registers and urgencies, may decide that such a shared facility will not bring them the reassurances that they seek. They will then hold their contingency facilities in-house and/or arrange with the outsourcing contingency service supplier to provide or manage for them a dedicated recovery site. This, is of course, much more expensive and the difference in cost would have to stand the test of a cost–benefit analysis in the light of the perceived impact assessment of not doing so.

As stated elsewhere in this book, the ability to sue a supplier for contractual failure is useless if the failure destroys, in effect, both organizations. It is down to the organization's own risk management processes to understand these residual risks and take a realistic view on their acceptability or otherwise, not least the contractor's own backups and alternatives.

Continuity planning will be explored further in a later chapter.

Information

Information can be stored technologically, on paper and in people's heads. With outsourced dependencies, the organization has a critical dependency that that information, in whichever formats, is not only held secure by the supplier but is also accessible by the principal in the case of the supply contract failing.

Technological processes are vital warehouses of very large amounts of information. This information is so important that it, and the ability to access or mine it in different ways, is a foundation of the whole organization. Loss can destroy the organization and, in some cases, human lives, too, e.g., medical *e.g.* records needed for ongoing treatments and some engineering safety records.

It is not enough to simply say that the files are 'backed up'. Is the backup readable in a way that makes the business needs achievable? Is the backup physically far enough away from the primary data that it really could not possibly be destroyed at the same time? Even then, this may not be adequate. Could a threat, say a virus, have damaged both backup and primary data at the same time? Physical distance in such circumstances would be irrelevant. How often is the backup taken? In other words, how much data is exposed to loss because it was input between the date of the last backup and the moment of the incident?

Case study

A subsidiary of a company provided back office services to the group's investment management business. This was a multi-billion pound group, managing investment portfolios for businesses, pension funds and private clients. Furthermore, this subsidiary earned additional income by also providing similar services defined by contract to other City institutions.

During the course of the business impact analysis, the consultant asked about backups to the computers. This was confirmed and an introduction was arranged with a senior member of the computer department. Assurances were given that backups were taken daily and a discussion began about the decision making that had led to backing up only once a day.

Further concerns were raised when the member of staff confirmed that he took the tapes home with him at the end of the working day. The warning lights were already on, and the concern deepened when he confirmed that he brought the tapes back in with him the following day. This in effect rendered both backup tapes and original tapes in the same building during the working day. This city central area had already suffered bomb damage.

It was after a long period of talking at cross purposes when it became clear that the member of staff had not been taking contingency backups at all. His backups were working backups that would help him if he had minor computer glitches to manage on a day-by-day basis. He was not aware that others believed that he was taking the main contingency backups and that he was the one thought to be taking on this wider responsibility. He saw no business-critical dependencies in what he was doing and thus stored and managed the tapes accordingly.

> The point of this true-life story is that everybody else thought he was making contingency backups, and because of this misunderstanding, in effect no one was doing so. It would be easy to cry stupidity but this is an organizational and communication failure, not one of personal inadequacy.
>
> (*A Risk Management Approach to Business Continuity*,
> Julia Graham and David Kaye, Rothstein, 2006)

Information on paper may also be a crucial risk issue when that particular information has been identified as crucial to a process. This is more difficult to protect by security controls, duplication and sharing, and the risk management measures demanded may be to insist that crucial elements are 'captured' technologically.

Information in people's heads is the most difficult to manage, both from a secrecy and from a protection point of view. Protection can only be gained by ensuring that crucial information is not just in one person's head alone, and perhaps also that there are manuals and other capturing of the working needs.

A full discussion around maintaining secrecy of identified sensitive information is a big enough subject for a book focused on that subject alone. For the purpose of this book, it needs to be said simply that the information security standards and the policing of those standards need to be agreed right across the supply chain where there is such sensitivity of information.

That sensitivity may be around the commercial or legal sensitivities of each organization, or the secrecy and use of controls that are imposed by such as the Data Protection Act 1998 (UK). The information may, of course, be simply valuable to third parties and as such the loss or theft can be very damaging to the organization.

> The Department of Trade and Industry (DTI) used PricewaterhouseCoopers to undertake an information security breaches survey. It revealed that in 52 per cent of breaches within large businesses, the cause of the most severe security breaches was people within the organization, not external organized crime. The experts interviewed, however, blamed ignorance and poor training for the growing insider threat.

The survey showed that only 49 per cent of organizations carry out periodic audits of their security processes, 49 per cent monitor activity for anomalies, and 38 per cent use software to detect any violations of security policy. Over half of organizations outsource their IT operations but only half of these companies have a formal service level agreement that embraces security standards.

It seems obvious to say that security breaches are only counted when discovered and it is likely that these figures seriously underestimate the problem and the cost. There does not seem to be a clear profile of the kind of employee who will misuse systems. The variance in motives and lack of uniformity in offenders makes them difficult to identify and anticipate.

These difficulties are being experienced within security managers' own organizations and yet are a fraction of the challenges in setting out to manage security of information in third party organizations.

The trust in the supplier's information security controls is therefore a crucial dependency that is, in effect, equally outsourced together with the ability to deliver goods and services. Information security is therefore an important risk issue that forms part of the due diligence undertaken before a contract is signed, as is setting into the contract the circumstances where and by whom that information is accessible.

'In the manner of a displeased schoolmaster, Britain's Information Minister last month served up a blistering denunciation of UK business practices in his annual report. With some incredulity, the Data Protection Watchdog marvelled at a slew of recent security breaches in which a "roll call of banks, retailers, government departments, public bodies and other organizations" had exposed private customer information to the public – and possible criminal – gaze.

… indeed if the data loss monitoring service Privacy Rights Clearing House is to be believed the global business community is not merely leaking it is haemorrhaging information – often without realizing the fact. Between 2004 and Spring 2007, reports the service, data breaches grew by 1,700 per cent with the known number of records lost or exposed growing by a staggering 50 million between December 2006 and April 2007.'

(Michelle Price, 'Inside Job', *Information Age*, August 2007)

Much of this information was entrusted to a third party within a supply chain and the loss had been from that custodian.

Other intellectual assets

The expression 'intellectual assets' embraces much more than the information database and the brand values that we have discussed.

It includes other 'soft' dependencies that have important ownership, access, legal and usability concerns for risk professionals. This is especially so when they are delivering entire sections of their organization into the hands, and under the control, of third parties.

Examples of such additional intellectual assets can fall within the three headings of copyright, trademarks and patents but there are even more intellectual assets, and thus dependencies. Additional ones can be organization specific or simply market positioning, licences, research, contract dependencies, effective business control, financial controls and audit trails, domain names, the right to royalties, regulatory approvals, legality and the confidence of its various stakeholders.

Such assets could be the most valuable possession that the organization owns, when measured by the consequences of loss or inaccessibility. Should any process re-engineering therefore affect the access, ownership and usability of any of these dependencies, any new risks and consequences newly incurred must be assessed as part of the initial and ongoing due diligence. The risk assessment must embrace not just existing intellectual assets transferred but also any new ones to emerge under the new relationship.

Patents particularly are formally registered by the national patent office of the country and can last for up to 20 years. It ensures not only use of that intellectual idea but the commercial value of exclusivity. If sufficient efforts are not maintained to protect such patents and brands they can be lost into the public domain. They are, of course, intertwined with brand and confidence, which have already been discussed.

The fact that these assets are untouchable, and measurable only with difficulty, do not make them any less important as crucial organizational dependencies. Risk managing any activity that passes them, or the control over them, to a third party is a crucial supply chain risk management challenge.

The audit and compliance trail

Another crucial and business survival dependency is to be able to show records of some decisions and actions taken and the facts that lead to that activity.

The interests likely to need this information include accountants, actuaries, regulators, financiers, credit agencies, stock market analysts, law courts, taxation authorities, safety inspectors and a host of other bodies that have a need and a power to demand access. Consequences of failure to deliver can range from financial penalties to damage to brand and confidence, and even to the use of some powers to demand closure of the entire organization.

Often that 'audit trail' of a responsibility has, effectively, been outsourced with the processes to a third party. Ensuring that that supply chain can deliver the information required and can illustrate its credibility is one more crucial dependency that may need managing throughout the supply chain.

If, for example, a UK life assurance company outsources the training of its sales staff to a professional training company, it will still have the need to always be able to deliver proof that the training has been delivered to the standards required by a financial services regulator. It will not be acceptable for the employer to say that it had delegated the training to another organization. It must therefore ensure that the training company's own 'audit trail' meets its own compliance needs and is accessible whatever else happens to the training company.

E-commerce dependencies

The risks around e-commerce fall primarily within the section dealing with computerized risks but the live-time dependencies are worthy of a few additional comments.

It is important to say again that any web-enabled or e-commerce activities are not distinct from the mainstream objectives and sensitivities of the organization. They are just one of the wide range of tools whereby these objectives are delivered. These carry, however, additional exposures to embrace in the risk assessment and impact assessment processes.

Domain names can be lost or abused. Damage can arise from inadequate management and controls, and the use of exclusive e-signatures could lead to fraud. There are 'new' crimes to anticipate including vandalism of the website, denial of service due to swamping attacks and viruses, phishing, website spoofing, hacking and Trojan horses.

E-commerce raises expectations to new levels and in new ways. Client businesses and direct customers are promised online, live-time deliveries of information and products. Failures are now measured in seconds. The web-enabled product can be the only way for customers and organizations to contact each other. Catastrophic delays can therefore be measured in just seconds.

In 2007, there were great concerns in financial markets as to where and on which institutions the final impact of the American sub-prime loans fiasco would fall. This was because of the habit of lenders selling on their loan portfolios to other organizations. Northern Rock had a business model that entailed the sale onwards of its loan portfolios. It became a perceived credit risk itself and suffered from a close down in credit availability. It needed to go to the Bank of England for 'emergency funds', adding to its reputational problems.

The problems deepened dramatically when millions of its internet customers were unable to access its overpowered website. The problem became a crisis as customers became extremely concerned about the bank's funds and began, in effect, a run on the bank, bringing the company to its knees.

There are new legality and compliance concerns, especially as e-commerce crosses international boundaries with ease. The laws themselves around e-commerce are evolving at a slower speed than e-commerce itself and when they do appear they do not cross country jurisdictions as easily. This leaves organizations exposed in their relationships with customers, third parties and governments.

The opportunities to commit crime wholesale, the remoteness of villain to victim and cross-border opportunities can cause large losses, and makes apprehension and recovery of assets or brand much more difficult.

Relevant to the subject of this book is the fact that e-commerce often brings with it a much higher and much more urgent dependency on third-party service suppliers than in other business models. This, as with all outsourcing, brings a range of risks and sensitivities even on calm days and additional challenges when an unexpected and potentially destructive incident needs managing through.

Virus attacks such as 'Melissa' and 'I love you' are infamous. IT security managers believe that there are more then 50,000 computer viruses existing at present and they are growing daily. Visa reports that 47 per cent of all complaints received are Internet-related, even though only 1 per cent of its European transactions are online ones.

(A Risk Management Approach to Business Continuity,
Julia Graham and David Kaye, Rothstein, 2006)

Legalities in an electronic age

The increasingly common practice of outsourcing electronic commerce to third parties makes life difficult for regulators and they have expressed concerns; especially where there are systemic implications resulting from a third party providing services to a large number of institutions.

These types of concern apply equally to all concerns to remain legal in circumstances where the 'players' are spread over many organizations and even continents.

It is beyond the scope of this book to delve into detail on specific legislation but the following are cameos of the laws around the world and the interested reader may wish to research further.

Financial Services Authority (UK)

Steps are being taken by the British Financial Services Authority (FSA) to monitor that firms and markets have adequate IT systems and controls to address the risks in their business (including, of course, e-risks).

The Electronic Signatures in Global National Commerce Act

This is a US federal law known as E-sign. It gives, *within its jurisdiction*, the same legal standing to e-signatures as is now available to handwritten ones. There is a parallel law in the UK: the Electronic Communications Act 2000.

ISO 27001

This deals with information security. There are sections dealing with the security of electronically stored and transmitted information.

There are numerous other legislative controls that are minefields for the risk and continuity manager. Some are designed directly for e-commerce, and some have implications that cannot be ignored. Further examples in the UK alone include the Privacy and Electronic Communications Regulations 2003, Electronic Commerce Regulations 2002, Regulations of Investigatory Powers Act 2000, the Consumer Protection (Distance Selling) Regulations 2000 and the Data Protection Act 1998.

An organization creating a web-enabled business model may be a new start-up business or it may be making major changes to an existing business. In either case it is likely to be a business model that could not be reverted back to erstwhile financial models and to old methods of communication and stakeholder relationships. The opportunities or the cost economics are too diverse and there will be no easy falling back on an old business model and its resources should the e-commerce driven supply chain fail. The skills and other resources are just not there, and the expectations raised by e-commerce trading cannot be supplied in any other model.

We must not forget the portals where technology makes contact with the real world. Orders or instructions taken over the internet must still at some point be delivered with the 'old model' world of people, warehouses, lorry fleets, call centres, aeroplanes, hotels, post rooms and countless other contributors. This point is more likely to be missed where the new technology – delivered by one external supplier – has to interface with 'old technology' – delivered by another – and, furthermore, where continuity risk is left for the technicians alone to handle.

The other easily forgettable ingredient is where the technology of e-commerce depends entirely on non-technological services being maintained. The inadequacy of Central Network's risk management exposed during the 2007 Gloucestershire floods brought the ugly fact to our attention that failure of one electricity distribution site had no bypass alternatives and much of Gloucestershire and beyond could so easily have been without electrical power for days or weeks. Most computer or server farms may have generator backup but still need diesel supplied by distribution centres with pumps powered in turn by electricity. Many 'end user' sites do not have even that luxury of backup generators.

Furthermore, where the technological applications are outsourced overseas, say into India, China or the Philippines, the infrastructure dependencies of power and water are even less developed and reliable than the Gloucestershire ones were found to be in the summer of 2007.

Other legalities

The need to remain legal and compliant is of course not just a technological one. Any organization must conduct itself within the laws of each and every country that it works within, whether they be employment laws, environment laws, safety laws, or customer protection and the laws around the products or services delivered. Some industries have their own compliance requirements imposed by statute.

Failure to do so can bring two types of damage. One is criminality with fines and even imprisonment of officials. The other is the imposition of indemnities by courts following a breach of duty that has damaged a third party.

Some penalties can be way above the ability of the organization to pay and certainly the costs of criminality are not insurable. Both types of damage can bring destruction of reputation that could be much more costly to the organization than the penalties themselves.

The activity of a supplier can render the activity of the distributor of a product or service illegal, e.g. in the case of Mattel selling toys allegedly with illegal levels of lead in the paint.

The ability to manage employees

There is a massive organizational dependency that is often overlooked. This is the ability to manage the workforce to suit current-day challenges and then divert them, if necessary, from one pre-agreed task to another one. In 'calm waters', the relevance is less important and no doubt the third-party supplier's employees will be quietly getting on with the job of delivering whatever was agreed in the contract. When waters are less calm, and the need is to change quickly to meet new urgencies, the ability to divert them is lost to the wording of the contract and also the supplier's ability (or willingness) to change the contract requirements.

Should that change be needed in time of major organizational threat and urgently, then of course the supplier's negotiating position is considerably threatened. One example could be a contract to supply something in a project that has an immovable deadline, e.g. the infrastructure for the Olympic Games. If that project is falling behind time, the contractor may not agree to move priorities, standards and planned intermediary delivery dates without a substantial cost premium or, indeed, not agree at all because of his or her work scheduling with other clients.

Where the workforce and its support mechanisms remain under the direct control of the principal, that principal, subject to employment law, of course, can divert this vital resource to meet the new and emerging urgencies. This is a vital ability when the organization is under exceptional stress.

We will explore this further under the heading of continuity planning.

6

Myths and realities

Realism in objectives

In this chapter we will explore some of the myths and realities of some commonly perceived risk opportunities, defences and tools. We will set out to test their values, strengths and weaknesses and measure them against expectations.

The first myth is that there are defences and tools that will remove all risk or impact. Even inactivity is not risk-free in a vibrant and changing workplace and market-place. This chapter should therefore still sit comfortably with the underlying message of this book: that it is just not realistic to expect risk management to remove all risk and impact. The best we can hope for is to reduce the likelihood and the impact of risk incidents down to a level that the decision makers and their stakeholders feel is acceptable, that is, within their informed tolerances for risk and also the measured risk/reward balancing act.

Whilst organizations have created desperately dangerous, single, catastrophic points of failure in modern business models, technology, conversely, has brought effective opportunities for continuity risk management and the wholesale duplication of data and the technology that enables its use. Furthermore, an external supply chain, if effectively risk managed, can be as much a continuity opportunity as it can be a threat. A dual access supply chain, or one where there are prepared and resourced alternatives ready to step in, in time, is a much stronger business model than the organization creating all the elements of a product in a single in-house facility. The very business models themselves therefore are risk opportunities as well as risk threats. The challenge is to be informed in risk issues, recognize both the threat and the opportunities and use them all in a commercially realistic way.

> The most realistic risk management objective therefore is to enable informed decision making that can at best remove or reduce the risks and impacts that had earlier been determined to be unacceptable ones. This chapter therefore does not set out to destroy expectations in the subjects discussed but to ensure that the expectations around them are based squarely on reality and not in myth or hope.

Insurance protections

It would be good to bear in mind, throughout reading this section, the potentially catastrophic risks that a large organization may face and then consider whether those risks are in fact insurable, either by the customer or the supplier. There are many slices that can be taken on this list but one for broad consideration is the ability to deliver on business-critical stakeholder expectations plus:

- brand value and credibility;
- retention of the customer and supply base;
- IT and other facilities that provide group-wide services;
- retention of an adequate skill base across the organization;
- regulatory and licence approvals and other legalities;
- business control – including financial controls; and
- solvency (cash flows, revenue and capital).

Traditionally, the entire boundary of risk management was perceived to lie within the purchasing of insurance products. Risk management has moved on significantly in seeing that there are more effective ways of managing risk and indeed many of the most destructive of risks are not insurable at all within the conventional insurance market-place. This is especially so in modern, primarily outsourced and hollow organizational models, where crucial delivery dependables are not even within the insured organization at all but repositioned into third-party organizations.

> One danger, because of the insurance roots of risk management, is overconfidence in the protections that the insurer can bring for the organization. Many a modern risk manager has had to respond to the suggestion that 'surely we don't need risk management, we're insured aren't we?'

Where then does a company's insurance programme and business resilience management meet? Do they meet at all, especially in risks to supply chain dependencies? An organization handling its first real-life, potentially destructive, risk incident will best see the real values and real differences between the insurance and risk management programmes. This particular learning curve is, however, best avoided where possible.

Insurance, indeed, has its values but it also has some major limitations. An insurance programme is of course a financial management tool and it will adequately finance the replacement of assets, whether those be damaged property or money demanded following an expensive legal liability judgment. It is, however, just that, a financial management tool, i.e. by definition constrained to managing only financial risks.

All insurable items must therefore be reduced to their monetary value, whether that be buildings, contents, machinery or indeed the financial cost of having to indemnify a third party that has successfully established a liability for negligence or other failure. The problem, of course, is that not all impacts of an unexpected incident can be so valued in hard cash terms. Nor especially can a cheque solve all of the insured's difficulties that emerge from an unexpected risk incident.

It is of no relevance to a material damage, or casualty, insurance protection that replacement machinery can take months to manufacture, deliver, set up and to train staff in its use. The policy wording does not offer an answer either to the fact that the damaged building can take months or years to rebuild. Consequentially, it is of no relevance either to such an insurance contract that customers may not be able to wait for the delayed deliveries and must go elsewhere for their products and services, probably never to return.

Furthermore, such a financial product is unable to provide a response for the variety of other potential disastrous consequences. They may include the loss of stakeholder confidence and support, destruction of brand values, the loss of the future commercial value of a whole range of intellectual assets, the loss of organizational controls, and the failure to satisfy a range of compliance and other legal requirements.

Insurers will offer risk advice but it is not always clear whether that risk advice is restricted to insured and insurable risks. It may not, by any means, be comprehensive risk advice designed to manage the organization's pre-determined critical exposures. This statement is not designed to belittle that advice. It has its important values but it is important to always be clear what the parameters are of that advice.

Material damage or casualty insurances

Damage insurance may be based around the traditional 'fire and perils' cover with additional protection available against the cost of various types of crime. 'Fire and perils' is usually around fire damage, riot, weather-related covers and impact damage. Even where an 'all risks' cover is granted, the insurer will usually demand that something sudden and unforeseen has occurred and caused damage. There will be numerous exclusions, important amongst them are war (other than marine risks), nuclear, chemical and biological, gradual damage such as 'wear and tear'. Significantly, for a supply chain business model, there can be an exclusion of 'system failure'.

The insurer therefore is concerned with the cause of the damage. Cause is in most legal jurisdictions precisely defined and the insurer will follow that local legal definition. Where UK law is the base, the definition will follow the description something like the following:

> Proximate cause of a loss is the dominant efficient cause that sets in motion a train of events that results in the loss and without the intervention of any new and independent source.

An expensive example of the application of such a definition was following the terrorist attack on the World Trade Center in 2001. A conflict on the cause definition between the owner of the building and its insurers was taken through the American law courts.

The question was whether the crashing of each plane into its building was a separate cause of loss, i.e. enabling two separate claims on the sum insured, or whether the proximate cause was a single incident, being the decision to attack the building complex. Was the second plane crash a 'new and independent cause' or just an evolution of one cause? In the latter case, the entire damage would be restricted to one, not two, payments of the sum insured.

> '*Swiss Re Wins in World Trade Center Insurance Trial (Update 4)*
>
> May 3 (Bloomberg) – A New York jury agreed with Swiss Reinsurance Co. that its World Trade Center coverage on Sept. 11, 2001, limited its maximum payout to $877.5 million, handing developer Larry Silverstein his biggest defeat in a 2 1/2-year court battle with his insurers.
>
> A 10-member jury found that Swiss Re, the insurer that provided about a quarter of Silverstein's $3.55 billion in coverage, issued a policy with language that defines the terrorist attack by two hijacked jets as one event. Silverstein, 72, said the policy was governed by terms that may view the assault as two occurrences, entitling him to double damages.
>
> 'We're gratified,' said Jacques Dubois, chief executive of Swiss Re America Corp., the Zurich-based insurer's US unit, in a courtroom interview. 'We're glad the jury has borne us out.'
>
> Silverstein's loss leaves the leaseholder of the trade center site with a maximum of $4.7 billion in insurance proceeds, short of the $7.5 billion he has said he needs for rebuilding at Ground Zero in New York. Jurors, who Friday said they were deadlocked on Swiss Re even as they found in favor of most of the 11 other insurers in the case, came to a decision after US District Judge Michael Mukasey ordered them to take more time.'
>
> ('Swiss Re Wins in World Trade Center
> Insurance Trial (Update 4)', Bloomberg.com.)

Where the sum insured is established on a maximum probable loss basis and not full replacement value of the entire building, such differences can be absolutely critical to the insured.

Loss of profits or consequential loss insurances?

There is a form of loss of profits, consequential loss or, as it is sometimes known, 'increased cost of working' insurance. The cover will reimburse the lost revenues and the increased costs incurred as a result of the reduced business activity within a pre-defined period of time following the loss. This period of time is called the 'indemnity period', and is designed to be the period of time the insured can expect to be recovering from the damage and has reduced revenues not meeting the costs that must still be paid.

Combined with the pre-set maximum sum insured, the indemnity period forms one of the two backbones of this additional protection.

The indemnity period within the loss of profits policy is therefore as crucial a driver in the claim payments as the sum insured. The protection will, of course, cease at the end of that pre-agreed period of time, regardless of where the organization is in its recovery cycle. The protection is primarily designed to protect cash flows where costs are still incurred even if trading is diminished. Such costs could be interest on loans and mortgages, salaries of skilled employees that are retained, property taxes and many other so-called 'standing charges'. Naturally, just after a disaster a business may wish to increase expenditure well above the norm to be able to move fast, and protect its stakeholder support and its distribution or supply chains. One example may be a heightened stakeholder communication and marketing programme to protect the brand name and retain as many customers as possible. This increased expenditure can also be insured.

The insurer, however, normally demands that to be indemnified such additional expenditure is economic *as far as the claim is concerned*, i.e. this extra spend needs to show its investment return *out of the other costs that are normally incurred within the policy indemnity period*. In other words, the increased expenditure on staying alive must reduce the claim payment by at least as much.

Working through a major disaster, however, the board's concentration is on survival over a much longer term, and indeed the investment in staying alive may need to be much more than simply maintaining revenues over such a short period of time. What is the value then of the limitation of a six-month, two-year or even five-year indemnity period on increased cost of working insurances? The differing horizons of the insurers and the insured can reduce substantially the indemnity offered and the insured may still have additional costs to pay from its own struggling finances.

As always, an important factor in gaining indemnity from insurance is ensuring the adequacy of the sum insured. This applies no less in consequential loss insurance. A frequent reason for inadequate sums insured is the failure to ensure that the calculation of the insured gross profit actually fits the policy definition of the same terminology.

A policy will normally define gross profit as the amount by which the sum of the amounts of turnover and closing stock exceeds the sum of the amounts of opening stock and uninsured working expenses (for example, purchases and discounts received). 'Gross profit' as shown in published accounts may be the figure after deduction of expenditures such as wages and others. This and other expenditure may not be stated as an uninsured working expense under the policy and there is a mismatch. Any under insurance can reduce payment of all claims as the average condition may reduce even small claims by the proportion of value at risk over the sum insured. In other words, if the sum insured under the policy is found to be half the value at risk, then the claim will be paid for just half the damage, even though that damage amount is within the total sum insured. If £2 million of value was under insured at only £1 million, then damage valued at £100,000 would receive indemnity only of £50,000. The average clause can also apply to material damage policies.

Insurance is of course vital – but is only one of the tools that help to achieve the very survival of a business. There are countless examples of the real value of insurance to businesses in troubled circumstances, and a real financial help towards those businesses and jobs surviving. Insurers will consider interim payments where liability is clear but the final claim is not yet quantified. These interim and final payments are especially important with small- to medium-sized businesses where it is not achievable to finance the cost of damage from current revenues, cash flows or balance sheets.

Liability insurances

Liability insurances are normally designed to protect the insured from any liability established in law to a third party. One key issue in this statement is that the liabilities must be established in law, usually following failure or other breach of duty, and that actual damage must have occurred to a third party. The liability may be as a result of an action taken or not taken or, indeed, that the service or product itself has, through failure of some sort, caused harm to another. Some liabilities, for example, those relating to products and employees, have a statutory or regulatory envelope of requirements within which liability is defined and the quantity of damage is established.

Indemnity is an attempt to reposition the damaged party back in the same financial situation as before the damage. This results in great challenges in finding the right monetary amount that equitably matches non-monetary losses such as death, personal injury and future losses. Some jurisdictions, notably North American, provide for an element of penalty, or punishment, over and above indemnity. These additional American court awards can be astronomical and insurers will exclude American risks in most liability policies effected elsewhere.

Contractual liability and insurable interest

Another crucial insurance implication for the supply chain risk manager is the underlying concept of insurable interest. The principle lies alongside the one of indemnity in that the insured must have an insurable interest in the insured event for the cover to be valid. With very few exceptions indeed, it is just not possible for anybody to insure against something happening unless that happening will cause that actual insured to incur loss. It is not normally possible to insure against a third party, even a contracted supplier, incurring a loss. The 'insurable interest' that enables cover to be placed is limited to any actual loss to be incurred by the person named as the insured in the policy document.

Those contracted to the insured in a supply chain, however, may not be third parties and have a special relationship in law, most often defined by the contract terms between them. Only very few contracts, however, must be in writing to be legally binding. A verbal agreement that embraces the requirements of contract may be enough to establish that it is a contractual, not a third party, relationship. Contractual requirements can differ amongst jurisdictions but embrace, in addition to the obvious ones of legality, achievability and agreement, the need for some 'consideration' (monetary or otherwise), however small, each way between the parties.

Often, too, the contract will establish where liabilities and losses will fall. If these contracted liabilities are to be insured, e.g. a financial bond, special contract liability policies will need to be negotiated. It is very unlikely, however, that the insurance protection will indemnify penalties (even where legal) and especially where the penalties are imposed by criminal law, such as corporate manslaughter charges. Fines in such circumstances can be unlimited and are always uninsurable.

'British Airways has been fined about £270m after it admitted collusion in fixing the prices of fuel surcharges.

The US Department of Justice has fined it $300m (£148m) for colluding on how much extra to charge on passenger and cargo flights, to cover fuel costs. It followed a decision by the UK's Office of Fair Trading to fine BA £121.5m, after it held illegal talks with rival Virgin Atlantic.

Surcharges were added to passenger fares in response to rising oil prices.

BA now faces the possibility of legal challenges by customers on both sides of the Atlantic who believe that they lost money as a result of the collusion.

The BBC's Adam Brookes in Washington said the airline could face multiple lawsuits for damages in the US from aggrieved passengers.'

(Source: http://www.bbc.co.uk, 1 August 2007)

Policy exclusions

Another minefield for the overconfident insured is that a standard policy wording will normally exclude the real value of an electronic database, which is, of course, its role as a business-enabling tool. Cover is normally restricted to the actual costs incurred in reinstating the database back into the technological storage format. This makes the somewhat extreme assumption that the database can be recreated at all, and also that this clerical cost is a significant concern at the time of the damage or inaccessibility. In reality, the clerical cost of reinstating an accessible database may be the very least of the problems facing an organization at the time. There is some special wording available for individual negotiation that may give an element of protection for reduction in turnovers following temporary loss of information.

Within conventional policy wording, the insurer is also unable to indemnify losses where the underlying or 'proximate' cause is an action taken deliberately by the insured and without the insurer's prior permission. That cause must be 'accidental' as far as the insured's role in it starting or evolving. A decision to concentrate the entire production line dependency into one link of a supply chain is a strategic decision. The impact of the loss of that link may therefore be described as the result of a strategic risk and not an accidental one.

The key point for this section remains, however, that the most crucial dependencies of a modern business are actually not insurable. These dependencies include client reaction and their ongoing trust, stakeholder support, effective business and financial controls and models, legality, brand values, position in its market-place, flexibility, contracts, its crucial employees and, above all, a whole range of owned and hired intellectual assets. Reinstating assets or money can of course help a little towards retaining these values but very rarely, if ever, are these undefined, high-value, low-frequency, exposures insurable in themselves. Indeed, some of the most crucial of exposures are singled out for exclusion.

An example of such an uninsurable loss would be a cruise ship sinking or suffering a terrorist attack that would lose thousands of lives. The resultant and reasonable media frenzy would have a massive impact on the whole cruise market-place and damage or destroy, not only the cruise line affected, but all others. It could even force some marginal players out of business as they face their standing charges with a massive reduction in passenger revenue. The loss to the other cruise line companies will not be insured by standard marine policies and may not even be fully insurable in the contingency insurance market-place. Another example is the damage to tourist and other industries as a result of controls introduced during a foot-and-mouth disease epidemic that closes off access to entire parts of a country.

Such a loss could happen anywhere in the supply chain. It is an important consideration that such a loss could equally be with the control or the influence of the supplier itself as it is with the risk manager's own organization's control. This lack of influence can be critical when considering litigation against a supplier that failed to deliver as contracted.

An opposing example of such potentially uninsured loss is when a disease or widespread flooding decimates crops, reducing supply and thus forcing prices higher. Those higher prices are not only driven by the market's demand/supply balancing but are also needed in cash terms by the farmer to meet costs out of a reduced turnover.

If that farmer is contracted over a period to supermarkets at fixed prices then that loss is felt entirely by the supplier farmer. Conversely, the supermarket is also damaged by the inability to obtain adequate shelf stocks at the time – even more so if enough farmers choose, because it has become unviable to do so, not to remain in that crop or produce production at all.

Bringing insurance and resilience together

Insurers, constitutionally, are driven by:

- proximate cause of the loss being anticipated beforehand and sitting comfortably within policy wording; and
- the amount of monetary loss incurred, again, as limited by the principle of financial indemnity and that wording.

The insured is, however, driven by neither. It is much more concerned by the holistic impacts of any surprises on the entire organization, its objectives, dependabilities and responsibilities to stakeholders.

Another underlying difference to be managed is that insurance is all about cure; risk management is all about prevention. Few chief executives and boards would argue that they have a preference for crisis management intruding into their already busy working days! Managing the interface between risk and insurance is, therefore, all about bringing together, as best possible, these fundamental mismatches.

Resilience risk management, in particular, is about all organization-threatening exposures, not just about the replacement of monetary assets or monetary liabilities. The fact that a potentially catastrophic risk is very high impact and very low frequency may indeed be difficult for the insurer to underwrite, but nevertheless it remains real and amongst the organization's own concerns and management needs.

Supply chain failure is difficult or impossible to insure adequately. Organizations are, conversely, concerned about failures within their supply chain. FM Global's 2006 survey, *Managing Business Risks in 2006 and Beyond*, named supply chain failure as topping the risks causing major disruption.

The organization's primary concern is, of course, about the impact of a failure, whatever may have caused that failure and certainly not just when that failure is caused by an insurable risk. Matters outside the supplier's control and with no insured damage or loss can as easily cause supply chain failure to the supplier. Just one example could be a change in government legislation.

Resilience planning is also about preparing staff and resources for the management of the incident itself as and when it happens. In some businesses, the most critical moments – especially in damage limitation and regaining confidence – are within minutes and hours, not days and weeks, after the disaster. The insurer is not equipped to support these needs and the others that are key elements of business resilience.

Trade disruption insurance

In recent years, an insurance product called trade disruption insurance (TDI) has been available for those organizations where it can meet a specific need. Its cover goes beyond the conventional range of insurance products and protects against disruption in the supply chain, even when there is no physical loss or damage to the policyholder's assets.

Disruption may be caused by political events (including embargo or terrorism) or physical events (such as closure of a navigable waterway) and natural perils (windstorms and the like). As such, TDI can complement or replace business interruption policies providing cover to businesses where a supply chain disruption can damage their trading operations.

Cover is still against specified perils only but it is much wider cover than business interruption covers. It can include the closure of a port or canal, protection against loss of a dedicated supplier or protecting a contractor against delay due to late delivery of key equipment. The original causes of the loss can include political events, physical events, natural events and commercial events (such as the bankruptcy of a key supplier).

The cover has some value in revenue or cash flow problems, such as loss of profit, loss of tax credits due to missed deadlines, loss of revenue, additional and/or increased costs of working, out-of-pocket expenses and the cost of executing contingency plans.

However, we remain as always within the constraints of the insurance industry, in that it provides valuable protection against defined financial consequences of an unexpected incident within its definition of insured causes. This cannot keep the organization alive should that incident have destroyed its ability to remain trusted, in control and with what it needs to get back fast enough into its market-place to remain 'alive'.

We have stated elsewhere in this book that the potentially catastrophic inability to continue can emerge more easily and quickly from many failures that are not financial ones. This is especially so with the brittle business models of the just-in-time supply chain.

The captive insurance company and pooling

A sufficiently large organization may decide to set up a captive insurance company that in effect is a subsidiary that operates in many ways just like a third-party insurer. This enables capital and cash flows to stay within the organization and also the ability to make use of tax-effective instruments and locations. It also enables the organization to gain access directly into the wholesale reinsurance market to protect exposures that are beyond the captive's own ability to absorb. Whilst such ownership enables the organization to underwrite risks often excluded commercially, and thus more suited to its own business, the protections offered by this instrument must still be commercially feasible and also be realistic enough to be able to attract reinsurance protections.

Furthermore, the use of an internal captive may enable a short-term method of diverting assets to prepare for future financial loss, but it is continuing to use the funds of the principal and so, net of reinsurance, it is the principal's funds that remain at risk.

Pooling is where a few organizations, often in the same trade, get together and share risks that may be impossible, difficult or more expensive to place into the conventional insurance market. The management of such a captive or pooling and its liabilities needs professional insurance management skills and a pertinent reminder is given in the following speech.

> 'As a result we saw a move away from risk management seen as a set of self-contained activities, carried out solely with the regulator in mind. For example, we were pleased to see examples where risk management information – including output from risk-based capital models – were actively being used to support strategic decision making.
>
> However, despite these welcome developments we concluded that a number of more difficult challenges remain. In our view, many firms in the insurance market still need to assess the effectiveness of their oversight of risk management, both at board and committee level, and to ensure that senior management have the knowledge and skills to sustain sufficient understanding of risk management processes. In a similar vein, we found some risk functions were merely acting as aggregators of risk at local and group level. Moving them towards a more strategic role in challenging and validating the risk information they receive would add greater support to senior management decision making.'
>
> (Speech by Sarah Wilson, Director and Insurance Sector Leader, Financial Services Authority (UK). A Reinsurance Practice & the Law event hosted by Barlow Lyde & Gilbert LLP, 18 June 2007. http://www.fsa.gov.uk/ pages/Library/Communication/Speeches/2007/0618_sw.shtml)

Indeed, in 2006, Standard and Poor's credit assessment agency added enterprise risk management to its list of separate assessment criteria for insurance providers.

Insurance and risk relationships

All effective risk management starts with a need to have a highly business-critical understanding of exposures that are potentially damaging. This is not just what may happen but quite precisely how such a happening could impact the organization, its people and its stakeholders. In doing so, some risks that are traditionally insured may be found to be within the board's risk tolerances and conversely, new, potentially destructive, currently uninsured risks may be discovered. This knowledge can be valuable, too, when reviewing insurance needs with the broker, insurer or captive.

There is a further benefit in beginning with such a critical understanding. Security and risk protection costs money. The best spend and use of resources on risk and security are where the spend exactly matches the organization's most critical exposures. Insurers can have a different view. The insurers may wish to advise, and focus protection spending, on where the highest insured values are at risk. The insured will wish to focus protections where there is greatest potential for destruction to the business model and thus its resilience. The business and its needs, after all, should be the driver.

Over recent years, there are two coincidental evolutions. The risk manager is increasingly looking beyond the insurance programme as the reason for, and value of, his or her existence in the organization. The continuity manager is increasingly looking beyond facilities replacement for the risks to, and opportunities for, resilience. They all begin to come together when the risk manager has evaluated risk and impact and identified those exposures that are unacceptable.

As stated in an earlier chapter, the choices then are from one, or a combination, of: reducing the risk, reducing the impact, transferring the risk to another and establishing continuity planning. The risk can sometimes be transferred by contract to counterparties other than insurers. Buying insurance is therefore just one risk tool option of four, and in view if its importance and implied promises, its strengths and weaknesses need to be understood very clearly indeed.

In summary, therefore, a business needs an insurance programme integrated with the process of identifying and managing risk exposures and business continuity planning right through any critical sections of the supply chain. All the risk tools are individually valuable and can feed on each other, but it is important to clearly understand both the value and the limitations of each. The real common denominator, however, is a business director-owned and -driven, careful analysis of not only the risk of an incident, but also exactly how that incident could affect the real business itself and the props and stakeholders on which it depends.

A word of warning may be valuable when the insurer will offer 'free' risk management advice. This may have many values but it does need to be clear what that advice sets out to achieve. It is likely that the insurer will offer advice on how to manage insured or insurable risk only and we have already established that often the organization's greatest risk concerns are not insurable risks. The insurer may not be setting out, nor indeed be skilled, to advise on the holistic risk concerns of the organization.

Above all, it needs to be understood that the insurance programme, however well crafted, will have critical limitations. This is no more visible than when the organization has successfully allowed an incident to totally and permanently destroy the real business dependencies by failing to risk manage exposures, or their potential impact, beforehand.

Only with the package of risk management opportunities and tools can there be some confidence that there will be a business left to manage. The directors can then make good use of insurance claims money to assist in keeping going a business that did stay alive (either by good management or good luck) throughout whatever it was that fate threw at them.

E-commerce and insurance

Organizations operating in the world of e-commerce are no less exposed to both insurable and uninsurable risks. These can include legal liabilities to others, physical damage and repair costs, loss of information and other intellectual assets and loss of revenues. They no less need to incur expenditures to retain their place in market-places whilst rebuilding is underway.

In the e-commerce model, damage can also be caused in entirely new ways, including the misuse of electronic signatures, cybersquatting, swamping, vandalism of websites and web page phishing. These exposures create new horizons of risk for insurance underwriters and are ones that they are struggling with.

E-commerce enables entirely new business models that in turn become critical dependencies, not least the massive operational cost savings and the ability to communicate and deliver instant and differentiated services to each and every customer. Any risk management that does not enable that ability to continue is valueless.

The damage can be instant, dramatic and worldwide, raising serious concerns about the adequacy of sums insured and, thus, the cost of insuring against adequate sums insured. Some losses, to which e-commerce businesses are particularly vulnerable, such as the instant, wholesale and international destruction of credibility and the brand name, are uninsurable.

All this makes the transfer of risk into the conventional insurance market very difficult, very expensive and sometimes not commercially achievable.

Insurances amongst the supply chain

It is logical therefore that a supplier's dependency on an insurance product can have the same values and face the same dangers as the customer's own insurance programme. An auditor's or purchasing manager's tick box that confirms that the supplier has insurance is no guarantee of resilience. Certainly any expectation that insurance alone can resolve conflicts between two contracted partners needs much further thought.

The principle that many believe is the answer to all insurance problems is for the supplier and the receiver to be named as joint insureds on the policy, i.e. the partnership is the actual insured named in the policy wording. This places each party separately as the insured and, of course, no third-party claim can be made by the insured against the insured. All litigation between the parties is therefore excluded. Furthermore, should either of the insured parties breach a condition or warranty the entire policy is invalidated.

If, for example, the supplier defrauds the principal, the insurer is very likely to see both the supplier and the principal as one insured, and exclude a claim on the grounds that one cannot defraud oneself.

If there is a failure to disclose a 'material fact' in the proposal to the insurer, the entire policy is invalidated. A material fact is any fact or circumstance that would affect the judgement of the insurer in considering whether or not to accept the risk, what premium to charge or on what terms and conditions. That material fact withheld may not be relevant to the actual claim, but any failure to disclose will invalidate the whole policy.

There is a policy extension available for both the material damage policy and the loss of profits policy: often called the 'suppliers extension'. Superficially, this means that if the supplier has an incident that causes a failure in supply, the frustrated recipient's own insurer will cover the damage to its own business. What should not be forgotten, however, is that this is an extension only of the primary policy cover, i.e. the supplier must have been damaged by one of the named perils and that none of the other exclusions in that policy must apply. The damage to the recipient insured must be, of course, within the indemnity constraints granted by the primary cover wording. It can be a help in certain circumstances, perhaps, but as an answer to all supplier failure, certainly not.

Cover can be arranged to cover business interruption on both a loss at a supplier's and loss at a customer's premises. Damage at a significant customer's premises, closing down orders, can be just as damaging to a supplier. It is normal, however, to name the individual supplier and/or customer although much lower limits can be arranged for unnamed suppliers or customers. The issue as always is the extent of dependency: if a supplier failure may cause financial damage then such insurance may be of value. If the dependency for survival is total because of the volumes or lack of alternatives, then it is unlikely that insurance can be the answer.

There is, in English law and elsewhere, a legal principle that a contract cannot be enforced against a 'stranger', i.e. a third party. An organization cannot therefore rely on, and demand protection directly from, another organization's insurance policy and insurer. It would in any event be a dangerous assumption as it would rely on premiums continually being paid, and the relationship between the actual insured and the insurer not being fouled by the failure to meet the obligations stated in that policy. The Third Parties (Rights against Insurers) Act, 1930 does enable a liability claim directly against another's insurer, but only with significant limitations, one being the insolvency of the insured.

We repeat that the purpose of this section is not to rubbish the insurance product, but simply to clearly see its values and limitations, especially with a heavily outsourced supply chain. At the time of writing, we see damage and liability losses assumed by the insurance and reinsurance industry following the World Trade Center attack measured in billions: Lloyds $3.1 billion; Munich Re US$1.959 billion; Swiss Re US$1.77 billion; Berkshire Hathaway US$1.5 billion; and Allianz US$1.233 billion. These are real hard cash contributions and bring real value to the insureds involved.

Internationalism

Spreading an organization across countries can be useful risk diversity and thus a risk management value. This is especially when the organization can retain supply options across different countries simultaneously, and thus retain these options for itself should one country's infrastructure fail. However, some economic dependencies, e.g. stable stock markets values, can fail simultaneously from Tokyo to New York. Some shortfalls in concentrated supply sources, from raw materials to computer chips, can also see a world supply failure. With these dependencies the exposure may itself assume a risk right across multinational boundaries, destroying hopes that multinationalism is a protection in itself.

It needs a structured risk process to begin to understand the range of international risks brought by the modern day supply and just how many different countries and thus transport systems are involved in getting the product into and through your own organization. Without that careful research, the scale and its risks may never be understood.

Just one example is the Intel premium processor that starts its life in Japan as a single crystal grown into a large ingot of silicon by Toshiba Ceramics. It is then sliced by Toshiba Ceramics and others into thin wafers that are flown to America. The integrated circuits are etched onto each wafer before they are flown back to Malaysia to be finished into sealed ceramic 'packages'. They then come back to warehouses in America before flying on again to supplier computer factories in America, Ireland, Brazil, Malaysia, China or Taiwan. These products then, of course, travel to customers' premises anywhere in the world (research source: *The Resilient Enterprise*, Yossi Sheffi, The MIT Press).

The myth therefore is that the last country of origin is the entire picture.

As if there are not enough surprises in the world of risk management, the international world brings its additional surprises to the table. By definition, the management of an organization crossing political and physical borders is entering less familiar cultures, geology, jurisprudence, regulations, weather patterns, crime patterns, cultures, transport, ethics, politics and other influences. Sometimes those differences are subtle rather than obvious and may come as a complete surprise from areas that had been considered familiar.

Supply chains that now routinely cross these borders have new risks of failure not even dreamed about in the familiar boardrooms of the receiving organization. Not only are there failure opportunities within each of the other countries but the very act of crossing borders brings new and interesting risks – often ones out of the control of both sender and recipient.

For smaller impacts, it is usual for the contract to establish which party will bear the cost of any delays or unexpected charges. There are important additional risk issues to address, however, where criticality and urgency means that unexpected costs and delays could destroy the very viability of the production line. The risk manager may take a view on the ingredient, the country and the route home and then take a view that a risk management expenditure on increased local stock levels is commercially justifiable. There are consultancies and embassies that will provide detailed country-by-country risk assessments to support the risk manager's own research. A risk manager will be cautious of advice from embassies and look for any political influence on the otherwise real-world facts.

In 2006 in a survey by Marsh, the responders viewed infrastructure risk as one of the highest areas of concern in Asia. A total of 54 per cent of respondents advised that such a failure in infrastructure would have significant repercussions for their business. The World Bank advised that in East Asia there is a need to spend some $165 billion a year over the next five years to bring its infrastructure in line with current needs. The implication, of course, is that some organizations are offering services and products without adequate infrastructure resilience.

The Marsh survey also found that, in Asia, measures taken to protect intellectual property are low. Only 33 per cent of responders had specific IT security protection, 19 per cent product tracking systems, whilst 12 per cent had no security at all.

The European Commission also reports that 71 per cent of counterfeit goods entering the EU originated in Asia, with 54 per cent from China alone. Counterfeit items not only cause reduced sales, they can bring real safety dangers (as in the cases of counterfeit aircraft parts infiltrating genuine supply chains) and can destroy confidence in the offerings of the real branded product – we illustrate the 2007 Mattel toys quality and safety crisis elsewhere in this book.

Reputation damage emerging from different overseas ethical and employment practices can rebound nastily on overseas organizations, whether the differences can bring damaging media attention or stakeholder reaction to corruption, environmental damage, employment practices and breaches of compliance.

As will be explored in another chapter, continuity of supply requires close and ongoing relationship management, often made more difficult by distance, culture and language differences. Sending a female engineer or relationship manager to some Muslim countries may create challenges for that relationship as will managers who are not totally fluent in another's language.

Malaysia, for example, has a well-earned status as a friendly and multi-ethnic society. This, however, means that it can be difficult to identify the characteristics and sensitivities that identify the different cultures within that one country.

> 'Business visitors from countries with a western secular tradition should take care not to underestimate the extent to which traditional Islamic values guide life amongst ethnic Malays, or the importance the Malaysian government attaches to the process of Islamization for the country as a whole.'
>
> (Culturewise Ltd, Business-Culture briefing Malaysia)

All these challenges are especially so when a crisis happens and the challenges created by that crisis are difficult, fast evolving and need to be handled very quickly indeed.

Suppliers' continuity plans

The supply chain brings the risk of destruction of the whole organization, whatever the potential reason for the supplier failure. The failure may be sudden or gradual, physical or non-physical, local or international, a failure in the speed, quality or quantity of delivery, or otherwise a failure to preserve a delegated critical dependency.

We discuss business continuity separately but it would be an important omission if we did not discuss here suppliers' own continuity planning in any section that has 'myths' in its title.

We have continually made the point that the management of the continuity of the supply chain needs more than a traditional 'business recovery plan' (BRP) and, most critical of all, needs much more than a due diligence tick box that states that the supplier 'has a recovery plan'. Of even less value is the tick box that says that it has 'exercised it'. A recovery plan may be of the technology alone or of only the bits of the business considered important to the supplier. A so-called exercise can be anything from telephoning a call tree to see who answers, to a full–blown, off site exercise. Even a so-called full-blown exercise will necessarily challenge one or a few disaster scenarios only, and the supplier is unlikely to want to list all the resilience failures found within that exercise.

Auditors' tick boxes do also miss the important point that the supplier may not see the risk manager's receiving organization as a priority in its own business impact analysis. As such, even a high-quality and trusted BRP or 'exercise' may not embrace the ability to deliver in volume, time and quality the particular products or services critically and urgently needed by the risk manager's own organization.

> If the supplier has one or more large customers that are business critical to that supplier, it would be naive for any other organization to believe that it can convince it to divert the diminished recovery energies and resources to meet their own business-critical needs.

It is a huge mismatch that continuity professionals, who have a healthy respect for whether their own resilience planning will work in whatever circumstances the planet and its occupants may throw at them, seem to be reassured by a third party's one-question answer. It does matter because the continuity manager's own organization only survives due to suppliers and their promises – those smooth promises that were made just as they were getting into bed together!

The lawyer's promises

This is another subject that needs a mention under the myths section.

The lawyer will be able, within contract wording, to place a risk with whichever counterparty will accept that risk. This does, though, bring in some important assumptions for business managers to embrace before contracts are signed.

The first dangerous assumption is that the supplier understands the implications of that risk.

> If you can keep your head whilst all about you are losing theirs it probably means that you do not understand fully the situation facing you.
>
> (Quoted from various sources.)

Even if the supplier does understand the implications, perhaps the supplier's risk tolerance level is different from its own counterparties, perhaps caused by a different risk/reward relationship applied to its quite different viewpoint on the contract to be signed. If, for example, the supplier is desperate for the contract to enable an escape route from a low trading cycle, it will accept higher risks to secure that contract. Such a risk level may not fit comfortably within the counterparty's risk tolerances.

The supplier may understand the risk implications and build its viewpoint on risk/reward balancing into the pricing and other terms. Again, if risk tolerances differ, one counterparty may be incurring greater costs of risk management than it would need to incur if it had retained the risk itself.

Finally, should the acceptance of a risk threaten the very viability of the supplier, and the deliveries are needed by its counterparty urgently, then the closure of that supplier will create a chain of events that may close the receiving organization too. Should a critical and urgent supply fail, and the receiver suffers disastrous market-place damage of its own, then any ability to sue the supplier for failure is only a corporate cry from the grave. The problems of the supplier's failure and the organization's own failure cannot, in such circumstances, be simply allocated to different legal boxes. They are one and the same.

This brings back the old saying about maintaining relationships with your bank: that you should always borrow enough money from it that your failure to repay is as much their problem as it is yours! This thesis can apply equally to any supplier/customer relationship.

Auditing supplier risk

The audit process is a natural subject development from the above sections as great dependency is placed on audits, whether they are internal audits, external audits or due diligence audits by such as supply chain relationship managers. Ensuring the ability to offer resilience is, of course, not just a matter for the time of signing contracts, but one throughout the entire period of the relationship.

The auditor needs to be clear whether he or she is auditing simply whether a management system procedure has been followed through, or whether he or she is taking a business view on the viability of the subject being audited. In other words, is the auditor offering assurance simply that he or she has seen a 'business recovery plan' document filed away, or is the auditor offering a view on the supplier's resilience? These two assurances are entirely different things. The latter assumes that the auditor is skilled in the subject being audited and is not just one who can follow through a management system framework document.

The difference in both expectations and responsibilities is huge, not least for an external auditing firm. If the board does not clarify and communicate those expectations beforehand it is taking some very high risks of its own.

People issues

One potential myth is that the employees of the supplier will be there fully to assist an organization that is facing a risk-related meltdown. Not many outsourcing contracts specify the contingency service levels that would be required whilst either organization is managing an emerging crisis. Such 'maximum time out' and 'minimum service levels' over periods of time are often pre-agreed within an organization's own contingency planning. It is remarkably difficult, however, to embrace every one of the potential exposures and consequences between contracting partners, and effectively to pre-quantify penalties for failures.

We have stated that one crucial resource removed during outsourcing is the hundreds or thousands of employees who had previously provided experience, skills and labour towards the organization's own objectives and needs. They are no longer there for the damaged principal to use as they have either been made redundant or transferred under the control of the other organization.

Certainly that supplier organization will direct all its new and existing employees tightly within its focus on its own business objectives. It will also manage them in its own style, with its implications on morale, training, skill levels, turnover and suitability for the tasks given. As said above, international supply chains may bring the organization unwillingly alongside employment practices, e.g. the employment of children, that are alien or illegal in its own environment.

Whilst there can be some contractual controls in the fringes, it is a myth to believe that any organization can fully impose its own agendas and objectives onto a third-party organization. It will simply have to live with this division on agendas and control as is best possible.

This diversity is at its most crucial during a crisis, or a potential crisis, caused by a risk incident or other failure. When the workforce is made up of employees, the employer, within the constraints of employment law, can redirect large sections of the workforce to meet the new and urgent priorities. This is not possible when that workforce is not under that direct control.

A request to a supplier to divert employees can be met by refusal ('I can't take them away from other contract commitments'), renegotiation ('We can do anything but at a price that recognizes your desperation') or even withdrawal of existing services as the damaged receiver's creditworthiness comes under question.

> 'A majority of respondents said that their weakest link in their business continuity planning and recovery efforts were their people risks. And yet, over 64 per cent are still not training their employees adequately on business continuity, crisis management and disaster recovery.
>
> It is critical that the people aspects get more focus ... organizations should link BCM to the organization's strategic vision, demonstrate it by developing training programmes to educate their employees on its importance and their role in the overall BCM, and exercise the people element more often.'
>
> (2006 Continuity Insights/KPMG Business Continuity Management Benchmarking Study)

During a crisis, it is often necessary to ask employees to work beyond the normal call of duty and the requirements that had been specified in the employment contract. Often they respond with magnificent support, either because of high morale levels, because they believe in the organization and want to see it survive, or just simply want to see their job preserved. None of these drivers are present when a third party's employee is unable to identify himself or herself with the struggling organization.

This vital human resource therefore needs to be recognized as an important value that is being repositioned into a legal or physical place where they are unable to assist when disasters create the crucial need for flexibility.

Pandemic

There are very special challenges, however, when the concern is that a pandemic will destroy the ability to retain the supply and delivery chains. The myth is that, with the readiness for people to work from home or be replaced by internet processes, this scenario can become a minor detour only.

The scenario could be that half or more of both the organization's and the supplier's employees have symptoms and are either sick or afraid of falling sick. Many other employees are committed to caring for sick family members, or to looking after children because their school has closed or childminder is not able to look after them. Healthy staff may be afraid to come in to work due to the fear of mixing with others during a pandemic.

Outside the workplace, transport, financial services and other utilities are having the same problem and, in an extreme case, the government may impose a state of emergency and curfew, keeping people at home.

The technological and other answers will need maintenance to enable them to continue to function and the maintenance staff may not be available. Home working has many challenges and is by no means an option for many organizations, not least getting work to home workers to do and the technological challenges to its effectiveness. A response scenario of a bank encouraging people to use cash machines instead of branches implies that there will still be people and transport infrastructures to keep them stocked.

The World Health Organization (WHO) has stated that it is impossible to estimate with certainty the economic impact of this unpredictable event in any given population.

The three major unknowns in predicting the possible economic impact are:

- magnitude and duration of the pandemic;
- psychological impact resulting in loss of consumer/investor confidence;
- supply side effects, resulting from a reduction in the workforce.

The effect on human health will depend on:

- unknown transmissibility and virulence of the strain;
- unknown epidemiology of the specific pandemic;
- rapidity and effectiveness of the response.

It is naive to trust that a vaccine can be made fast enough and in sufficient numbers for a pandemic, partly because the type of vaccine needed will not be known until the pandemic has already arrived. Furthermore, governments are likely, in a severe outbreak, to impose a ban on the sale of the vaccine until they are satisfied that emergency services, health service staff and other critical infrastructure staff have been prioritized and supplied.

It is also naive to believe that it will not happen. The Spanish Flu (1918) killed 40 to 60 million people; the Asian Flu (1957) killed 1 to 4 million and the Hong Kong Flu (1968) killed 1 to 4 million (WHO figures).

The implications are not just in keeping the supply chain moving; perhaps even in conflict with that objective, would be the risk that an employer may not be taking reasonable care over the safety of its employees and visitors. This will become a liability issue both for employees and third parties and of such a scale that it could exceed the policy limits of liability. Certainly, deliberately putting people at risk, say for commercial considerations, may be a cause for the insurer's refusal to meet the liability. Other costs, such as specialist clean-up costs, may be the subject of specific exclusions.

The myth here is that a pandemic is the government and the health service's problem. If only it was that simple.

However, in concept, the risk approach remains the same as in all other risks. It starts as ever with an understanding of the likelihood and the facts and then relates these to the precise sensitivities and objectives of the organization, coupled with a clear understanding of the dependables that enable those sensitivities to be safe and objectives to be delivered. With a pandemic, the worst-case scenario is that the reduced services normally considered adequate to keep the organization alive in a crisis situation may need further downsizing for this particular risk.

Product recall

One of the most expensive challenges, in terms of cost, reputation and brand damage, is when it becomes clear that a product needs to be recalled. This may be for legality, safety, or unsuitability reasons and whenever a product recall is triggered, the reasons and impact could easily be organization threatening.

Recalling products is a major challenge when the organization has manufactured and distributed products and services from within its own infrastructures. The challenges multiply when the cause of the recall is sourced deep within the supply chain and the distribution has also been handled by others. The stakeholders and the media have little interest which organization is at fault: it is the named brand that is being damaged.

The first question is – who is to take the hit? The named brand is necessarily taking the reputational hit but who is to absorb the additional financial and operational damage? Any public statements that 'it's the supplier's fault' leave the obvious point unsaid that the brand named has still failed, either by choosing the wrong supplier or by failure to manage the relationship effectively. The financial hit includes potential litigation, and the fact that products identified as failing cannot now be sold or released into the delivery chain. Costs include lost revenue and the cost of having to store, dispose of or destroy those products.

The recall itself brings the world's spotlight on the organization. How it is seen to respond to the challenge will redeem some of the damage done or alternatively cause much more damage to the brand. This is especially so where the opinion makers believe that the organization is sacrificing the safety of others to the great god of profit and expediency.

One of the most expensive and high-profile recalls in recent years was when Ford Explorers were having problems with their Firestone tyres. A total of 20 million tyres had to be recalled by Ford and Firestone and the financial cost was alleged to be over $3 billion. We can only guess at the reputational damage.

There was clear allegation that both companies took too long to understand – or admit – the problem and that they could have reduced the hundreds of deaths and injuries. Ford sales certainly dropped by over 10 per cent the following year.

E-distribution via the web brings its own challenges and difficulties in recalls, especially where it is not easy to trace back the recipients. The database of individual clients may not be immediately accessible to the damaged organization, and although it may fulfil its duty to inform the relevant authority, it faces a major task in making public announcements of the recall when dealing with an international, web-based community of customers.

The UK's General Product Safety Regulations 2005 (GPS) impose a statutory responsibility on both producers and distributors to place onto the market only those products that are safe in normal or foreseeable use. This replaces earlier legislation and applies to both new or second hand products used by consumers, whether originally intended for them or not. Product liability in any event is not easy, in law, to avoid:

In *Britvic Soft Drinks and Others* v. *Messer UK Ltd and Another* (2002), the defendants, Messer UK Ltd and Another, were advised that they could not rely on a term in the contract between them and their customers that limited liability. The drinks had been contaminated with benzene and the customers could rely on an implied warranty as to quality and fitness. To do otherwise would not be reasonable under the terms of the Unfair Contract Terms Act 1977.

(A Risk Management Approach to Business Continuity,
David Kaye and Julia Graham, Rothstein, 2006)

The failure may be in a physical product or in a service. Financial service companies in the UK were accused of misselling pension products, i.e. the advice that potential customers should transfer their existing pensions to their own products was not in the interests of those customers. Many were sold through independent financial advisers.

As the regulator, the Financial Services Authority (FSA) demanded that pension companies and advisers contact all customers and proactively seek out those who felt that they had been harmed, and then indemnify them. The regulator's role in this case protected the public interest but increased dramatically the cost of this failure. The regulator's demand placed the companies in direct conflict with their professional indemnity insurers, which demand in their policies that insureds do not set out to find claims against them. Pension companies had to follow the FSA's instructions and were placing at risk any recoveries they might subsequently have been able to make under their professional indemnity insurance policies.

The best answer, obviously, is to get the product right first time. There is a principle in law that requires a product to be of 'serviceable quality for the purpose of use' and this is the starting point. This definition acts as a useful reminder that quality is a variable and that the product should meet the purchaser's reasonable expectations that it will fulfil its purpose. It is not necessarily good if something is over-engineered and is thus too expensive for its chosen market-place. As in most business decisions, the real answer lies in getting an effective balance between any conflict of choice and cost. However, if an organization has chosen to distance itself from its competitors through an image of greater quality, it is business critical that this greater quality is sustained. One key word here is 'sustained'. Variable quality is poor quality. Furthermore, as said, late delivery is also a poor-quality delivery.

The risk manager's contribution could come in one of two ways, depending on the structure of the organization and the need for other specialists. The risk manager will bring a commercial feel for the damage that may be caused by delivering lesser-quality products and, through the use of fault trees and similar, can establish the sort of dependencies that may fail.

The risk manager will also ensure that any product recall plans are in place and exercised, and he or she will almost certainly be asked to work with factory managers, product designers and others in the supply chain to ensure that quality is delivered in the first instance.

Even the best-run organization can still have problems with its products, with criminals or lobby groups that threaten to make them unsafe in order to extort money or for publicity for their cause. A common risk management requirement against such extortion is to demand that suppliers design packaging, for example, food packaging, that is unable to be opened without the package then showing clearly that it has been opened.

This assists in quantifying threat and moves some of the risk management onto the purchaser who routinely will not purchase a food container that clearly has been opened.

Planning for product recall

Even a basic recall plan would need to embrace the many aspects and decisions as listed below. There just will not be enough time after the incident to negotiate and create a response as safety, legal and brand needs dictate visible and great urgency. Each of the organizations involved will no doubt be first wishing to protect its legal position, its brand and the cost implications.

It is a myth to believe that any product recall is a straightforward and mechanical process. The recall plan needs to prepare people, equipment resources, communication tools and information sources that deliver very quickly the answers and resources around a range of decisions to be made and actions to be taken. In each of the questions in Table 6.1, there is the need to know who is responsible in the supply chain and who will take the responsibility for the answers.

It is hoped that presenting the issues involved in a recall in this way will reinforce the point that it is a myth that, after the crisis has occurred, such plans could be evolved in time. This is not least within an atmosphere that may be diverted by accusation, searches for ownership, indemnities and worries about potential litigation.

Table 6.1 Supply chain decision making

To recall or not?	• Whether a recall is wise or necessary at all is the very first decision to be made, needing someone with the knowledge and authority to make the best possible decision, understanding the implications of what is known at the time. • The person making the decision needs to take a view on the credibility of the information or the threat received. • These are difficult decisions with far-reaching consequences, perhaps differing consequences for each of the counterparties of the supply chain.
Who needs to be reached?	• Suppliers, distributors and/or customers who may have already purchased the product? • Distributors who may have stocks for sale or distribution? • Is the organization able to gain legal and physical access to use the customer information?
What is the message itself to be broadcast?	• Clear and consistent messages and instructions must be given.
How best is the recall message to be delivered?	• What is achievable? Which method is best? • The media can be both an opportunity and a threat and will need proactive and reactive strategies and messages.
What practicalities need to be managed?	• Receipt of the returned products and the logistical arrangements for storage, repair, replacement or destruction. • Managing customer enquiries, refunds, complaints and litigation. • Product development and change to enable a resupply of the market-place and recover lost revenues.
Who monitors the recall and analyses the success or otherwise?	• Progress will need to be monitored throughout and from the point of view of different interested parties. • Some decisions may need to be changed in the light of the unfolding circumstances.
Who leads the debrief?	• The lessons to be learned about the original failure and the recall process that can overcome vested interests and bring useful business intelligence values.

7

Business continuity – both a science and an art

Introduction to business continuity management

The purpose and positioning of this chapter is to introduce the reader to the opportunities and skills and tools usually employed by business continuity management professionals.

This arena of business risk management can be known by different names within different organizations: business continuity management, business resilience management, recovery management, contingency planning, crisis management, disaster management, crisis risk management and emergency response planning. Some of these titles deal with different aspects of preparedness and recovery but one of the minefields of the profession is that the boundaries and thus the stakeholder expectations are not precise and are often unclear.

For the purposes of this book, we will use the expression 'business continuity'. We will, however, make the important assumption that this expression embraces all aspects from risk managing potentially catastrophic exposures right through to pre-prepared incident response planning and the response itself.

We will also embrace the importance of building in flexibility, so that the crisis teams can have the options to handle a wide range of surprises that did not feature beforehand in the 'blue-sky' scenario planning.

BS 25999-1:2006 defines business continuity as follows:

'2.3 business continuity management (BCM)

holistic management process that identifies potential threats to an organization and the impacts to business operations that those threats, if realized, might cause, and which provides a framework for building organizational resilience with the capability for an effective response that safeguards the interests of its key stakeholders, reputation, brand and value-creating activities

NOTE Business continuity management involves managing the recovery or continuation of business activities in the event of a business disruption, and management of the overall programme through training, exercises and reviews, to ensure the **business continuity plan(s)** *stays current and up-to-date.'*

(http://www.bsi-global.com)

The function sets in place owned, and understood, recovery plans that are designed to maintain effective control and to enable the organization to manage through the unfolding, potentially catastrophic, incident. The need is to ensure that the organization can retain organizational control, communications, reputation, legalities and priorities, maintain urgent service delivery and also accelerate the return to an acceptable normal situation, whatever shape that 'acceptable normal situation' then becomes.

Continuity management is not different to risk management. Failure to survive is just one risk – it just happens to be a crucial one. There is, other than the unreasonable risk to human life, no more important risk than the closure of the entire organization.

There are potentially catastrophic continuity threats lying, of course, within the whole range of the organization's activities and responsibilities. Every single operational manager may have lurking deep within his or her own day-to-day process engineering the most dangerous exposures and, conversely, the most effective answers and opportunities for resilience.

So who carries the responsibility of continuity? Enter the risk manager! Or perhaps the compliance manager? The business continuity manager? The health and safety manager? The internal auditor? The non-executive director? The brand manager? The supply chain manager? The insurance manager? The counterparty relationship manager? The customer services manager? The design engineer? The project manager? The lawyer? The security manager?

If we add externals such as the external auditor, the regulator and the media, maybe we have just about brought in Uncle Tom Cobley and all?

Losing the life (or lives) of a key person or team has important ramifications for business continuity. 'No, no!' says the health and safety manager, 'it's an H&S matter'. Retaining intellectual assets is a crucial continuity matter. 'No, no, it's ours!' says the brand manager, the IT manager and that man Cobley again. The insurance manager may have convinced the board that 'they are covered' and do not need to worry about risk anymore (gulp!).

It is thus easy to see that individual facets of this organization-wide continuity requirement are sometimes managed separately within organizations, often dangerously so, if silos of activity and understanding do not communicate with each other. Risk incidents do not respect these organizational boundaries and only too often find the gaps in-between.

Certainly, no serious-minded manager of any part of the organization can accept only the responsibility for what's happening today and thus not also have the implied responsibility for ensuring that his or her division's contribution will also be around tomorrow. Those concerned with continuity recognize that the hidden devil of discontinuity, especially within a modern, low-cost, web-enabled, tight-margined, outsourced and thus just-in-time and brittle organization, can come not only from failure of the strategic big picture. The risk of destruction can equally come from within the detail of critical and urgent dependencies within any one of the operational and strategic arenas.

Let's add to this minefield the fact that even the people who carry the same job titles may not have the same job to do for their employers, nor have imposed on them the same expectations. The business continuity manager may be charged only with keeping the IT going. The risk manager may be charged only with arranging insurances or balancing the risks within the investment portfolio. The expectation on the brand manager may only be to undertake carefully worded 'surveys', to plant good news stories in the media and treat journalists and key clients to corporate entertainment at sports events.

It is no wonder that the people who carry the primary responsibility for the continuity of an organization need not only to know what they are talking about, but also need to have highly developed people skills. Their task is certainly more akin to an orchestra conductor than it is to first violin, as it is all about recognizing the value of all of these roles, then professionally bringing all their concerns, skills and opportunities together to raise that resilience confidence.

In the same way that risk management has moved on from being the purchase of insurance products, business continuity is emerging from its own historical silo of workstation replacement and increasingly sees itself as part of the much wider risk and strategic management framework. Business continuity risk management, when used to its full extent, as in all risk, is as much about opportunity as it is about damage. It is about good management, enabling the balancing of risk rewards on risky activities to be informed, and is an enabler when otherwise profitable opportunities are avoided because of an anecdotal fear of the risks that they may carry.

In an outsourced supply chain model, the critical and urgent dependabilities on which survival is based are spread, not just within the one organization, but across many. The number of separated key delivery sources of course multiplies the challenge of continuity, as does their independence of control and agenda and, mathematically, by the multiplication of their dependencies on each other.

Continuity risk tolerances

A common risk decision could be that the identified and measured exposure is acceptable, and is documented as such. This is a reasonable decision if the carefully assessed worst-case consequences could not possibly have an *unacceptable* impact on the organization's own people, viability, stakeholders and business models.

Boards that consider the risk/frequency matrices that bring together risk and frequency feel comfortable in accepting risk when it is clear that worst-case scenarios may bring difficulties to manage but nevertheless difficulties that, overall, are manageable ones. They may also accept very low frequency as a reason for risk acceptability, although this book has already brought out the danger of giving impact and probability the same decision weightings.

> If that potential impact, however, is the total destruction of the organization as currently recognized, then it is unlikely that a simple risk/frequency balancing act will be adequate to establish risk priorities, as it can usefully do in lesser-impact incidents.

A well-maintained computer mainframe in a fire-proofed, flood-proofed and secure building with its own IT security, water and power supply is very unlikely to fail for more than a few hours at a time. That mainframe farm may be a single risk dependency, however, on which the entire worldwide organization depends for its survival. In such a case, it would be a hard task to convince regulators and other stakeholders that the risk/frequency matrix had caused a decision neither to have a computer recovery plan nor to duplicate off site the data and the software.

Continuity risk choices

The usual risk manager choices are constrained a little by the potentially destructive nature of the impact of a risk incident. The choice to manage downwards the risk of the incident occurring would have to be extreme and well trusted to make the catastrophic impact acceptable. Reducing the impact is always the big opportunity in continuity planning, such as when there are duplicated centres of delivery, each capable of picking up the lost delivery of the other. Clearly, the centres would need to be entirely separated in infrastructure and location – even perhaps overseas. The simplest information impact management is the simultaneous backing up of data and downloading it concurrently across a secure intranet to a backup site many miles away.

Another common risk management choice is to transfer the risk to a third party, but this simply moves the risk to that of the counterparty failing, thus bringing the same impact back round in a circle. We have already described the limitations of transferring risk into insurance products.

This list of choices now takes us into business continuity management – the subject of this chapter. In effect, the chief executive or the board decides that, with careful preparation, the organization has the strengths and resilience to manage the incident through without potentially destructive damage. That 'careful preparation' is, of course, no less than a business continuity cycle, but, as said, a cycle that reaches way beyond facilities renewal and also ensures the identification, impact measurement and then protection or duplication of all crucial dependencies.

Business continuity deliverables

When setting out on the stepping stones of effective continuity planning, it is worth remembering throughout that the board or senior management team, when facing a potential meltdown, is not only worrying about how fast information, workstations or people can be reinstated. It is asking other urgent questions too, of which just a few are:

- Can we, immediately, keep the confidence of all our stakeholders, even those now with conflicting demands?
- Will our suppliers and distributors stay with us?
- Will the suppliers be willing to respond to our urgent and changing needs?
- Will our best staff stay with us?
- Can we stay in control of our business?
- Can we stay legal and satisfy our regulators, not only with secured audit trails but also during our activities whilst the crisis is unfolding?
- Do we still have all our intellectual assets (knowledge, paper, internal and outsourced databases, software, market positioning, licences, confidence, patents, research, contracts, etc.) available to us and can we access them and use them?
- Will our critical business and financial models remain valid?
- Can we be effectively closed down because we are unable to deliver on time and in quality on existing contracted obligations?
- Can we keep enough of our presence in our market-place and secure our position there before someone else steals it, probably forever?

Clearly, a recovery plan that only offers four weeks' access to an alternative site may be nowhere near enough!

Therefore, business continuity forms just a part of a much wider and co-ordinated risk management programme that sets out to clinically understand the organization's business objectives and how it is exposed to potentially catastrophic damage. Discussion of the 'recovery plan' can only then begin.

Business continuity: the process

For a more detailed summary of the process cycle that makes up the business continuity cycle, the reader can best read in full the British Standard BS 25999-1, *Business continuity management – Part 1: Code of practice*. This standard takes its readers through the six processes of the business continuity management (BCM) lifecycle as follows.

'a) BCM programme management...

Programme management enables the business continuity capability to be both established (if necessary) and maintained in a manner appropriate to the size and complexity of the organization.

b) Understanding the organization...

The activities associated with "Understanding the organization" provide information that enables prioritization of an organization's products and services and the urgency of the activities that are required to deliver them. This sets the requirements that will determine the selection of appropriate BCM strategies...

c) Determining business continuity strategy...

Determining business continuity strategy enables a range of strategies to be evaluated. This allows an appropriate response to be chosen for each product or service, such that the organization can continue to deliver those products and services:

- at an acceptable level of operation; and
- within an acceptable timeframe

during and following a disruption. The choice made will take account of the resilience and countermeasure options already present within the organization.

d) Developing and implementing a BCM response...

Developing and implementing a BCM response results in the creation of a management framework and a structure of incident management, business continuity and business recovery plans that detail the steps to be taken during and after an incident to maintain or restore operations.

e) BCM exercising, maintaining and reviewing BCM arrangements...

BCM exercising, maintenance, review and audit leads to the organization being able to:

- demonstrate the extent to which its strategies and plans are complete, current and accurate; and
- identify opportunities for improvement.

f) Embedding BCM in the organization's culture...

Embedding BCM in the organization's culture enables BCM to become part of the organization's core values and instils confidence in all stakeholders in the ability of the organization to cope with disruptions.'

(BS 25999-1:2006, http://www.bsi-global.com)

This is equally about embedding the process right throughout the organization, having a clear understanding of the organization's criticalities and coming to the informed and best strategy for each exposure. It is then about developing response strategies and mechanisms and exercising those views so that there is some credibility in the decisions made and the resources that have been positioned. Above all, the standard brings out the important need to embed business continuity management right throughout the organization's culture and values and this brings back the 'orchestra conductor' metaphor used earlier.

The business continuity management lifecycle

If it were necessary, hopefully not, to choose between effective risk management of business-critical dependencies and a sophisticated recovery plan, the greatest safety will always be with the former. Otherwise, the risk is that the latter could become no more than an expensive weapon to beat an already dead horse. Critical and urgent dependencies still in place and accessible will at least give the managers half a chance of keeping the organization alive.

We can effectively return again to BS 25999-1 for an effective summary of the business continuity process, or cycle. The process is described by Figure 7.1.

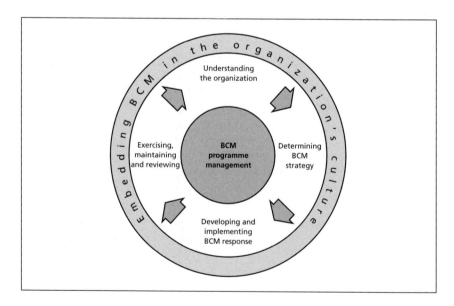

(Source: BS 25999-1:2006)

Figure 7.1 The business continuity management lifecycle

Business impact analysis (BIA)

This is the generic title often given to the process of setting out in a co-ordinated and consistent way to understand what are the critical objectives and responsibilities of the organization. This leads directly to recognizing the activities that enable those objectives and responsibilities to be delivered. Once the activities are identified clearly, the research will go on to embrace the wide range of resources that are needed to enable that activity.

A useful definition can again be identified within the British Standard BS 25999-1. This definition is as follows but needs some clarification within the context of supply chains and the context of this book.

'6.2 Business impact analysis (BIA)

6.2.1 The organization should determine and document the impact of a disruption to the activities that support its key products and services. This process is commonly referred to as a business impact analysis (BIA).

6.2.2 For each activity supporting the delivery of key products and services within the scope of its BCM programme, the organization should:

a) assess over time the impacts that would occur if the activity was disrupted;

b) establish the **maximum tolerable period of disruption** of each activity by identifying:

- the maximum time period after the start of a disruption within which the activity needs to be resumed,
- the minimum level at which the activity needs to be performed on its resumption,
- the length of time within which normal levels of operation need to be resumed;

c) identify any inter-dependent activities, assets, supporting infrastructure or resources that have also to be maintained continuously or recovered over time.'

The borders with what are called risk assessments are not always clear. The reader will see that this particular BIA template has a main focus on the amount of time that an organization is able to stop production without, presumably, destroying itself. This is extremely valid but understanding the potential for corporate failure goes beyond this and takes on board the things that the organization needs to give its recovery teams half a chance of keeping the organization alive.

Subclause **6.2.2c)** sets out to embrace these. These can be a wide range of dependables from links deep in the supply chain, workforce skills, contracts, and relationships, to capital and cash flow adequacies, technological hardware and software and other equipment, and information and other intellectual assets in all its formats. The activity, of course, needs to be able to stay legal, satisfactory to regulators and meet all the stakeholders' quite diverse and sometimes conflicting expectations. If any of these – or any other critical abilities or dependencies – are lost or become irrecoverable during the incident, the organization has completely failed and no amount of recovery planning will bring it back to life.

Identifying these structural dependables, understanding precisely what that reliance is, and risk managing the unacceptable exposures is as crucial to business continuity as is deciding the maximum tolerable period of disruption.

Whether that process is embraced within a separate risk assessment or embraced within a business impact assessment is less important to the absolutely crucial need for all the intelligence obtained to be brought together before the decision making and the business continuity process cycle moves forward.

One occasional confusion is to use the expression 'risk assessment' to look at, say, buildings and contents that have been identified as survival critical by the business impact assessment. The purpose is to see whether fire, security, safety, weather or other risks can be improved by localized risk prevention methods. This again is a valuable exercise to undertake. It should not be confused, however, with the early strategic and high-level setting out to understand the organization's weaknesses and exposures to catastrophic damage that is the starter in the process of risk and resilience management. What these individual processes are called by individuals and their organizations is less important to the fact that they themselves, and their own audiences, are clear what their individual objectives are and that, somewhere in the organization, the wide and holistic needs of business resilience is embraced.

With critical dependabilities risk managed, duplicated or otherwise secured and available for use, organizations then need to anticipate incidents that have the potential to destroy the organization altogether and so ensure that a response is planned that will:

> - 'enable an immediate, authorized and visible control of the incident and its aftermath;
> - ensure that damage is contained as far as is possible;
> - ensure that security and safety is reinstated;
> - ensure that damage assessments are received with confidence and acted upon;
> - ensure that financial and operational controls remain in place;
> - protect the brand value and other stakeholder confidences;
> - ensure that the immediate responsibilities and urgently expected deliveries are deliverable; and
> - accelerate the return to "business as usual".
>
> Individual organizations will no doubt add their own survival needs.'
>
> (655: Risk Management. David Kaye. © The Chartered Insurance Institute 2007 http://www.cii.co.uk/downloaddata/655_Syllabus_2008.pdf)

A suggested baseline format for a supply chain risk BIA appears at the end of this chapter.

Crisis management

The normal organizational systems and communication routes are very likely to have failed as a major risk incident unfolds, or they may no longer be appropriate. Fast unfolding crises need dramatically shortened chains of command and much faster decision making. The incident may demand entirely different ways of communicating, either because the crisis-driven new playing field applies new pressures or because the normal communication infrastructures have failed. These special communication needs are across the organization, external to the organization and also to and from the crisis teams themselves.

As crisis managers focus on the specific impacts that are threatening survival, new urgencies may need to cut right across routine management structures, subjects and even individuals who otherwise would be considered important. In a crisis within or to a supply source, these crisis management and communication challenges multiply.

The key issue remains that however good the recovery plan, it can be no more than a boot to kick a dead horse should the organization have allowed itself to be irrecoverably damaged even as the incident is unfolding.

By way of example, the organization may have failed to duplicate crucial urgent information and other intellectual assets. It may have failed to prepare some urgent and vital supply needs that could not possibly be sourced and set up after the incident fast enough to keep the organization credible and in its market-place.

Potentially catastrophic risk

Organizations face a range of strategic risks and in this wider context an organization may consider that, in addition to operational risks, killer risks include the following:

- failure to innovate against the competition;
- poor reputation and brand value management;
- poor employee and motivational performance;
- poor management of major projects; and
- failure to respond to market-place and competitor evolution.

These failures may destroy more slowly than a sudden catastrophic event, but will destroy just as effectively. As always, organizations will have their own individual killer risks, which may be either an operational risk or one of these wider strategic risks, sometimes known as speculative risks.

Sometimes, however, there is no clear division between the two disciplines. Indeed, in a disaster they can come together and compound the impact. A poor response to a damaging incident can directly affect the way the public sees the organization and the branded products that it distributes. If an organization, for example, handles communication with staff badly during a crisis, morale and motivation can be damaged for a long time afterwards. We have already discussed the dangers in responding to media attacks and thus the opportunities for making the problem much worse than it was.

There are a number of generic failures that could threaten survival. These include:

- failure of the web and market-wide or organization-central computer and communication infrastructures and their support needs;

- critical failure of divisional and workplace computer and communication structures and their support needs;
- destruction of buildings and other equipment that are needed for processing and delivery and their support needs;
- destruction of crucial information, whether it is on paper, in individuals' personal knowledge or within computer databases;
- loss of any other of the wide range of intellectual-type assets that are essential ingredients in the organization's ability to continue;
- failure to comply with regulatory or other legal frameworks;
- where there is an exposure to serious damage through the loss of one employee, or a team of key employees, in one incident; and
- breakdown of internal or external essential service supplier and product distribution chains. This would include transport, power, water and fuel.

Individual organizations will no doubt have additional potentially catastrophic concerns.

All risk and continuity managers had to reconsider their scenario setting following the terrorist attacks in America in September 2001, not least around the risks carried through from their just-in-time, outsourced supply chains.

'We're probably looking at everything in terms of how do we run the business in a mode of crisis?' said Dan Flores, a spokesman for General Motors in Detroit. The additional outlay on less cost-efficient, but more resilient, systems of sourcing and storage were described succinctly by Jorge Gonzalez, Chairman of the Economics Department of Trinity University, San Antonio, as a 'terrorist tax'.

Business continuity: computerization

Within the context of this section, it is of value to delve a little deeper than we have done into the need to ensure continuity of computerization. The computer and communications contingency plan will usually entail copying the latest data and software onto backup media, simultaneously or at agreed regular intervals, and storing it somewhere where the working data and the backup data could not possibly be destroyed at the same time. The file management systems always need to remain in sync and any common exposures to both sets of data, e.g. viruses, will need careful management.

Stand-by equipment will be positioned to enable end user computer services to be reinstated quickly. That 'stand-by' equipment may be available elsewhere from within the organization and be held ready for emergency use. Where this is not cost effective, the organization may contract with specialist disaster recovery companies that will supply equipment and workstations to an agreed location, to the required specification, in adequate numbers, and as fast as is contracted. The descriptions used of a 'hot site', a 'warm site' or a 'cold site' relate to the degree of readiness maintained and thus the speed by which they can become fully operational in an emergency.

The stepping stone described in BS 25999-1:2006 as 'Understanding the organization' will, by the use of a BIA, have brought operational managers and computer managers to an agreement on the maximum amount of time the computer network can be down without critical operational damage. This period is sometimes referred to as the 'maximum time out' (MTO) or 'recovery time objective' (RTO).

Computer recovery planning that delivers too much too fast for critical and urgent operational needs is a waste of money. Too little or too slow is fully destructive and is thus also a waste of time and money. There is, therefore, great danger in operational managers fully delegating technical continuity to technical managers. Effective protection can only come from a partnership between the two that ensures that crucial needs and responses are matched precisely.

Plans to use any alternative 'workaround' options (such as doing the work on paper until the computer network is reinstated) in business continuity planning should consider whether that alternative could fulfil each and every one of the functions, audit trails, communications and credibilities that are presently part of the computerized delivery. It needs to be able also to fulfil the new needs of modern business, financial and communication structures that have emerged as a result of the opportunities offered by computerization, outsourcing and the web.

The technology BIA, therefore, considers a number of issues including the following.

- The frequency of backing up the software changes and the data. This frequency sets the amount of processed data that can be lost between the last backup and the disaster itself. This lost information would need to be found again and then re-processed again, not by technical staff but by operational staff. This could be especially difficult if computers and paperwork were lost in the same incident and major backlogs were already emerging due to reduced facilities being available and following a period where there was no production computerization at all. Different businesses, of course, will have different stress levels when computerization is inaccessible. The MTO can be measured in weeks, days, hours, minutes or even seconds.

- How soon could the required computerization and all the communication systems be available and credible for end user operational use?
- The number, location, power and speed of the contingency machines. This, of course, includes not only central computers and servers, but also communication equipment and all the local and desktop equipment required by the operatives.
- The need still to ensure that sufficient employees, customers and others can continue to access the technology through end user equipment and the internet. In other words, to reinstate the ability to actually complete all the processes that have been identified as crucial and urgent. Recovery is not just a technological process.

An example reporting format is given at the end of this chapter.

An insurance company scans all incoming claims correspondence and the claims department responders handle this correspondence on screen.

The screen and its process trails are part of company-wide software. That software (including a database) records and supports decisions, responses, reservations, reinsurance implications, the audit trail, accounting, cash flow management, management information and credit control. It also communicates directly with the claimant and any third-party contracted suppliers that provide building, vehicle, property replacement and other recovery services.

The wide range of information on screen pages is so extensive that 21-inch screens are essential for staff to be able to do their work. They are certainly not just a luxury.

The technology BIA would need to pick up this need and ensure contingency arrangements are provided for those 21-inch screens. The view is that staff would be able to operate the system on smaller screens for only a very limited amount of time, if at all.

Should a BIA fail to pick up this detailed but crucial need, the entire recovery process could be rendered useless.

Meeting all technology contingency needs is, of course, expensive and the faster and more powerful the recovery, the more the need for pre-positioning of equipment and then ensuring that that equipment and software is kept up to date. Pre-incident risk expenditure is not recoverable as part of an insurance claim, whereas post-incident consequential costs are – another reason for getting the balance of preparation and response just right.

It is important to remember that the agreed and planned MTO in the plans should be acceptable, not timed from the incident originally occurring, but from the authorized decision to trigger the recovery plan. The inevitable gap between the two as authorized decision makers are reached, and the scenario is assessed, can be crucial in some businesses.

A bank, for example, will have special continuity needs for the service that enables customers to access cash 24 hours a day, every day, from cash machines. Its technology will also enable businesses internationally to verify their own customers' credit cards at all times. Call centres and card-authorizing software may be offering a 24-hour, seven-day service across continents. Failure of that computer or communications technology would create immediate and very widespread damage, not least to reputation. Clearly, there is a need here for very sophisticated – and expensive – contingency plans around both computerization and communication tools.

An organization that deals with its customers by mail, promising delivery of a product within weeks, would not need the same speed of recovery and, therefore, will spend less on before-incident costs. The need to protect current and historical information about customers and payments, however, is just as important.

Crucial information

Information is stored in many formats: in central computer databases, on localized computer drives and laptops, on paper, deposited with third parties and even in the heads of key employees. It is much more difficult to secure this information than the information in even the largest of computer databases.

Duplicating all information is not commercially realistic. The process of continuity management needs to identify all crucial information and ensure that it is still available during the disaster. The need is not just to protect but to also enable fast, credible access, as the information may be needed both to handle the disaster itself and then as the organization needs to continue to deliver its goods and services.

The key questions are therefore: is the information crucial, and/or is it needed urgently? Where the answers are positive, the information becomes a crucial risk issue to be managed. The next question is whether there is *sufficient* information available from elsewhere, i.e. not exposed to the same and simultaneous loss, to meet these urgent and crucial responsibilities?

For example, an organization may have thousands of staff record files. They provide current and historical information about each member of staff. Duplicating or otherwise protecting every document on every file is unlikely to be realistic. Fireproof cabinets will only delay fire damage to the contents for a period defined in the safe's specification.

The BIA may reveal that there is sufficient information to continue to meet the contractual, legal and other operational needs of managing those staff on the (backed-up) computer database. Therefore, the organization may take the decision that it could lose those paper files and still meet the contractual, regulatory, taxation, motivational and legal responsibilities to those employees.

The risk decision therefore is that the loss of those paper files is an acceptable risk. Such a decision will, of course, be taken with great care. The organization would not necessarily destroy those files. However, it could relax in the knowledge that, if they were lost accidentally, the business-critical needs could still be achievable.

Case study

A major life insurer was concerned about the loss of a warehouse containing over a million life assurance files. The long-term nature of the life assurance business meant that these files went back as far as 50 years and held massive amounts of information. Most of this information was simply routine adjustments and queries that had been satisfactorily dealt with over the years. To scan all these files would be a massive and costly job.

The business impact analysis report advised that current computer databases carried much of critical information such as payment records, names, addresses, policy covers and amounts, due dates, bonus allocations and periods. The primary contractual details were intact.

There were, however, two issues demanding a management decision:

1. The original files had the proposal forms that in turn held the original signatures of the policyholder.

---

2. The files had information about mandates going back many years where policyholders had instructed the assurer to pay named individuals on the life assured's death. The computer files recorded that there were mandates on individual old policies but did not record the precise instructions and the name and relationship of the payee.

As such, there were two issues calling for risk management decision-making.

The decision was that the assurer felt it could convince regulators and auditors that it could retain control over the portfolio and the subsequent claims without the policyholders' signatures. Signatures do vary over such long periods of time and as an essential claims control they had a value – but not a crucial one. Managers could anticipate from experience how many claims there were likely to be where the presence of the actual policyholder is disputed. There were other ways identity could be legally established and the cost and resource demands of these occasional disputes could be anticipated and accepted. The decision was therefore to accept the risk of losing the policyholder's signature. This decision was checked with auditors and recorded in a board vote.

The assurer could not, however, lose the names and details of a significant number of payees within its policy portfolios and continue to profess business control over future claims and maturities. The decision was therefore to create a project to go though the named files and capture this additional information from the old mandates onto computer databases.

When this project was finished, the assurer felt that it had put itself in a position that it could lose all these files in a fire, say, with only negligible or marginal impact. The costly alternative of fire resistant safes, sprinklers, etc. (with their own risk of failure) or other risk diversions was averted.

(A Risk Management Approach to Business Continuity,
Julia Graham and David Kaye, Rothstein, 2006)

Finally, it would be a mistake to assume that the most important information lies progressively in the most senior people within an organization. The issue is not seniority but the single point of information in which a crucial organizational process depends.

Minimum resource levels

An organization may decide that, should a potentially catastrophic situation occur, it is able to move its diminished resources away from non-urgent and non-crucial activities as it concentrates on its new survival-driven urgencies.

The BIA will enable managers to pre-agree the minimum service resources that they need to meet those urgent responsibilities over windows of time. These timings could be, say, from the decision to trigger the plan + 24 hours, the decision to trigger the plan + 5 days and/or the decision to trigger the plan + 2 weeks. This can lead to more cost-effective arrangements for contingency workstations that will not try to accommodate the entire organization, but only those responsibilities that need to be met urgently and progressively.

It is the context of this book, of course, that the risk manager will need to look beyond the employer's own organization for potentially catastrophic exposures. If the organization has a total dependency on a supplier, or indeed a distributor, then the loss of that link in the chain can be as destructive as a loss within the organization. The same principles of risk and impact apply, although the direct operational control over a third-party workforce during a risk incident will be more difficult or even impossible.

Unexpected and untimely loss of key employees or teams can prevent the achievement of operational objectives. There is the need to urgently find a replacement of those skilled resources and knowledge.

That person may not be the highest paid nor normally considered to be the most important member of staff. When a Provisional IRA bomb devastated the City of London, one insurance company found that just one of its problems was the destruction of its communications room in the basement of the office. This node received and directed some 5,000 internal and external telephone calls a day throughout its offices from Southampton, through all the London offices to Reading and Norwich.

The skilled person best and quickest able to divert calls through the system was not available. His marriage had failed and he was living at a new address, not even known by his previous wife.

The recovery plan was out of date in this tiny matter of detail and caused delays in reinstating services. A lesson learned was to ensure that human resources were charged to feed contact updates concurrently.

The other learning point was to ensure that this single dependency was removed by emergency succession planning or detailed procedures and other information documented so that replacement personnel could pick up the pieces as quickly as possible.

Even then, dangers remain:

An organization had a major mainframe, divisional computers and server farm with a 'hot site' facility contracted to IBM. The recovery plan was routinely tested and regularly to good effect with only small details requiring change, such as changed file management systems since the last exercise.

The risk manager required, however, that the next exercise recovery would be delivered not by internal staff but by IBM staff. The recovery manual would be made available to them and the organization's own staff would be observers: a role reversal from previous exercises.

Highly skilled IBM staff were unable to complete recovery on five different stages, requiring an explanation of the manual before they could proceed. The exercise was valuable in addressing clarity of the recovery manual, should the author not be available for interpretation during a real disaster.

There may be company rules about numbers of key employees travelling by the same transport, e.g. one aircraft. It is not necessarily rank that decides, but also whether important skills or information is contained only within that team of people.

Some organizations will conduct risk and impact assessments beforehand where large numbers of employees meet, say at an employee convention or celebration.

Employees are, of course, no different from other people in that they have the same propensity for crime, or indeed to be blackmailed or threatened into criminal damage. It is a naive organization that believes that the only damage or crime threat will come from outside the organization. Where the potential loss or disclosure is organization threatening, the issue becomes a continuity issue to be addressed.

Recovery plans

With the catastrophe risk analysis completed, the organization has a clearer idea of the crucial and urgent needs that will enable it to manage the organization through a potentially destructive incident. It then builds a recovery plan to fulfil the quite distinct need to:

- limit damage, including the immediate reinstatement of security, environment and safety, and protect remaining assets;
- immediately be able to reassure and protect reputations and relationships;
- accelerate the response through the use of trusted, authorized resources;
- create a speed, order and priority to the recovery process;
- immediately be able to respond to the new disaster-created challenges, e.g. a media, stock market, regulator or credit agency reaction;
- communicate immediately to a wide range of stakeholders within and beyond the organization;
- meet urgent customer and other contractual needs;
- protect the formal brand names; and
- keep the organization firmly within its 'market-place'.

Communication is a vital subject for continuity planning, with the following needing to be kept informed: employees, customers, regulators and all existing and potential stakeholders. This importance cannot be underestimated in maintaining trust and co-operation, not least amongst the various players in the value chain that pass through the damaged organization. This need is no less important because the usual communication challenges may have been damaged, in fact it is even more so as the challenge is to get to the stakeholder with information and support before those concerned stakeholders find themselves trying, unsuccessfully, to contact the organization.

The plan not only needs to pre-position contingency facilities and other options. It needs to ensure that the organization can effectively take immediate control of the incident. This latter need applies throughout the organization, and throughout the supply chain, wherever the cause or impact of the incident may be.

Where a supply chain is critical, the planning needs not only to be able to manage these issues during the crisis but also to have established beforehand where alternative supplies are to be obtained that are in the quality, speed, specification and volumes needed. However professional the crisis team response, in many organizations it may be too late then to set out to find alternative crucial supplies.

Contingency plans do not only deal with physical crises such as fire or bomb damage. They can be designed to cover all types of incident that the organization itself has decided could be disastrous for it and in need of structured, resourced and co-ordinated responses.

Plans could be prepared for specific risk incidents, say a hospital preparing for a power failure. Other plans may be required to:

- recall unsafe or illegal products from distributors and customers;
- respond to actual or threats of kidnap, ransom, industrial disputes, etc.;
- respond to a media attack;
- ensure a potential major fraud is handled professionally and securely in the early stages to protect assets and evidence, and adhere to employment law;
- verify and respond to a 'dawn raid' by revenue authorities;
- handle an epidemic such as bird flu or other widespread disease;
- take control, assess and respond to, at the time, just a threat, such as a terrorist bomb threat to the building or nearby;
- deal with pollution damage;
- handle the failure of technological processing ability and information security;
- handle supplier failure; and
- deal with the death or loss of an employee.

The very essence of recovery planning, however, is that it is need-based rather than scenario-based. It is rumoured that, in 1987, British Rail had 20 plans for 20 scenarios, but not one for a hurricane of the type that devastated services for a while…

The recovery plan document

The shape of business recovery plans will vary, organization by organization, but they are very likely to include sections that deal with certain key ingredients. These are detailed in the following sections and will be base points from which we can consider the additional needs of any crisis that spreads across an external supply chain.

Plan objectives:

Objective 1: speed of reaction to ensure:

- damage assessment;
- retaining of control;

- damage limitation, both physical, supply chain and brand;
- security.

Objective 2: predetermine, train and authorize trained teams to:

- set short-term and long-term objectives;
- set priorities;
- enable central control and co-ordination;
- enhance channels of communication;
- achieve the set objectives;
- monitor the recovery process.

Objective 3: to anticipate and position the resources and information that are likely to be needed and ensure timely access to those resources, perhaps over 24 hours/7 days a week.

Crisis management and crisis communications

The prepared response will include a named crisis manager (with deputies in case of unavailability) who will make important early decisions about the need and level of response. 'Do we or do we not have a crisis?' It will also include an authorized crisis management structure that is understood and accepted by all that are likely to be affected. The plan will also enable 24/7 access to trusted people, information and tools and trusted damage assessments.

There is a crucial need for a meeting place for crisis managers with pre-notified address, telephone, fax, email, website and other communication information. This would be used if usual meeting areas, say, the boardroom, were destroyed and not accessible nor safe. Any secondary or tertiary crisis meeting rooms would be far enough away to avoid simultaneous damage and be outside the likely areas of police cordons.

This section of the plan will empower the crisis managers and establish a chain of responsibility and communication. Code names may be used to establish levels of authority and responsibility. Normal communication methods may have been destroyed by the incident and immediate, new and perhaps increased replacements are needed. Separate, suitably manned telephone lines can respond to worried colleagues and families where there is loss of life and injuries. The sheer volume of calls and enquiries may demand additional resources and the use of the media, email, websites and call answering services.

Pre-advised crisis contact numbers and secure web access can provide information periodically to dispersed employees. Employees' home numbers and possibly their next of kin will be included in the plan document or be otherwise available off site.

Facilities

An off site store can be set up to store, away from the target building, anything that may immediately be useful. Contents may include hard hats and other safety equipment, information, urgent stationery, copies of plans, tools, communication equipment, laptops and printers, address books and a host of other tools that may be useful.

The IT, workspace and communications equipment will have their own plans that list the facilities that will be available, where and when. Their plans will be the detailed, step-by-step, technical rebuild and configuration actions.

Business managers will need at least a summary of facilities that will be available to them and the speed and the service levels they can expect. There is a crucial difference between having a 'hot site' and using an 'as and when' approach. With a 'hot site', facilities managers pre-position technological and other infrastructures so that they are in place and maintained ready for use. Where the planning, however, saves cost by requiring the team, subsequent to the disaster, to set out to buy the equipment and then configure it and install it, the risks to continuity are very different. The risk is that in practice the second approach proves unrealistic and the replacement times are just not achieved. The expression 'best endeavours' is sometimes used to differentiate between reality and hope but the difference should be clearly brought out and the risks assessed against the criticality of failing to meet the recovery targets.

Occasionally, the expression 'best endeavours' should be seen for what it can be: a spin expression for organizations not fully committed to continuity planning and an excuse not to adequately invest in the need.

Business managers will also need the names and contact information of those persons who have the responsibility to recreate these environments. This summary information will be in the organizational recovery plans for all other managers so that they can clearly see the delivery limitations that they had earlier agreed.

Documentation

- A range of prompts, checklists, reminders, priorities, pre-prepared 'workaround' options, etc.
- Pre-agreed minimum service levels of staff, workstations and equipment needed to maintain urgent service delivery
- Crisis teams, other staff, supplier and other key contact names, with mobile numbers, websites, addresses, email addresses, etc.
- Staff records, which may include next of kin information
- Service levels expected of technology and other facilities managers
- Location, access and contents of the off site store
- Location, access and directions to the crisis meeting room choices and alternative workspace opportunities
- Critical information and how to gain access
- Special features
- Perhaps, all staff phone contact information
- Other useful third-party contact information

Media

The media offers a wonderful opportunity to gain assistance in communicating to a wide and dispersed audience. It is also a dreadful threat.

There is a crucial and always immediate need to manage the information flow to the media and through it to the public. It is necessary to respond immediately and factually to the media's reasonable need for information and to get the current facts to the media that may help to meet the need of different stakeholders for information.

Achieving this entails pre-prepared, authorized and trained spokespersons. Media conference rooms, periodic press conferences and dedicated media lines will be needed if the media interest is likely to be large scale and international. The spokespersons need to be available at all times and have access to the latest information even as it emerges.

Urgent instructions may need to be circulated to all staff and suppliers to avoid unauthorized, possibly incorrect, information being released by staff or others. Such instructions should include how and where to direct media enquiries 24/7 to obtain exact, up-to-date information.

> **Case study: How not to do it**
>
> A *Sunday Times* article discussed a dengue fever alert in Central America and some Caribbean islands. It asked Thomson Holidays why they were not warning their tourists:
>
> *'Thomson told us that it was a matter for health and safety, which had been outsourced to a separate firm.'*
>
> ('Caribbean on dengue fever alert', by Chris Haslam
The Sunday Times, 14 October 2007)

Customers and other stakeholders

Arrangements may be needed to ensure that key stakeholders are kept informed, sometimes individually. This must be a proactive task and means getting facts to them before they feel concerned enough to ask.

One challenge is that different stakeholders will be looking for different information; indeed one information requirement may conflict with another. Shareholders are looking to preserve value and investment returns, competitors are looking for opportunities, supply chains are looking to their interests, not least creditworthiness, customers are looking for an assurance of service continuity, environmentalists may be looking for environmental damage and the media may be looking for villains as it already has the victims. These are just a few!

Crisis management structure

We mentioned earlier that a fast-moving and threatening crisis would need a faster, shorter, decision chain than the more normal ones within large organizations. Organizations will adopt the structure that best fits their needs but one example, adapted from police and military emergency structures and readily adaptable for a non-emergency organization, is given in Table 7.1.

Table 7.1 A crisis management structure

Code name	Members	Tasks
Gold	A quorum of the board or most senior management	• strategic and financial control; • empowerment of key players in the recovery; • high-level decisions and priorities; • arbitration between departments that are competing for resources; • monitoring; • media and other stakeholder information management.
Silver	The facilities managers and representatives of the business managers	• rebuild the operational environment according to the objectives and priorities set by Gold; • report to Gold and communicate with Bronze.
Bronze	The most senior person available at the time of each department potentially affected	• to carry individual responsibility for maintaining urgent services from his or her department as is best possible; • to meet as a team in order to receive and give information and to co-operate with each other where there is a clash of priorities between departments and where otherwise there is value in so doing; • to communicate, both ways, to all levels within their departments and to Silver and Gold.

Exercises

Exercising the crisis management teams, the contingency decision making and resources that have been positioned, is an essential. It introduces all, in a non-threatening way, to circumstances and possibilities that may not be part of their usual life or job experiences. The exercise can also:

• raise staff awareness and commitment;
• check decisions made about the resources needed and their speed of availability;

- reveal mistakes that may, in a real disaster, be destructive; and
- check that planning and risk decisions are still current.

For example, a typical exercise might set out to achieve the following objectives:

- raise awareness and exercise business continuity concepts, plans, opportunities and individual roles;
- convey the importance to participants and the need for ownership;
- test that all the internal and external technological and infrastructure planned solutions work – and also that they meet the business need;
- measure both risk and the impact understanding against the BIA and recovery plan;
- capture the learning points evolving;
- allocate timed action points to named individuals and thus develop and update risk and continuity work previously undertaken.

There is also value in exercising all staff who may be needed in a crisis response so that they can become aware of circumstances and the expectations on them, and also of the support and resources similarly available to them.

The exercise therefore delivers the objectives of preparing staff, checking the adequacy of prepared resources and developing further – and raising confidence in – the work of continuity planning.

The word 'exercise' is used widely, however, with a variety of different meanings. It is proffered as a route to credibility and confidence, but is it really, if it only exercises the ability to call out the gold team and to time the rebuild of an internal workplace? An exercise that will offer confidence is much more difficult to do and will also entail the critical measuring of all the decisions and activity around the whole of the risk environment, as it will around disaster response structures. Does the organization have fast enough access to *all* that it needs to ensure survival?

The simple tick boxes that say an organization has 'exercised its recovery plan' are a genuine worry, not least when relationship managers and auditors accept such tick boxes on face value from critical and urgent suppliers.

Exercising can, importantly, take many forms, from a simple brainstorm of continuity needs to a full-blown exercise using large numbers of people acting through scenarios over longer periods of time.

> 'The choice of exercise is important: it should provide the most appropriate and cost effective way of achieving its aim and objectives. There are basically four types of exercise, although there are variations on the theme of each:
>
> **Seminar** – also known as workshops or discussion based exercises;
> **Table top** – also known as floor plan exercises;
> **Control post** – also known as training without troops; and
> **Live** – also known as practical, operational or field exercises.
>
> New plans or players would normally be involved in seminar or table top exercises before a control post or live exercise was planned.'
>
> (Home Office exercise planners guide, http://www.homeoffice.gov.uk)

One example of a large-scale exercise is the annual tripartite market-wide exercise of London financial service organizations. A recent exercise involved 80 organizations across the UK together with the Bank of England (BoE), The Treasury and the Financial Services Authority (FSA). The FSA designed and delivered the exercise supported by the BoE and The Treasury, and by the project consultants KPMG and Crisis Solutions Limited. More than 50 market specialists also advised and helped throughout.

The complex exercise was designed to be realistic and international in scope, and entailed news broadcasts and web-based information. Organizations taking part included Canary Wharf Management, City of London Corporation, City of London Police, Leeds City Council, London Resilience, London Underground and Transport for London.

The scenarios scripted included incidents in London and other major centres, with the potential for damage to people, buildings and infrastructure, and demanded that participant firms considered both humanitarian and business concerns.

Another example of a large-scale exercise was when federal officials in Connecticut staged a mock chemical weapons explosion on the New London waterfront that was designed to exercise the Homeland Security response system.

It lasted for almost a week and involved public safety officials from local fire departments up to the US Department of Homeland Security itself. The US$16 million, week-long exercise involved more than 10,000 people. No real weapons or bio-agents were being used, but officials responded as if it was the real thing, flooding the area with investigators and emergency service staff in protective suits, sealing off the area, preserving evidence and dispatching fleets of ambulances to hospitals. Mock 'patients' presented themselves at hospitals with a range of medical needs. They underwent triage assessments, some were 'treated' in emergency rooms and admitted, and others were dealt with in outdoor decontamination in parking lots.

A total of 8,500 people participated in similar exercises in Seattle and Chicago in 2003 simulating a 'dirty bomb' explosion and a bio-terrorist attack.

Business Continuity Institute (BCI) six standards for certification

One effective summary of the business continuity process could also be simply to refer to the six certification standards of business continuity as established by the BCI. They are:

- BCM policy and programme management;
- understanding the organization:
    - *business impact analysis (BIA),*
    - *risk evaluation and control;*
- determining business continuity management strategies;
- developing and implementing a BCM response;
- exercising, maintenance and review;
- embedding business continuity management within the organization's culture.

Trusting third-party suppliers' continuity management

We need now to take these important concepts and explore the role, values and difficulties where a disaster spreads across different legal entities within a supply chain.

Risk and continuity professionals have a healthy respect for whether their continuity planning will work in situations that can only be guessed at at the time it was developed. Taking a view of, and trusting, a third-party organization's work is much more difficult. It has additional challenges that are not only in understanding the ongoing sensitivities of that other organization, but also whether it is up to date or, indeed, whether its planning embraces the needs of the counterparties as well as itself.

The reality is that many of these suppliers' so-called recovery plans will not work in some scenarios, and the ones that do may only protect the interests of the supplier, not individual customers. Not many exercises seem to include in their debrief the list of dependabilities and scenarios that they have not exercised, and also state, post exercise, where uncertainties still remain that have not been exercised.

Most important of all, the supplier may have decided as part of its BIA that it must prioritize between suppliers to ensure that the organization has a chance of remaining alive. We have already established that it is not commercially achievable to build recovery plans for major disasters that will enable the delivery of 100 per cent of all services immediately to all customers. The obvious result of this is that some customers will be let down. The supplier may also consider customer vulnerability and select those that will be damaged most by non-delivery. However, the latter vulnerability will still fit well within the organization's first need, to stay alive by first meeting its own range of most important survival and stakeholder needs.

Those needs may not just be financial. A supplier of drugs to both the private health care business and a public health care system may decide to prioritize the latter because of the further damage caused by a disproportionate media interest in the second of the two failures.

For either reason, one customer may not feature quickly in the work to continue deliveries.

Continuity management of the supply chain

Talking through the above business continuity headlines may have helped to gain an understanding of the issues involved in trying to ensure business resilience. To meet the agenda of this book, we need to translate these into the additional challenges where a supply chain link is under the control of others, is critical and is urgently needed.

The reality is that, however well constructed to normal business continuity standards, the supply chain dependencies will have additional challenges. Continuity risk management of the supply chain starts with the initial collaborative relationship building and the effectively risk managed common system requirements.

It is also about getting risk and continuity management right into the contract negotiations and well before signatures are added. It is also about anticipating the suppliers' own reactions where their confidence of future relationships and payment is shaken by a receiving organization that is seen to be facing difficulties.

Relying on the fact that the supplier is safely maintaining the distribution database is valueless if that outsourced supplier has lost confidence in the organization's ability to pay for the service. It is also useless if the suppliers themselves fail and the contract wording, legal ownership, mismatched software or even the Data Protection Act 1998 denies the counterparty's ability to step in and use that database productively.

It is no less a crisis when the receiving organization finds that its brand is being destroyed by gradually diminishing quality from a key supplier. But at what moment is a crisis declared, and what, legally, electronically and operationally, are the choices? Certainly, ensuring all of the legal, physical and operational usability of that database and software, and a whole range of other needs, whatever happens to the principal–supplier relationship, is no less a business continuity issue.

Especially with modern day business models, the true business continuity package particularly needs to:

- ensure that ongoing business relationships are collaborative, supportive and wherever possible ensure common interests and agendas;
- ensure that the common and interdependent management systems are included in the continuity planning and that the collaborative business relationships embrace, not only the good days, but also other scenarios that could be disastrous and the crisis management itself;
- ensure that no business-survival dependency can possibly be lost – the organization must be in a position to be able to tolerate any possible loss of dependencies, whether the potential loss is sudden or is unfolding gradually. In other words, the alternatives beyond the supplier must be pre-identified and known to be available in quality, volume and in time;
- ensure the promises to replace (supplier or internal) workplaces, intellectual assets, people, hardware and data quickly enough to avoid unacceptable damage to the organization can be trusted. Do supply chain service level agreements (whether internal or external) also document the service levels

being guaranteed during a primary failure? In addition, check how often these catastrophe service level agreements are formally signed off, not only by the facilities staff but also by the managers of all the departments, suppliers and distributors that could be affected;

- ensure continuity plans are established beforehand so that incident management teams are known and fully authorized, skilled and resourced adequately to retain effective control, and can communicate widely and deliver urgent products and confidence. A crisis that is caused, or needs to be managed, across two or more independent organizations needs, crucially, for this response planning to interface closely with each other.

A business continuity cycle that does not embrace this wider strategic exposure of dependencies is just lip service to the need for continuity. Such a part process creates new risks in itself, because it will raise expectations of resilience among its stakeholders, and as such is more dangerous than having no 'business recovery' position at all.

There are benchmarks produced by various organizations such as the British Standards Institution, regulators and trade institutes. Some are still in the process of catching up with the changes in organizational logistics and operational models of 21st century organizations. Some of these will be discussed in a later chapter.

Recovery facilities companies

No discussion about supplier continuity exposures is complete without a reference to those companies that provide, specifically, contingency facilities for clients to move into when their own facilities are inaccessible. Companies such as SunGard Availability Services, IBM Resilience and continuity services, ICM and others will contract to have ready, at an agreed lead time, stand-by facilities. The facilities supplied will, of course, be as contracted and the lead time again as contracted. This lead time may be measured in just a few hours starting at any time of day or night when the contract is triggered by the client's crisis managers. The contract could be to provide, say, 100 workspaces within 5 hours fully resourced with telephones, computers configured with the client's software, backup data and communication technologies with adequate bandwidth, and other business-critical tools that are needed.

They are therefore an extremely critical supplier to the organization, and just at the most critical moment for their survivability. Almost all contracts will include the client regularly exercising access to, and the use of, the facility.

Therefore, all the discussions about due diligence and the right choice of supplier to meet the need apply, as does the right relationship management that will ensure the arrangements remain constantly up to date and meet the most critical of requirements.

These suppliers will maintain these suites in different parts of the country with the ability for each of them to communicate between them and provide overflow facilities. It is, however, normal for the companies to 'sell' the workspaces many times and there is the risk of a large-scale disaster causing a greater demand than the supply available. In such a case, the contract is likely to say that supply is on a 'first come first served basis'.

The risk, therefore, of them failing an already damaged organization is a risk to be managed. The obvious risk management strategy is to contract with the supplier for exclusive use of a dedicated facility. This is, of course, a cost–benefit issue that will evolve from the client's perceived criticalities and risk comfort levels. Normally, a dedicated suite will cost between 15 to 25 times the cost of shared facilities.

The next stage of risk management is to engage fully with the supplier and understand its own risk management of the overpowering risk. The companies will not normally contract with more clients in one perceived area of risk, say a central area of a city, than they feel could overpower them. We have already, however, talked about risk's ability to surprise and bring unexpected scenarios. All scenario setting carries with it a risk of new surprises.

The BCI Good Practice Guidelines 2008 describes the exclusion zone as:

> 'The exclusion zone is the distance within which the recovery supplier will not resell the resources you have subscribed to another potential customer. The organisation's definition of exclusion zones should be clearly defined within the corporate BCM Strategy e.g. within the City of London a 800 metre exclusion zone (vehicle size bomb) is a minimum acceptable standard for this specific threat but may not be appropriate for other types of incident.'

This suggestion has already been made obsolete by the multiple bombing of London Underground in July 2005 and the current worries about a CBNR (chemical, nuclear, biological or radioactivity) terrorist threat.

The third level of risk management is when the larger suppliers have other contingency suites in other parts of the country. The long shot response is that a customer will be directed to a site further away than they expected. Whether this is acceptable depends on the organization and the ability to bring staff easily to those more distant sites.

The Financial Services Authority (FSA) has stated the following:

'Does the firm know the total number of additional claims per syndicated seat, details of the provider's back up plans and arrangements for providing alternative space?

Before contracting with a provider, the firm should be fully aware of the risk and using syndicated space (e.g. competing claims). The firm should check the providers back up plans to cope with multiple invocations; consider the adequacy of the provider's exclusion zones; and press for information regarding seat ratios. Without this information, execution of BCP may be seriously compromised.'

(FSA: *Risk Focused Review of Business Continuity Management in Major Financial groups post September 11 2001*)

All this simply reaffirms what has been said before about relationships within the supply chain. The 'client' cannot delegate the responsibility for facilities continuity to the supplier and the need remains undiluted, therefore, for the client to ensure that the supplier's risk tolerance and risk management profiles precisely match its own. If a supplier is unable to offer transparency of risk, then the 'client' needs to look elsewhere for such critical services.

Managing Risk and Resilience in the Supply Chain

BIA Base Document – Dependencies on Service Suppliers and Systems

1   Do you depend on third parties to supply services or information to enable you to meet your fundamental responsibilities to stakeholders?

YES	NO

2   What is your dependability and alternative assessment category as defined? If critical, crucial and with an urgency, please identify.

SUPPLIER	DEPENDENCY ASSESSMENT	SPEED NEEDED
a) Other internal company department		
b) *Third-party* suppliers		

3a   Has anyone discussed business continuity issues with them?

DO NOT KNOW	YES	NO

3b   If Yes: are you satisfied with their resilience to disaster and are your needs adequately covered by their recovery plan?

DO NOT KNOW	YES	NO

3c If the answer to 3a or 3b is 'No' or 'Do not know', are you satisfied that you can still meet your key responsibilities entirely in-house in the event of a disaster at the service suppliers' location?

	YES	NO

3d If you now have remaining exposures please identify an action point in paragraph 5 to check the facts and review.

Not necessary	Action point established

4 Please use this section to clarify your answers above.

SUPPLIER	CLARIFICATION

5 Risk management action points, including those emerging from the answers above and any further investigation necessary.

ACTION POINT	NAME	TARGET DATE
(offsite store?)		

Dependencies on Service Suppliers and Systems, continued

6   Prompts and priorities emerging for the recovery teams to be included in the recovery plan. (Please write these as you would wish to see them in the recovery plan document itself.)

1	
2	
3	
4	

Please confirm that the corporate relationship management standards are in place,

including:

Yes	No

- board and relationship managers have agreed the contingency supply policy and delivery arrangements;
- recovery plans embrace liaison with suppliers' plans and also any contingency suppliers as agreed to be necessary;
- frequency these arrangements are updated;
- exercises undertaken and planned. Please explain what is being exercised.

Please copy these pages for each dependency identified.

Anticipated Disaster Recovery Service Levels: Template for discussion

This section should detail premises, telephony, IT, etc. service levels that can be expected or needed in the event that the IT and facilities recovery plan is invoked.

THE SCHEDULE SHOULD INCLUDE AT LEAST THE FOLLOWING.

Please complete two schedules:

A. Services delivery from contingency site
B. Services delivery if primary site remains accessible, serviced and safe

- Please advise frequency these are updated and confirmed to be available.
- Please advise frequency that operational needs are researched and updated.
- If recovery is progressive, please explain the progression.

	In place? Internal/contracted?	Best endeavours? (Please define)
Maximum loss of current production data and process software?		
Maximum loss of any archive data and process software?		
Maximum loss of current development data and process software?		

Maximum delay in reinstating processing?	
Maximum delay in connectivity to existing and/or any business contingency site?	
Maximum delay in reinstating servers?	
Maximum delay in emergency cabling?	
Maximum delay in replacing end user equipment?	
Estimated downtime time needed to reinstate computerization to a rebuilt office site?	
Maximum downtime for web-enabled activities?	
Time delay before incoming calls can be transferred to emergency answering?	
Time delay before staff have full working communications?	
Availability of contingency workstations and the facilities available?	
Quantum and list of facilities available at workstations as confirmed acceptable with operational managers?	
In summary, therefore, when can the business staff start processing again in any numbers?	
Please quantify risks of failure to deliver these service levels.	

8

Third-party relationship management

Managing third parties

Managing third parties carries all of the usual challenges of managing internal staff: in other words, getting the best out of employees by ensuring motivation and identity with the organization's widest objectives. That motivation at least includes that each and every player involved understands and buys in to the objectives, their own roles and the importance of their own delivery towards meeting those objectives.

Where labour and skills are not within the organization's own control structures, however, there is a wide range of additional management challenges caused by the fact that the relationship is one of partnership and not authority. Furthermore, that partnership is two way, with each party bringing its own agendas, objectives, pressures, stakeholder needs, demands on the other and, not least, problems.

Each party will also see the particular partnership under discussion as only one amongst a further wide range of employee, partnership and other stakeholder relationships, many of which, in the grand scheme of things, could be much more important to it. All players are therefore performing a balancing act of some type or another.

> 'The art of management consists of issuing orders based on inaccurate, incomplete and archaic data, to meet a challenge which is dimly understood and which frequently is misinterpreted; to accomplish a purpose about which many of the personnel are not enthusiastic.'
>
> (Anon)

These words are worth quoting again within the context of this chapter. Even though he was perhaps just having a bad day when he penned this classic, he does make good points in turn about incomplete data, old data, real understanding (not just lip service), misinterpretation and enthusiasm. He was probably also talking about the military people over whom he had absolute power to demand activity precisely to his orders. If only it was that simple in the employee/employer relationships within civilian life. If only it was as simple as employer/employee business relationships when operating with an outsourced supply chain!

That partnership will be designed, primarily and hopefully, to bring added value to each participant. That value will be required continually within one's market, business model, and financial, political or risk environments that existed, and had been envisaged, at the time of the agreement.

Each organization will know that the only thing it can guarantee in organizational life is change of some sort or another, even without an externally caused risk incident. The values in the partnership will need to survive those changes, be flexible if necessary or, in the extreme, be able to trigger a very clearly envisaged exit process with acceptable levels of pain to all players.

> A young journalist asked Harold Macmillan, when British Prime Minister, after a long dinner, what can most easily steer a government off course. 'Events dear boy, events' was the answer.

However many controls and contractual clauses are added, the relationship will only continue to satisfy the original hopes whilst all parties continue to perceive value to their own organization as they, and their own environments, continue and evolve.

If all that is not enough of a challenge, the relationships, both ways, will need the flexibility to manage through any crisis that emerges; some of these crises may be potentially destructive to one or both of the parties. When the threat of destruction is to one partner only, the temperature rises dramatically, and it brings under critical view, with great force, any perceptions of remaining values in the particular relationship. Above all, it asks the question whether the extra effort and cost now asked by the struggling party is not overpowering the value of the ongoing relationship to the other. This is, of course, *if and whether that counterparty survives.* However much personal sympathy may be offered, it is unrealistic to ask any organization to put sympathy for another before its responsibilities to its own wide range of stakeholders.

This chapter will explore these relationships, from a strategic level and also from the aspect of integrating common management systems and, finally, the need, if separation is a must, for as least painful a divorce as can be achieved.

As has been discussed earlier in this book, ensuring that an acceptable pre-agreed nuptial agreement is in place does need the enthusiastic project personnel to face up to the fact, and even admit to their audiences, that their career building idea could just go wrong in the future. This may be the greatest challenge of all.

Collaborative business relationships

The British Standards Institution's Publicly Available Specification PAS 11000, *Collaborative Business Relationships*, has a framework that is useful to structure the first part of the chapter. The specification, in turn, discusses:

- the wide scope within which collaboration is needed;
- awareness to ensure the right basis for what follows, in knowledge gaining, internal assessment, partner selection and working relationships;
- the creation of added values from the collaboration;
- staying together; and
- the exit strategy should that be the only remaining choice.

We have discussed some of these things elsewhere in this book and so we will focus here on any points that are additional ones, or worthy of another mention within the broad context of third-party relationship management.

We mentioned the need to ensure that there is continuing mutual value for each. This was evidenced by Land Rover's experiences with the manufacture of the chassis for its Discovery model.

There were deep sighs of relief all around at Land Rover's Solihull factory in the UK (and many neighbouring suppliers, too, no doubt) when it was announced that the company had reached an agreement with administrative receivers to end the deadlock over Discovery chassis supplies. Land Rover agreed to buy the chassis makers, UPF Thompson, for a reported £16 million.

> Had the parties failed to reach agreement following UPF Thompson's financial collapse, Land Rover's chief executive, Bob Dover, had threatened to close Discovery production until a new chassis supplier could be found. The resulting job losses can only be estimated, but many thousands would have suffered.
>
> Curiously, the receivers, accountants KPMG, suggested that Land Rover was in some way itself responsible for UPF Thompson's demise by driving down the price it would pay for the company's products. Land Rover had also previously refused to pay out £62 million to take UPF Thompson out of receivership.
>
> (Richard Howell-Thomas, *Land Rover Monthly*, April 2002)

Whether KPMG's allegation is true or not, it makes an important point. This is that for any organization to use its relative power and negotiating strengths to drive the counterparty towards a position of no value can only lead eventually to the destruction of the partnership. In an outsourced, just-in-time, objective-critical supply chain on which the receiving organization depends, such corporate bullying is only a form of delayed suicide. There is blatantly no help either available from the usual comfort blankets of lawyers or insurance.

The BSI specification includes a chart that gives an overview of the principle components of a successful collaborative business relationship, which is worthy of repetition here (see Figure 8.1).

For the purpose of this chapter, we will assume that the best choice has been made in the right choice of the counterparty for the role in mind. To be the best choice, the process of deciding will have included the recognition, measurement and reporting of the risks within that choice. The risks, when identified, can, of course, trigger their own risk management before partnership commences and also continuing as a part of the ongoing relationships. Common examples are credit terms, continuity planning, quality controls, audit access, change reporting, information and other security, financial guarantees or assets secured against outstanding balances.

Awareness

PAS 11000 brings out the importance of clear communications and ownership within these collaborative working relationships. What the awareness phase entails is shown in Table 8.1.

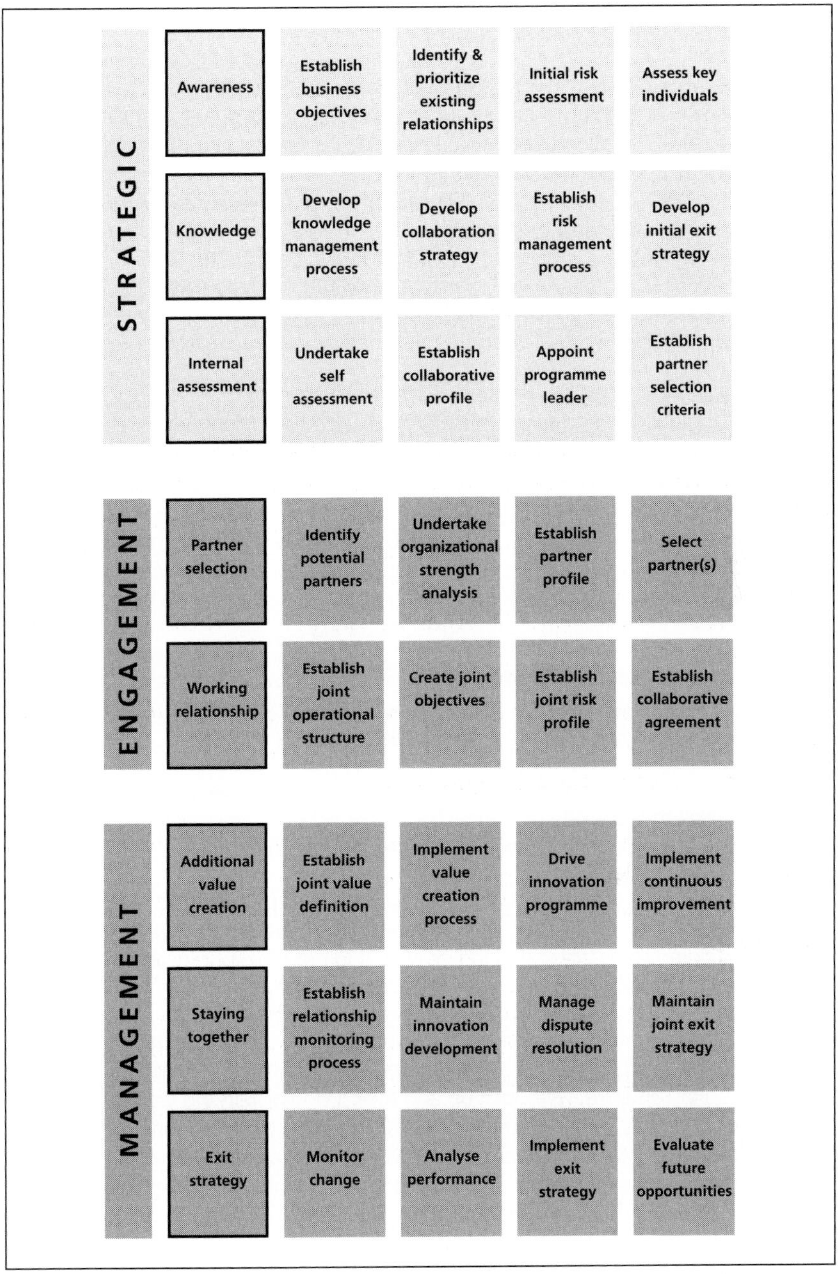

STRATEGIC					
	Awareness	Establish business objectives	Identify & prioritize existing relationships	Initial risk assessment	Assess key individuals
	Knowledge	Develop knowledge management process	Develop collaboration strategy	Establish risk management process	Develop initial exit strategy
	Internal assessment	Undertake self assessment	Establish collaborative profile	Appoint programme leader	Establish partner selection criteria

ENGAGEMENT					
	Partner selection	Identify potential partners	Undertake organizational strength analysis	Establish partner profile	Select partner(s)
	Working relationship	Establish joint operational structure	Create joint objectives	Establish joint risk profile	Establish collaborative agreement

MANAGEMENT					
	Additional value creation	Establish joint value definition	Implement value creation process	Drive innovation programme	Implement continuous improvement
	Staying together	Establish relationship monitoring process	Maintain innovation development	Manage dispute resolution	Maintain joint exit strategy
	Exit strategy	Monitor change	Analyse performance	Implement exit strategy	Evaluate future opportunities

(Source: taken from PAS 11000:2006)

Figure 8.1 Overview of the principle components of successful collaborative business relationships

199

Case Study: Heathrow's Terminal 5

BAA, the airports operator, adopted what was considered to be a different approach in building the Terminal 5 extension to Europe's busiest airport, Heathrow. At a cost of £4.3 billion, it embraces the largest free-standing building in the UK plus two satellite terminals, 60 aircraft stands and a new air traffic control tower. The project encompasses a 600-bed hotel, 8 miles of tunnels and a multi-storey car park.

BAA set out to achieve cost and quality control that could be managed centrally and agreed, unusually for such a large project, to retain all the risk itself. More commonly, carefully worded contracts pass much risk onto contractors.

BAA clearly understood the risks in the tendering process itself where a contractor is encouraged to put in a low price, and has incentives to recover cost throughout the job and even raise claims and disputes to recover additional sums. Such disputes can delay the overall project completion. This is especially so where the finishing date is critical, such as preparing a site in time for Olympic Games. There were suspicions in Greece that some Olympic Games contractors were deliberately delaying work so that they could use increasingly powerful negotiating positions to revise quality and cost agreements and even access contingency budgets.

BAA chose contractors with which it has long-term relationships, and created an atmosphere that enabled – collaboratively – the early identifying and thus addressing of individual risks, well before damage was caused.

When, for example, a wet winter delayed the work, they were able to catch up by changing the sequence of works. Traditional subcontractor contracts would have made this difficult or caused additional charges to be made.

Major risks in such contracts lie in the very complexity of the project and the interdependencies of various contractors and their own supply chains. Risk was considered to be integral to the delivery and not a peripheral aspect to be separately managed.

One result of this viewpoint was the decision to test and pre-assemble as many components off site as possible. The single-span roof over the main building was tested in Yorkshire. 'We put it up and took it down, with the architect, the engineer, the safety people and the crane driver,' says Mr Wolstenholme, the project manager. 'We took away about 120 lessons we would otherwise have encountered on the critical path on the main site.' 'So many other programmes leave the risk of testing and commissioning very late,' he says.

Quotes from Mr Wolstenholme as reported in the Financial Times, October 16 2006.

Table 8.1 PAS 11000 awareness headlines

Specification headline	Author's comment
Identification of one senior executive with the responsibility for the collaboration	The 'seniority' adjective assumes power or influence to redirect any element or division that is diverting the relationship away from the overall strategic values of each organization.
Identification and segmentation of existing business relationships	It is too late when something has gone badly wrong for the criticality of an individual relationship to the wider organization to then be grasped. We are talking here, of course, of the wider organization objectives and responsibilities, and also the wide expectations of stakeholders, not just those directly relating to the individual relationship objectives.
Prioritize business relationships	We are here, of course, in the familiar arenas of the risk assessment and the business impact analysis. The prioritization question being addressed is: 'Where do we start in assessing and thus prioritizing the risks within our business relationships?'
The risk assessment	Because the outsourcing risks themselves can be different ones, it does not mean that the risk assessment is separated from the routine risk standards, control procedures and cultures currently in place across each organization. It will need to fit comfortably within wider risk controls, reporting, tolerances, self-assessments, and compliance needs.
Formal and informal relationships	The supply dependency can be either formally contracted or informal, e.g. making routine purchases when required from one supplier. Furthermore, there is a need to recognize those individuals within the organizations who are in the front line of the relationships and who, day to day, make the relationship work. These people and their roles in turning contract wording into meaningful activity need recognizing, encouraging, supporting and, if necessary, training.

For example, an organization will have a risk register and an accident register with the latter document capturing learning points from accidents and near misses. The most public of accident and near miss registers are in the air transport industry where a near miss is defined and must be reported. It then triggers a formal investigation to learn whatever can be learned to avoid a repetition. Where there is a genuine common objective to avoid disruptions there can be real value in suppliers and principals sharing this information, and opportunities for learning.

Clear objective setting

This seems an obvious prompt but it is surprising how often objectives can be less than clear, even at the outset. This is especially so when the changes are being forced on an organization by outside pressures such as when facing a significant new disadvantage emerging over competitors. The clarity of objectives can also be lost as the project unfolds and as new objectives start to slip into the project. 'Project drift' is a clear ongoing risk in the minds of professional project managers as a repositioning of a supply need can impact, and bring other opportunities for re-engineering, right across the organization. The supply chain project is therefore particularly at risk of side agendas creeping in and fogging the initial clear objectives.

It is suggested that this has happened in the UK's National Health Service computerization project.

PAS 11000:2006 usefully brings out the critical arenas of business environment, organization, people and processes and goes on to discuss and recommend individual assessments of resources, manpower, customer value and capability.

With this awareness, clear goals can be established that are specific, measurable, achievable, realistic and time bound. Furthermore, there is clarity to be found in assessing what the prospective partner can and cannot bring to the relationship in the critical areas shown in Figure 8.2.

We make no apologies for raising these issues in a book about risk management of the supply chain. Without these foundations clearly in place right from the beginning all the subsequent efforts of the risk manager could become futile.

We remind yet again at this point that risk management is not about removing all risk from a venture. This is just not an achievable objective; indeed, we have said elsewhere that doing nothing is not risk free in a competitive and developing market-place.

	Importance of partnering attributes
1	Level of commitment
2	Level of capability
3	Dynamic culture
4	Appropriate organization
5	Level of communication
6	Commercial model
7	Quality programme
8	Commitment to vision and values
9	Customer focus
10	Attitude to collaboration

(Source: PAS 11000:2006)

Figure 8.2 Establishing the profile of the potential collaborative partner

This of course brings out the corollary that the knowledge sharing embraces an understanding of the joint and individual risks being retained, by which party and whether those retained risks are within each party's documented risk tolerance levels.

Knowledge

Knowledge and the sharing of that knowledge may be perceived to be a 'soft' dimension to a relationship but it could probably be the most crucial. The need to make the best use of skills, now available to both organizations, is often the primary value of collaboration. That knowledge is not only useful to work new opportunities, but also to retain a clear focus and, not least, to see threats emerging.

Access to knowledge, skill, experience or other intellectual assets owned by the counterparty, of course, can often be the primary, maybe only, objective of the collaboration. The loss of that knowledge, either by staff resignations or by the counterparty failing to ensure that the intrinsic value of that knowledge is maximized, destroys the whole relationship value. Should that skill base objective not be risk managed, and then lost, the organization has not only failed to gain from the collaboration but may also have removed the alternatives that it had available at the time of the choice to proceed.

Certainly due diligence enquiries on copyright, patents and ownership of research material, etc., and also on the counterparty's succession planning, are especially crucial in such circumstances.

That knowledge comes in many formats, informal and formal. The value can be found, or perhaps developed, in the team building and informal mixing of employees from the different organizations. The knowledge can be in the partnership-wide use of centres of individual excellence within each organization, through to the more formal patents, research, software, databases and experiences that have been brought to the table.

PAS 11000 usefully discusses the importance of knowledge sharing in setting up the relationship but it reaffirms the importance of knowledge sharing continuing right through each day of the ongoing relationship.

The problems of integrating two diverse organizations, following mergers or acquisitions, are subjects of many a learned treatise. The issue is not just one of merging production lines, capital, finance and marketing. It is often as much around the creation of an overall management that has the support of the entire, combined organization. It is as much about the mixing of cultures and all of the personnel's comfort or discomfort with the new arrangements.

At least with a merger there emerges (hopefully) one overall management control and style. Placing a strategic part of the organization's value chain into the hands of a third party, however, provides all of the challenges of a merger without any of the overarching cultures and controls to sort out any emerging difficulties. Furthermore, both mergers and outsourcing arrangements must sit equally under the harsh spotlight of the promises made to stakeholders at the time the new arrangements were sold to them.

Collaboration risk management

The principles outlined elsewhere about the risk assessments and the business impact analyses will be integrated within the ongoing control and governance procedures within each organization. There is a further layer, which is the risk assessment and business impact analysis of the partnership itself and its crucial objectives.

It needs to start at project planning stage – it is too late when the contracts are signed. Completing risk assessments and business impact analyses bring their own challenges when completed within one organization, but there are even more challenges when undertaken in collaboration with a third party that may wish to put a 'spin' on any risks that might prejudice the chances of the contract being signed. There, is therefore, a special challenge of credibility, and one not easy to resolve.

To deliver credible risk and impact assessments there is a crucial need for clear and common risk objectives and risk definitions across both organizations. The objective of the risk assessment needs to be clear to all of its stakeholders, and have common definitions. One example of 'business critical' is as follows but this may vary organization by organization:

'The information needed and the ability to undertake processes that will ensure that the business unit can:

- Meet the need to retain control of the business and the business portfolios
- Retain all necessary compliance and regulatory approvals
- Retain its distribution base and place in the market place
- Meet essential and urgent customer needs
- Maintain financial control
- Retain and potentially continue to develop the brand value
- Meet any requirements in civil and criminal law
- And does not lose money – nor fails to meet targets – to the point that, in any stakeholder's opinion, a 'disaster' has occurred.'

(*A Risk Management Approach to Business Continuity*,
Julia Graham and David Kaye, Rothstein, 2006)

The practical but quite difficult challenge of the risk manager is to gain credible access to information around which he or she will make recommendations to the board or chief executive. There are many ways of doing this; indeed, different sources may need to be cross-checked to ensure that credibility. Views as to what a risk is, and its acceptability or otherwise, are very personal opinions and those personal views are carried forward into the corporate risk cultures of each organization. One challenge with risk managing across outsourcing relationships is the different agendas that each bring to that risk researching.

This may be simply a strategic difference or it could be contradictions in the detailed requirements of different regulators or legal environments. An organization requiring to report within the Sarbanes-Oxley Act may have different criticalities to one needing to report to the Monetary Authority of Singapore or within the UK's Financial Services Act. One organization may have particular stakeholder requirements such as the security demands within military contracts, or liability and insurance issues such as when components are provided to aircraft manufacturers. Furthermore, an organization's other contracts may be demanding all sorts of individual quality, risk, speed of delivery, transparency and control management requirements.

Communicating risk information back to the risk manager's own stakeholders is also absolutely crucial to the risk management process. This needs to be full and frank, and in a clear format that enables informed decision making about the acceptance and management of risks. When that information is market sensitive, perhaps even share price sensitive, however, either to the wider market-place or just to the current negotiations, there are real challenges to overcome to get this right.

We repeat that the failure of a just-in-time, objective-critical supplier can be equally destructive and cause failure, too, to the receiving organization. This is especially so where there is no adequate alternative source available quick enough to minimize damage. The receiving organization does itself only short-term favours by hiding risks from the supplier during the contract negotiations. The legal principle of 'let the buyer beware' may stand up in court, but it fails to comfort the organization that lets its supplier fail and then falls down itself as a result.

Continuity management

Continuity management includes the preparation of plans to inform, guide and resource crisis teams as they set out to manage the organization through a potentially disastrous situation. The principles are discussed elsewhere in this book but a couple of additional issues are worthy of mention under this heading.

Where the organization has been bombed, flooded, burnt or destroyed by a hurricane, it is quite easy to see immediately that a disaster has occurred and that the recovery plan needs to be triggered. A gradually evolving potential crisis is, however, much more difficult because someone has to make, at some point in time, the decision that there remains no choice left but that the exit, or continuity plan, needs to be brought into play. This is never an easy decision as switching into crisis mode brings all sorts of cost, brand, employee and other relationship damage as well as media interest, and also can close down routine operations. Such a step will most likely bring the entire relationship to an end with all that that implies going forward.

A gradually declining quality or consistency of delivery issue with a supplier can be a problem but it will, at some point in time, begin to damage the brand values of the receiving company. There may either be a problem that can be resolved within the relationship management or, on the other hand, it may be the first sign of a crisis that cannot be resolved. Brand confidence and trust are, of course, crucial business dependencies for many commercial and public service organizations.

All of the collaborative relationships will no doubt have been exploited but the hard decision may still have to be made. Someone has to make the hard decision that this is the moment in time that the 'contingency plan' must be brought into play. The decisions are whether to trigger the exit strategies that are available to the organization and, if so, at which moment in time.

Another continuity issue worthy of mention again here is that an organization may be able to redirect its own workforce and other resources to meet such a new and increasingly urgent challenge. It is much less likely to be able to redirect the workforce and resources of a third-party organization.

The supplier may simply not have the needed resources to bring to the problem. As said elsewhere, the supplier organization will have its own objectives to deliver, not least to its other customers. These other customers may, indeed, be much more important to the supplier than the struggling one. Finally, the supplier may take the view that the struggling customer becomes a risk to itself, for example, a credit risk, and wish to renegotiate the relationship to the further detriment of the struggling customer. A classic supplier, a bank supplying crucial working capital, could wish to engage in such a debate.

It is vital, in continuity planning of an outsourced relationship, to ensure that the continuity planning, its resources and its communications spread across the two relationships. It is equally important in the BIA and the resultant action plan to consider the supplier not only as deliverer of crucial dependencies, but also as a stakeholder and thus likely also to react as a stakeholder.

Building incentives into relationships

We can, of course, discuss contractual and other agreements between members of a supply chain, but, as stated elsewhere, this will only create the required activity when the counterparty is financially and physically able to deliver as promised. There may also be a view on whether the result of complying as promised is less expensive to its stakeholders than the alternative of not doing so. This is especially so when the counterparty, for any reason, sees no beneficial reason for continuing the relationship into the future.

There may be, in the real world of relationship management, a recognition that contract wording is inadequate, and that there is the need to ensure incentives are maintained to reduce variances and to both deliver on a day-to-day basis and to continue to deliver the required strategic relationship.

A supermarket establishes with its logistics and delivery supplier that, in the event of a lorry load of frozen food stock not arriving within a defined variance of a certain period of hours, the supplier is considered, within the contract wording, to have purchased the contents of the lorry. The cost of that lorry load is simply debited within the inter-company accounting.

A risk manager had major cost concerns because a subsidiary had extremely poor claims experience on its 4,000-vehicle car fleet. The motor insurance was purchased by the group and there was no internal debiting back of the cost. There was no penalty on the subsidiary, therefore, which resisted requests to control the types of cars purchased, ages of employee and family drivers. Nor were there any penalties imposed on individual employees with regular claims experiences.

The risk manager then agreed with the group board that all insurances on the cars would be cancelled other than the minimum required by law. Costs of claims would be debited back to the individual managers' departments and would thus become a deduction from the divisional results on which the managers' performances and bonuses were measured. An incentive had thus been created, resulting in concentration on the problem by managers. The claims experience fell dramatically.

Troubleshooting and dispute resolution

We are not going beyond the risk management agenda when we consider here the subjects of troubleshooting and dispute resolution. Troubles and disputes can be expected almost as 'normal operations' and prepared structures for mediation and handling the issues is as much a risk management issue as it is a relationship management issue. The risk being handled here is the risk of disputes developing into objective-destroying crises.

It is so much easier to address a problem before it turns into a crisis and this brings us first into relationship monitoring. The weaknesses and threats perceived by both parties do need to be kept under continuous review just as much as the strengths and the opportunities. This is not an annual task to be done over a pleasant lunch, nor the subject exclusively of auditors' tick boxes, but should be built right into the ongoing, day-by-day, relationship management and reporting.

A pre-agreed dispute resolution process that sits comfortably with both parties can be a vital risk management tool. Its first value is to establish clearly who owns the problem, who addresses the problem and how. The process can pre-agree:

- how the problem and its causes is analysed, including access to information;
- how the problem is assessed against individual and joint objectives;
- the mediation process and its players;
- the establishing of agreements and action plans;
- the monitoring of the resolution agreed;
- the measurements by which the problem will be considered resolved;
- sign off of the problem and by whom within each organization.

The arbitration clause can pre-establish: 1) the designation by the parties of an actual person or company of professionals as arbitrator, 2) that whomever the arbitrator is, he or she must have experience/be qualified in the issues under dispute.

The exit strategy

This leads us neatly into the exit strategy, as the risk of divorce is a clear matter for risk management understanding and management. Should over-confidence encourage a glossing over of the need for a clear exit strategy, Dun and Bradstreet figures bring sobering statistics: 20 per cent of outsourcing relationships fail within the first 2 years and 50 per cent within 5 years. A Diamond Cluster International Survey reported that 78 per cent of responding executives had had to terminate agreements early due to poor service, a change in a strategic direction or costs.

As part of the risk assessment the risk manager will have suggested to the board that the sudden – or even gradual – closure of the relationship is one of a negligible, marginal, critical or catastrophic risk. The underlying deciders will be to what extent that dependency is business critical and/or urgent. That assessment will guide the board to the decision of whether the risk being carried is tolerable and requires no action or, otherwise, whether a degree of risk management and continuity management would be good management.

A key risk assessment factor, of course, will be whether the risk manager believes that an alternative supply, able to be fed right into the production line, can be arranged, quickly enough, with fit for purpose specifications, volumes, quality and cost. The obvious primary management strategy is to avoid placing the organization in the situation whereby these options are no longer available to it should they be needed. The additional cost of retaining relationships with duplicate suppliers, or maintaining reserve stock levels, may not please those managing the accounts, but those extra costs may be considered by the strategist to be cost-effective risk management expenditure, and a part of the strategic exit strategy.

Conversely, such a decision could also be to enable effective risk management by outsourcing in the first place and thus avoiding the single dependency on in-house processes. This is where an outsourcing strategy is a risk management opportunity in itself.

Such a luxury of avoiding total dependency on one supply, however, may be unachievable for many cost and practical reasons. Some supplies, such as power, water and governmental services simply do not have alternatives available other than local, somewhat short-term, backups, such as generators.

There may also be dangerous dependencies of supply that could affect a worldwide supply of one product. Hurricanes Katrina and Rita had a significant effect on the supply of oil because of concentrations of oil extraction in the regions affected. Consequentially, the hurricanes affected the supply of liquid hydrogen, causing a 35 per cent shortage of liquid hydrogen supply in North America. Liquid hydrogen can be a crucial dependency for some organizations' production. Suppliers of liquid hydrogen declared a force majeure which was defined as an 'act of God' and thus beyond the control of the firms. This enabled them to cease meeting customer-contracted demand requirements.

Lean inventories and the timing of the year created their customers' own major supply problems.

We discuss elsewhere the advisability of a contingency service level agreement in the contract that defines the minimum or priorities that are acceptable to the receiver in such a case of a force majeur incident. That clause would then establish those levels as contracted requirements.

A supplier which is itself a monopoly or near monopoly presents additional risk to its customers by the fact that it has less incentive, in troubled times, to put energy and resources into protecting its place in a competitive market-place.

The agreed exit agreement, sometimes known as transition management/ transition continuity will cover notice, period and format of the termination/ transition to the other party. It will deal with records, data and reports, including the provision for regular/daily providing of these records, data and reports on an ongoing basis, and not just in the event of a termination or expiry of the term of the agreement.

Recovering dependencies

The ultimate risk in such circumstances is an organizational divorce, and we can usefully bring back to the table the various dependencies that may have been passed over to the supplier.

Earlier we listed the key elements of a modern 'hollow' company as simply the sum total of:

- the business and financial models;
- a wide range of stakeholders and their expectations;
- the small control and entrepreneur teams;
- legality and compliance;
- brands and wider confidence;
- other intellectual assets;
- the ability of the (mostly outsourced) supply chain and delivery chain to meet its expectations in cost, quality, speed and volume.

There is value in keeping these headline abilities and assets in mind as we explore the exit strategy and the chain of activity that will need to emerge from the decision to exit. Any organization or individual within the supply chain who currently owns or manages these key elements of operational survival remains at the centre of survival needs.

The process of divorce brings many service delivery problems, but in addition can bring in to question many legal issues: compliance, brand, human and ownerships of both physical and intellectual property. Process engineering a structured and calm separation can be crucial to survival as it enables these elements to be positioned and managed throughout the process and without residual damage to any of them.

It would be particularly helpful if the detailed dependencies are defined from the beginning and a clear agreement made as to their ownership, transfer, access and operability should divorce become necessary for whatever reason. The exit schedule can usefully include a statement of supplier and customer responsibilities during the exit process and also how that transfer will take place.

Separation may take weeks or months to fully complete. The transfer agreement can usefully embrace, therefore, the responsibilities and activities of each party whilst that separation is underway, as well as the reimbursement of cost and lost revenues during that period.

The detailed schedule of activities and legalities can also include the agreement on ownership and access to intellectual assets and physical assets remaining in secure, good, accessible and useable order. This may not be as straightforward as it sounds. The transfer of technology hardware or software may need to include the skills and manuals to maintain these tools and any code words that will enable technicians to do so and to develop them further.

The transfer of hardware, buildings and their contents may be best agreed beforehand, and to include agreement of the method by which such assets will be valued. The financial market value, even if there is one, is unlikely to be the only consideration.

Ownership and use of an electronic database of personal client information may require pre-registration as custodians and for purpose of use under the Data Protection Act 1998 (UK) (or similar elsewhere). Information is not just constrained to that which is on electronic databases. Even in modern businesses there is a whole range of crucial information kept on paper, in employee heads and within their own separate counterparties' organizations.

There is a whole range of other intellectual assets that may have formed part of the relationship, not least: patents, copyrights, trademarks and their exclusivity, brand names, domain names, and website and email addresses. There can be research materials and the implied right to use that material, and the positioning of any ongoing liability claims to or from third parties and between themselves. Inherent within this is the agreed positioning of any ongoing insurance claims. The relationship itself may have created new trademarks and enhancements to any intellectual property by the service provider, and establishing the ownership of these is an important risk management task.

The future position of employees will need to be agreed, whether just the responsibility for redundancy payment and pensions, or the fight to retain the most useful skills and experience. There may also be expensive and difficult repatriation, training, retraining, security and safety concerns. Ensuring continuing employee motivation is also a communications challenge to be carefully undertaken perhaps through both organizations, recognizing that both organizations may not have the same incentives to do so.

Audit trails and reassurances may be vital to enable each party to illustrate compliance and legality to its regulators and legal jurisdictions. The announcement to shareholders and other stakeholders is best engineered beforehand in a spirit of co-operation and (hopefully) a mutual protection of reputations.

The ownership or value setting of work in progress will need to be agreed, especially if the separation makes that work no longer marketable.

Opportunity costs are a real issue, especially for commercial organizations, and the breakdown of a relationship may destroy them, particularly if the split causes a delay to market long enough for competitors to fill the gap. The process of calculating that, again, may be usefully agreed beforehand, especially in circumstances where one counterparty is believed to have failed the other.

Any process of major re-engineering will need its own change management and control processes to be followed through and that process again should be clear in the exit strategies agreed.

Finally, there can usefully be a contracted provision requiring the service provider to act in good faith and use best efforts during the transition phase, and provide required information to the customer and also to the new service provider.

The loss of the original outsourcing values

The decision made in the first instance to outsource was for one or more strategic reasons. We have already stated that outsourcing is not just about subcontracting but is also a strategic placing of key elements in the business model into the hands of third parties.

The reasons have gone well beyond just cost saving. The objectives could be many and certainly often include the need to be flexible and order-based rather than supply-based in its deliveries, to spread delivery risk. The reasons may include access to the specialist knowledge not available within one organization or from where an organization can gain more expertise and/or resources than the business has itself.

The business model may have enabled multinationalism, best use of different tax and legal environments, customer product differentiation and the maintenance of a market positioning advantage over customers. It may have enabled entirely new market-places to be created.

These may be just some of the details to be considered as we also ensure that the strategic values are still remembered and also embraced in the preparation to engineer an exit from an outsourced supply chain contract.

Making separation happen

The reality, of course, is that, however carefully a contract is worded, it does not mean that the contract clauses that agree a calm and mutually supportive exit will be directly translated into action as expected. This is especially so if the separation is hostile or caused by the operational or financial failure of one of the parties.

One party may be alleging that another party has failed to deliver on its contracted promises, and thus that the other party has in effect nullified the entire contract, exit clauses included.

That reality also may be that one of the parties will be simply unable to proceed to exit as hoped, or appointed liquidators may be searching out and securing anything of value to meet their own legal responsibilities to their failed principal's creditors. The organizations themselves may use the exit procedures and possessions as negotiating strengths to argue a quite different dispute that had caused the separation in the first place.

Legal rights are only useful if enforceable and enforceable in time to stop destructive damage. The counterparty is unlikely to have the time, where its market-place and stakeholder support requires urgent attention and is threatened, to begin legal proceedings in the courts for contract liability, nor are the indemnities achieved likely to keep the organization alive.

The informal maxim, 'possession is nine tenth's of the law' may not be legally enforceable. It can be very valuable, however, and especially in the short term, if the counterparty that has been let down knows that it has retained throughout the legal and operational ability to gain possession and use of these critical dependencies. This applies equally to the possession of data and highlights the need to obtain up-to-date information on a regular basis from the service provider.

This exposure of the counterparty not delivering as contracted in the exit clauses is equally a risk management issue, as is the original failure of the supplier to deliver the primary objectives of the relationship.

Common management system requirements

Carefully establishing common management systems, whether they are of production line machinery, specification matching, or management controls and cultures, will reduce the risk of failure. A key risk, therefore, must be the failure of those management systems to mesh and work together.

We need to begin with ensuring measurability of those management system requirements and there can be value in using external standards and documented best practices as a foundation, to which the individual system requirements are added. There are a whole host of organic-, trade- and product-specific standards to use and even the choice of which standard to use is an important starting point towards agreed measurability.

Again we have an organic, Publicly Available Specification, PAS 99:2006, that offers a *Specification of common system requirements as a framework for integration*. This prompts a measurable standard in such matters as general requirements, management system policy, planning, implementation and operation, performance assessment, improvement and management review.

This and other standards set by other standards bodies, governments and trade organizations can be vital starting points. They do not, however, replace the organization's own risk management care.

PAS 99:2006 does not, for example, cover the value of a clear and pre-determined exit strategy as advocated above. Organizations could, for example, demand that an organization meets the standards documented by the Business Continuity Institute and Disaster Recovery Institute International. Even these will not provide full reassurance that the supplier's business continuity management planning will identify the particular counterparty as 'business critical'. It will not, thus, ensure that that counterparty's needs and urgencies are embraced in the supplier's own 'maximum time out' decision making and prioritization.

Indeed its BIA may have caused the decision, as part of its crisis prioritization, to shed some customers that it considers 'non-critical' to its survival needs. It can then focus on those large but few clients that could still give its business model a critical mass customer base, and thus ensure its own best chance of survival. That business continuity management decision, however carefully it meets BCI, DRII and other standards, will not protect the less important customer – even if that supply had been a survival issue for that customer.

The organization's lawyer(s) will find it much easier to defend allegations of failure if the organization can illustrate to the satisfaction of the court that it had adhered to accepted standards.

Contract wording

There are almost as many different types of contract wording as there are contracts and many larger organizations will have purchasing and legal departments that set the organization-wide standard wording, demanding that managers obtain individual approvals to divert from that wording.

'The Out-sourcing Agreement covers a number of key areas including manufacture, quality control, packaging, storage, insurance, pricing and confidentiality. At the parties' option, this agreement can also cover the packaging of products by the Contractor (manufacturer).'

An Out-sourcing Agreement may contain the following headlines:

'1. Definitions and Interpretation
2. Grant of Licence
3. Manufacture of Product
4. Indemnity
5. Liability
6. Quality Control

---

7.   Pricing of Orders and Forecasts
8.   Packaging Materials
9.   Packaging
10. Disputes
11. Restrictions on the Contractor
12. Title and Risk
13. Storage
14. Insurance
15. Pricing
16. Payment
17. Intellectual Property
18. Confidentiality
19. Term and Termination
20. Consequences of Termination
21. Force Majeure
22. Assignment
23. Entire Agreement
24. Rights etc cumulative and other matters
25. Costs
26. Invalidity
27. Notices
28. Relationship of the Parties
29. Set off
30. Law and Jurisdiction

And Schedules:

1.   Product Specification
2.   Packaging Specification
3.   Pricing'

(Source: http://www.simply-docs.co.uk)

To which, of course, we must add the different service level agreements.

The UK Ministry of Defence provides a commercial toolkit including contract administration on its website: http://www.aof.mod.uk and has an 'authoritative guidance summary' on risk that begins with the following:

'1. The project strategy, which includes the contract strategy, should address risk assessment.

2. Project risks may include programme, technical and commercial risks. Commercial risks include pre and post contract performance risks (e.g. those arising from loss of property or defective equipment).

3. Risk assessment is fundamental to the management of risk. The aim is to identify risks and prioritise them against the probability of occurrence and likely impact. Commercial Risks should be analysed for probability and impact and the result recorded in the Project's Risk Register.

4. Risks should be allocated to those best placed to manage them which in procurement invariably means the contractor. There is a greater risk associated with being a supplier (seller), and the risk management systems and interfaces are often different. Where risk is associated with Sales Contracts, the separate guidance entitled "Sales Contracting" should be read in conjunction with this guidance. The remainder of this guidance, while addressing general risk issues, primarily relates to procurement projects.

5. Where Risk Questionnaires and Risk Identification Prompt Lists are used it is important to make clear who has accepted responsibility for a particular risk or risks. To this end a narrative condition is provided under Authoritative Guidance for inclusion in the Invitation to Tender (ITT) and contract.'

(Source: http://www.aof.mod.uk)

Many other industry bodies and their supply chain managers set such standards and then detail the requirements to meet those standards. The Institute of Chartered Engineers (ICE) has, for example, a family of standard conditions of contract for civil engineering works.

The ICE Conditions of Contract, which have been in use for over 50 years, were designed to standardize the duties of contractors, employers and engineers, and to distribute the risks inherent in civil engineering to those best able to manage them.

Generic matters for consideration within contracts are, of course, to ensure that the contract, however carefully drawn up from a legal point of view, no more nor less reflects the agreed objectives and strategy in hand. It is clearly illogical to accept unlimited liability where the benefit of being contracted is of limited value. There are legal restrictions on excluding liability, as introduced in the Unfair Contract Terms Act 1977, more recently expended by the Unfair Terms in Consumer Contracts Regulations 1994 (more widely applicable to consumer contracts). Other UK legislation such as the sale of goods and services legislation and the General Product Safety Directive may be applicable, as will other related legislation overseas.

Contracts to agree are usually unenforceable because of the uncertainty, for example, of statements such as 'specification to be agreed' or 'specification to be advised by the buyer'. On the other hand, a 'material adverse change' clause may enable one party to move away or make changes should there be such a change in the environment.

> The Royal Bank of Scotland lead consortium had such a clause, enabling it to lower the price of its EUR70 billion offer for ABN AMRO if market conditions worsened. Such a clause would enable RBS to reduce the agreed price or walk away if it could prove that there has been change that has had a material impact on the value of the purchase.
>
> The interbank credit squeeze in the summer of 2007 could be offered as such a change. Such clauses, however, are not often invoked and are difficult to prove.

Service level agreements and terms and conditions

Some would say that the heart of supply contracts is the service level agreement. This is of value to both parties and defines and agrees expectations. It sets terms, and defines those terms, to make service deliveries measurable in an objective way, and also to verify performance. They may include allowable failure and error rates, reporting requirements, problem response times and penalties.

The service level agreement may include the ways in which the relationship is to be monitored, both proactively and reactively.

Unfortunately, what is rare is to see the service level agreement define the level of service that the other can receive in exceptional circumstances, say, following the accidental destruction of the primary worksite or technology. This may be part of a modified force majeure clause.

In other words, the service level agreement defines precisely any reduction in service levels that can be expected following the implementation of any contingency plan. The counterparty can, when such an agreement is produced, then take a view as to whether that contingency service level is fast enough, and with quality and capacities that will enable it to retain its own crucial continuances. Also that service level agreement becomes integral within the contracted relationship, with all the clarity of expectation and acceptance or otherwise by the counterparty and, indeed, the consequences of failure.

9

Benchmarking and gaining of confidence

Gaining confidence

There are many ways that confidence can be gained, to a greater or lesser degree, in the risk management work undertaken. Confidence can be offered by exercises, by illustration that the work undertaken satisfies industry best practice, by third-party assessment and by measuring the activities against documented standards and legislation.

There are dangers, however. A standard or industry best practice will indeed provide guidance but will never be able to achieve the strategic vision of one organization's own sensitivities nor indeed specifically address the organization's own view on what are acceptable and unacceptable risks.

Furthermore, it can be extremely misleading to hear an assurance from one division of the organization, be it facilities management, supplier relationship management, information technology or another operational team, that it has, single-handedly, satisfied the requirements of a standard or audit requirement. These silo views on risk and continuity, however careful within those silos, may not have taken the organization-wide sensitivities as their drivers. Such ticking of customers', auditors' or regulators' tick box formats can be even more dangerous than doing nothing. This is because of the false confidences they can raise amongst their various stakeholder organizations and third parties, removing the incentive for these stakeholders to enquire and then engineer their own risk protections.

This audience may not always agree, of course, with the decisions made about risk tolerances and risk management. However, if those activities and opinions are communicated and clear, that audience can simply then decide on its own response. They can raise demands, or decide whether they wish to deal with the organization at all. They could price the remaining risk in their negotiations and/or bring in their own self-protection measures such as duplicity of supply.

There is no substitute for the ability to illustrate that a structured process has been set out with a clear agenda to understand and continually 'own' risk at the very highest strategic level within each organization. This is followed by a visible process of decision making about those risks and consequences, finally a process of controlling those unacceptable risks and potential consequences. The evidence will include a 'sign off' at that level of their comfort, and comfort also that the process in place will continue to manage future change. This not only brings together the responsibility and the ownership of that responsibility, but also ensures that the crucial strategic and organization-wide stakeholder views are brought to the party.

Some standards and compliance requirements do demand such a visible process and this is of real value, but it is in the quality of that process, not the compliance headlines, that the difference between risk management and window dressing can be found. Furthermore, as stated elsewhere in this book, a supplier can meet all the requirements, say, of BS 25999 (British Standard on business continuity), then survive as an organization but not see the risk manager's own organization as a strategically important customer.

It is worth repeating here that it is a wild assumption that a supplier or a distributor, confirmed to be BS 25999 compliant, has decided that the risk manager's own organization is a crucial customer to be protected at all times in its own survival interests. It could be that the supplier, having to prioritize its customers to protect its own reputation and cash flows, will have taken the decision to sacrifice its responsibilities to some that would impact these dependencies less than others. In a potentially destructive situation, any organization must make hard and commercial decisions about the limited choices available to it, and it is a naive customer who relies on a tick in a box on a matter that could mean the very survival of its own organization.

Types of published standards

A full standard in the UK that has the consensus of the relevant industry is known as a British Standard. It has the prefix 'BS', and can take the form of a specification, method of test, vocabulary, code of practice or guide. A European Standard has the prefix 'EN' and an international standard has the prefix 'ISO' (International Organization for Standardization) or 'IEC' (International Electrotechnical Commission).

It can take time to develop a full standard so there are other documents and guides, including a Draft for Development (DD), a Technical Specification or a Technical Report.

Other publications, perhaps en route to becoming full standards, include:

- Published Document (PD);
- Privately Subscribed Standard (PSS);
- Publicly Available Specification (PAS);
- International Publicly Available Specification (ISO/PAS);
- European or International Workshop Agreements (CWA/IWA/ITA).

There are, of course, many other standards around the world, and some are listed in the appendices.

Auditing of risk management or a business continuity plan

We need to start with the objectives of the audit itself. Is the auditor charged only with checking that a governance process has been undertaken, or is the auditor charged with delivering an assurance that the organization is resilient? These are two entirely different messages but they are often dangerously combined in many audit reports. The latter responsibility – 'this organization is or is not resilient' – imposes a dramatically different demand on the auditor for experience and also strategic and operational understanding. Caution should therefore be exercised surrounding the skill base used, and the wide organization and strategic experience needed, to deliver such a real assurance of resilience.

Audit reports are both internal and external, of course, and are not just for the published accounts and the risk statement within those accounts. Another expectation is that the 'auditor', perhaps even a purchasing or supply chain manager in the day job, is confirming resilience or otherwise of an existing or potential supplier. However carefully the so-called auditor aligns the report with the headings of published standards or internal governance procedures, such a mismatch of skill and responsibility as described above is a fundamental flaw that should destroy confidence in the message delivered.

The auditor of a supply chain dependency will need an agreement within the contract to undertake an audit in third-party premises. The messages on contracts in Chapter 8 are integral to this, as is the relationship that will insert or remove barriers to an open audit atmosphere. The auditor will at the very least wish to become satisfied that service level agreements and key performance indicators are being met, that adequate controls are in place to give confidence into the future, and that there is adequate and open communication between the audit and the function being audited.

In some organizations, the risk function reports into audit, which places the chief internal auditor in the conflicting role of both manager and auditor. This cheapens both functions and in particular removes that vital role of the auditor of being distant from the management structure and with a clear responsibility to provide an independent view on the activities undertaken right across the organization. The independence of the auditor and the audit committee from line management responsibility is a crucial foundation stone of the credibility of that department.

Any limitations of the audit's objectives therefore need to be clear and communicated to all 'stakeholders' of that audit. The auditor needs the modesty to reaffirm the limitations well as the values in the report, and the board or other stakeholder readers need to be realistic in responding to the information provided.

George A. Zsidisin, PhD, CPM, Assistant Professor, Michigan State University in the Critical Issues Report of January 2007 for CAPS Research suggests the following key audit questions.

1. Do you understand your core business vulnerabilities or potential failure points during a major, extended crisis? This would include:
   a. How do we redirect production and/or distribution capacity?
   b. What capacity is available and how quickly can we redirect?
2. Do we have emergency management structures and defined roles and responsibilities in place to respond to a crisis?
3. How do we procure direct and indirect materials? Manually? How are supply chain disruptions accounted for?
4. Who is responsible for business continuity and crisis management at your site?
5. What immediate action must we take to minimize loss and liability?
6. Do you know your key support groups and business continuity plans? Are your plans in alignment so that you would be able to continue operations?
7. Do we need to prioritize customer demand? If so, which customers will be prioritized?

---

8. What is the worst-case financial loss and legal exposure? Do you have a key contact list for individuals required to respond to the crisis?
9. How long will it take to resume operations?

To apply the same questioning process to the supply base, this firm created a supplier business continuity discussion framework that facilitates discussions with key suppliers regarding their operational resilience and business recovery capabilities.

Questions asked during these discussions include:

1. What kinds of business functions are considered critical and have business continuity (BC) plans associated with them?
2. What kinds of impacts are considered by your risk mitigation and recovery planning activities?
3. How does senior management support the BC program? What management review and corporate governance mechanisms exist?
4. Does your BC program ensure that all business processes and functions that are 'critical' to your company are identified and documented?
5. Does the BC documentation cover the components that make/support critical processes to an appropriate level of detail to ensure that single points of failure can be identified?
6. Does your BC program ensure that business interruption risks are understood and prioritized and their impacts comprehended? Have your business groups taken steps to reduce risks? How frequently is the risk and impact assessment refreshed so that changes to your business are reflected in the BC program?
7. Does your BC program ensure that the BC plans in place are well documented and current? Do these BC plans provide an effective crisis response and ensure that critical operations continue during a crisis?
8. Is the BC plan documentation readily available to the people who need it and maintain it?
9. What kinds of exercises and drills are done to ensure the completeness of the plans? Is the organization prepared to perform effectively during a crisis?
10. Can your senior management confidently answer 'yes' when asked if everything reasonable and prudent has been done to be able to respond to and recover from an emergency?

Change management

Whilst this has been mentioned elsewhere in the book, its importance is worthy of another brief mention within the scope of this chapter.

It is a very rare organization that does not change quite frequently or find that its market-place or its other environment has not changed around it. The devil of potential destruction lies both in the holistic view of the organization and can also lie deep in the detail. Change can affect either its internal or its external sensitivities. It could simply be a market opportunity that changes the quality, urgency, resilience or volume dependencies on one supplier. A risk management programme and continuity management that do not move on to continually embrace these changes may be totally useless when needed.

All effective risk management will ensure that there is a continual review of the foundation stones around which earlier risk decisions were made. The need is to be proactive and reactive.

The internal division, or external supplier, will be required to review its risk registers and impact analyses frequently. The parent organization may dictate a frequency, depending on the perceived pace of change within that division or supplier organization. There is a danger here, however, that that local management team may feel that it only needs to consider risk at those frequencies.

Proactive change management is when an organization will not consider any suggestion for change until any new risks or sensitivities evolving from that change are formally evaluated. All change management processes within the organization will formally embrace a formal statement of the impact on risk policies and tolerances, and the change recommendations will include a risk change statement to that effect.

The changes may be major or detailed. There could be a market opportunity in a new country and legal jurisdiction, or a different supply chain availability may change dependencies elsewhere across the chain. There could be competitor movement, or mergers or acquisitions within the change or parent organization.

There can be tiny detailed changes that can be traffic stopping in times of strife, perhaps simply the changed contact details of urgently required members of the emergency response team. All of these need 'capturing' and brought into the risk and response envelope in a structured way.

Exercises

This subject is covered in Chapter 7 and is worthy of a brief further mention under the heading of gaining confidence in the risk management and continuity processes undertaken.

It is also relevant to remind ourselves that the exercise, if done well, can be used to check the currency of risk and continuity planning.

'Do you exercise your recovery plan?' is another common question in supplier negotiations. Risk and continuity professionals are aware that the word 'exercise' covers a multitude of activities, and the exercise so confirmed may not, in fact, have adequately tested the supplier's recovery plans.

The most professional of continuity managers will understand the challenge of fully effective exercising and will have a healthy respect for both the values and the limitations. Exercise debriefs will always communicate the constraints of the exercise undertaken and caution about other non-exercised risks. Communicating all this through a mark in a tick box alone should be considered unachievable.

It is again a useful tool but, as said, one whose values can be overstated. The scope and precise objectives of the exercise do need to be clear beforehand and the exercise report needs to restate those objectives and thus be clear on both their values and their constraints. It is, of course, just a view of the resilience position at a particular moment in time and change will no doubt continue to evolve thereafter.

Corporate governance

Internal governance

Clearly, the risk manager and the senior executives, having established a comfortable level of risk for the organization, need to be reassured that, throughout the organization, the divisions then conduct their business in accordance with those risk standards. They also need to know that the divisions will inform them when there is activity that varies that risk profile.

Any well-managed organization will have established corporate governance standards that its executives will continually use as a framework for their activities. They will embrace not just risk but a whole wide range of subjects from money laundering to employee recruitment. The risk manager can have a significant contribution in establishing that the governance control processes embrace risk issues. The objective can then remain throughout that the governance process will reduce the risk of future unpleasant surprises.

The risk management governance controls need to be indivisible from the routine governance processes within the organization. One set of governance controls will set a consistent standard for employee management and the measurement of their performances against pre-defined key task objectives. One generic key task objective can include the requirement to be able to illustrate risk awareness throughout all other activity.

Risk governance will fundamentally ride on the risk policy statement and, through this, lead down through all of the processes and standards that have been introduced to deliver the risk environment that is described in that statement.

The risk manager will also make use of the organization-wide audit processes and standards that are already in place and will co-operate with corporate governance managers, security managers, audit managers, the audit committee and others to agree the risk standards that will lie within their own agendas.

Whilst practicality demands that the risk manager cannot – nor would wish to – second guess every risk decision in the organization, he or she will need to be assured that risk is on the agenda whilst decisions are being made. He or she will also need to be assured that organization-wide standards are being maintained as those decisions are being made.

A shopping list for business continuity governance standards could include the following amongst other more organization-specific requirements:

- appointment of a business continuity manager and supporting structure;
- identification and prioritization of business functions and recovery speed objectives;
- identification of all internal and external resources needed to support business functions and applications;
- off site storage procedures to protect critical materials, data and other information;
- establishment of notification procedures at the time of business interruption and the designation of an individual and deputies to authorize the execution of a contingency plan;
- a clear and resourced strategy to communicate, internally and externally, with all affected parties;
- design and implementation of continuity plans that ensure the continuation of critical business functions within agreed scenarios and co-ordination between interdependent departments, suppliers and distributors; and
- completion of an agreed programme of reviews, updates and business continuity exercises.

There are likely to be additional detailed guides and recommendations behind these statements available to assist and guide managers.

It may seem possible on the surface to move these standards out to outsourced supplier organizations. In practice, the lack of day-to-day control over these organizations, the differences in cultures, longer communications and differences in risk tolerances, objectives, stakeholder needs and environment makes confidence much more difficult to achieve.

External governance

There was a particular mood change in the 1990s triggered by the recognition that a lack of adequate, effective internal controls was an important cause of failures amongst business corporations. Partly in response to some individual scandals, but also because companies are getting bigger and more multinational, and shareholders are becoming more aware, the demand emerged that they be seen, even more clearly, to be conducting their affairs in a fit and proper manner.

There are thus a host of individual Acts and other regulations in the UK and elsewhere in the world that set standards of behaviour in a whole range of organizational and employment situations. In the UK, company directors' duties are outlined in the Health and Safety at Work Etc. Act 1974 (and subsequent regulations), the Companies Act 2006, the Company Directors Disqualification Act 1986, the Insolvency Act 1986, the Financial Services and Markets Act 2000 (FSMA), the Banking Act 1987 and others. There are also provisions in law for corporate manslaughter.

Other countries have their own set of regulations, laws and standards, for example, the Code of Corporate Governance (Germany) and the Sarbanes-Oxley Act in the USA. Some European regulations apply across the individual countries that make up the European Union.

Many of the regulations deal with matters of ownership structure, relationships with financial markets, transparency, standards of disclosing information, and board structure and the behaviour of the board in relation to its employees, customers, stakeholders and others. More specifically, they can relate to one or more of employee regulations, company regulations, financial and taxation regulations, insolvency, intellectual property controls, buying and selling businesses, environmental protection, start up regulations and trading. Risks find themselves at the core of these areas of interest.

As stated elsewhere, the fact that an organization has positioned key elements of its organization into the hands of third parties does not enable it to also pass over the responsibility to satisfy these regulations. This applies not just to profit-making businesses: a government or a government body has the power to demand that a public service or charity organization meets specified product, service, behaviour and audit trail requirements as well.

An organization's failure to comply with these legal standards, when made public, has wide-ranging brand and confidence impact. It can cause employee, customer and other stakeholder reactions that can in themselves be very damaging indeed. Once again, this reaction and the unexpected stresses that it causes can be as damaging to a monopoly or public service organization as it can to a competitive, profit-making business.

One of the objectives of risk management and continuity programmes is, before any problems emerge, to be able to satisfy these regulators that have the legal powers to fine an organization for failure to do so, and in extremis, demand that the organization closes down. It is only one of the objectives, however, of risk management to make the narrow satisfaction of the regulator the sole objective of risk management. The purpose of risk management is no more nor less than good business management and satisfying the regulator is a by-product and not the only driver. To get this the wrong way round takes the organization directly into the auditor dangers already outlined above, about the auditors' commercial awareness and the constraints of the audit's own agenda.

It is not possible to discuss here every compliance requirement of any organization operating anywhere in the world but by way of Appendix 2 we list a selection and what they set out to achieve.

The risk manager, however, needs to be aware of the wide-ranging powers of many government departments, not least (in the UK) the Financial Services Authority, the Serious Fraud Office, the European Commission and Her Majesty's Revenue & Customs, together with their equivalents in overseas countries. Their powers can include the 'dawn raid', whereby they can raid an organization, demand and take away papers, information and even the technology on which the information and audit trails are stored. The organization may therefore need not only to handle the damage to its reputation, but also the disruption of its ability to continue to operate whilst the investigations are proceeding. This may be over months or years.

Civil Contingencies Act 2004 (UK)

The Act and accompanying regulations provides for a single framework for civil protection in the UK. The Act is separated into two substantive parts: local arrangements for civil protection (Part 1) and emergency powers (Part 2). The Act moves civil defence on from defence of a hostile attack to preparing for a civil emergency such as floods and major transport accidents.

The Act focuses on three types of threat:

1. an event or situation which threatens serious damage to human welfare;
2. an event or situation which threatens serious damage to the environment; or
3. war, or terrorism, which threatens serious damage to security.

Part 1 establishes a new statutory framework and expectations and responsibilities for front line responders in the event of a threat posing serious damage to human welfare or the environment in the UK. Part 2 sets out the situations in which it may be possible to use emergency powers if thought appropriate.

It divides local responders into two categories. Those in Category 1 (local authorities, some government agencies, health service bodies and emergency services) have duties imposed to:

- assess local risks and use this to inform emergency planning;
- put in place emergency plans;
- put in place business continuity management arrangements;
- put in place arrangements to make information available to the public about civil protection matters and maintain arrangements to warn, inform and advise the public;

and, in the event of an emergency, to:

- share information with other local responders to enhance co-ordination;
- co-operate with other local responders to enhance co-ordination and efficiency; and
- provide advice and assistance to businesses and voluntary organizations about business continuity management (local authorities only).

Category 2 organizations are placed under the lesser duty of co-operating with these organizations and sharing relevant information. Those to be included at present include utilities, communications, transport companies, and the Health and Safety Executive and other government agencies where existing legislation is insufficient.

In Part 2, the emergency powers section allows the making of special temporary legislation to create emergency powers, an instrument of last resort to deal with the most serious of emergencies where existing legislation is insufficient.

Further information can be obtained at http://www.ukresilience.info.

Other regulators

Financial Services Authority (FSA)

The FSA in the UK and its equivalent bodies elsewhere are worthy of an individual mention in view of the special need to regulate the financial services industry. This industry has quite a few additional sensitivities over other types of business, not least its opaqueness in the eyes of the customer unskilled in this industry, and also that it takes money, often substantial amounts, from individuals and offers in return only a promise on paper that it will, sometime in the future, hand the money back precisely as contracted. Some of the dependencies created, for example, in pension fund management, are fundamental to the individual customer's livelihood. The sheer scale of the industry and the dependencies by other industries also means that it is one of the core infrastructures of national economies.

In the UK, the FSA is an independent, non-governmental body that exercises statutory powers under the Financial Services and Markets Act 2000 (FSMA). It is an important regulator, therefore, of financial services businesses within the UK. Under the requirements of the FSMA, the FSA has been given four objectives, namely:

1. maintaining market confidence;
2. promoting public understanding of the financial system;
3. protection of consumers; and
4. fighting financial crime.

The FSA states in its Business Plan 2008/09 that its aims include 'promoting efficient, orderly and fair markets' and 'helping retail consumers achieve a fair deal'. It has wide-ranging powers relating to information gathering, investigations, intervention and enforcement. Key documents include the *FSA Handbook of Rules and Guidance* and its risk assessment frameworks.

The FSA also has control of enforcement of the Money Laundering Regulations 2007. From 2004, the FSA has integrated the responsibilities for the regulation of insurance companies.

Prudential Standards on Outsourcing, 2006 (Australia)

This standard was released by the Australian Prudential Regulation Authority (APRA) on outsourcing for authorized deposit-taking institutions, general insurers and life companies (regulated institutions), general insurers and life insurers. Practice guides were released in support.

They apply to the outsourcing of 'material business activities'. Material business activities are defined as those that have 'the potential, if disrupted, to have a significant impact on the insurer's business operations or its ability to manage risk effectively'.

The standards expect to see an approved outsourcing policy and demonstrated assessment of options: legally binding outsourcing agreements, access to service providers, notification requirements, monitoring and audit.

We include in the appendices a mention of other UK and other countries' equivalent bodies.

Registration, Evaluation, Authorisation and Restriction of Chemicals (REACH) 2007

The supply chain exposures, however, are not limited to ensuring the smooth flow of required materials and services. The organization may find itself responsible in both statute law and civil law for the activities of its suppliers or distributors. One example is the EU's REACH legislation. This imposes an onerous duty of care over chemicals right through the supply chain and records of that care must be maintained for 10 years.

Certification

A step beyond meeting the standards requirements of bodies such as BSI is to get a certified verification by a trusted third-party arbitrator. There are a few such certification schemes available.

Law (P.L. 110-53 – Title IX, Section 524) USA

This law provides for voluntary certification of the emergency preparedness of private sector organizations – including disaster/emergency management and business continuity programmes. Interestingly, it will engage key stakeholders to participate in the development of the programme and will embrace small business needs.

The programme will be administered outside of government by third-party organizations with experience and expertise in managing and implementing voluntary accreditation and certification programmes. The certification will designate one or more preparedness standards, e.g. Standard NFPA 1600.

Business Continuity Institute (BCI) certification (UK)

The UK-based BCI has six certification standards that apply, not to organizations, but to individual practitioners. These standards demand competence under all of the following headings:

- BCM policy and programme management;
- understanding the organization:
  - *business impact analysis (BIA)*,
  - *risk evaluation and control*;
- determining business continuity management strategies;
- developing and implementing a BCM response;
- exercising, maintenance and review;
- embedding business continuity management within the organization's culture.

Disaster Recovery Institute International (DRII) (USA)

This industry body provides education to and certification of individuals practising in risk and continuity roles.

DRII provides four levels of professional certification, again directed at the individual professional's standards rather than the corporate achievement. These progressive levels are Associate Business Continuity Professional (ABCP), Certified Functional Continuity Professional (CFCP), Certified Business Continuity Professional (CBCP) and Master Business Continuity Professional (MBCP).

British Standards Institution (BSI), BS 25999

BS 25999 is discussed elsewhere in this book but relevant to this certification section is that Part 2 of BS 25999 provides for steps that need to be taken to enable certification. This is corporate based rather than for individual practitioners, and it provides a specification for use by internal and external parties, including certification bodies, to assess the organization's ability to meet regulatory, customer and the organization's own requirements.

Part 2 deals with the requirements of BS 25999 that can be objectively audited. Those organizations requiring more general guidance on a broad range of business continuity management issues are referred to BS 25999-1.

Demonstration of successful implementation of this British Standard can therefore be used by an organization to assure interested parties that an appropriate business continuity management system is in place.

Institute of Risk Management (IRM) (UK)

IRM is risk management's professional education body and has strong links to leading universities and business schools across the world. Recognizing that risk management is a multi-disciplinary field, it also works closely with universities and business schools and many other specialist institutes and associations. Members have backgrounds in many different risk-related disciplines: accountants, project managers, insurers, chartered surveyors, health care professionals, lawyers, bankers, auditors, health and safety professionals and engineers are among those represented.

Again, the different levels of certification follow examinations in a wide range of risk management subjects directed at the individual's ability to illustrate professionalism and experience.

The IRM's International Diploma in Risk Management is a broadly based postgraduate-level qualification.

ISO 28001:2007 Security management systems for the supply chain

This standard guides organizations in international supply chains to design and implement their supply chain security processes and thus establish and document a minimum level of security within perhaps a segment of a supply chain. The standard details the documentation requirements that would permit verification.

'Users of this International Standard will

- define the portion of an international supply chain within which they have established security [...];
- conduct security assessments on that portion of the supply chain and develop adequate countermeasures;
- develop and implement a supply chain security plan;
- train security personnel in their security related duties.'

(ISO 28001:2007)

Other institutes

There are many other institutes and trade bodies around the world offering awareness, assessment and certification of professionalism in subjects that can be related to supply chain management challenges. Some are industry specific, as in the Chartered Insurance Institute or the Institute of Bankers. Others are more generic, such as the Project Management Institute and the Institute of Directors.

Contract requirements

A supplier may find that the contract will demand certain quality and performance standards, either defined in detail in the contract or by a demand that the supply meets, and continues to meet, one of the advisory or regulatory standards.

This may be a problem for small businesses supplying to larger ones and the cost of compliance may deny them an opportunity to tender for the contract. However, as part of the wider relationship management and support, the counterparty may best offer guidance and resources to the small supplier towards meeting these standards.

Appendix 1

BS and ISO standards

PAS 99:2006 Specification of common management system requirements as a framework for integration	See comments in Chapter 8.
BS 6079 (all parts) Project management	This standard aims to draw attention to the management problems encountered in different project environments and to present possible solutions to these problems. The guidance given and the principles of project management described are applicable to all sizes of project.
BS 7799-3:2006 Information security management systems — Part 3: Guidelines for information security risk management	Gives guidance to support the requirements given in BS ISO/IEC 27001. This includes assessing and treating risks, ongoing risk monitoring, risk reviews and reassessments. Applicable to all organizations, BS 7799-3:2006 is intended for those business managers and their staff involved in ISMS risk management activities.
ISO 9000:2000 Quality management systems fundamentals and vocabulary, and in ISO 9004:2000 Quality management systems guidelines for performance improvements	There are eight quality management principles defined in ISO 9000:2000. The principles are: 1. the focus on the customer; 2. leadership; 3. involvement of people; 4. the approach to the process; 5. management systems; 6. continual improvement; 7. the use of facts in decision making; and 8. supplier relationships.

BS ISO 10006:2003 Quality management systems – Guidelines for quality management in projects	This International Standard provides guidance on quality management in projects. It outlines quality management principles and practices, the implementation of which are important to, and have an impact on, the achievement of quality objectives in projects. It supplements the guidance given in ISO 9004.
	These guidelines are intended for a wide audience. They are applicable to projects which can take many forms from the small to very large, from simple to complex, from being an individual project to being part of a programme or portfolio of projects. They are intended to be used by personnel who have experience in managing projects and need to ensure that their organization is applying the practices contained in the ISO 9000 family of standards, as well as those who have experience in quality management and are required to interact with project organizations in applying their knowledge and experience to the project.
PAS 11000 Collaborative business relationships — A framework specification	See comments in Chapter 8.
BS ISO/IEC 16085:2006 Systems and software engineering — Life cycle processes — Risk management	BS ISO/IEC 16085:2006 describes a process for the management of risk during systems or software acquisition, supply, development, operations and maintenance. The purpose of this standard is to provide suppliers, acquirers, developers and managers with a single set of process requirements suitable for the management of a broad variety of risks.
BS ISO/IEC 17799:2005 Information technology — Security techniques — Code of practice for information security management	Recognized and adopted by industry professionals worldwide, this universal code of practice provides a complete set of guidelines and principles for an effective information security management system (ISMS) and information security policy.
	This standard has 11 sections supported by a clear introduction and relationship with risk assessment/treatment; the main clauses are as follows:

	• security policy; • organizing information security; • asset management; • human resources security; • physical and environmental security; • communications and operations management; • access control; • information systems acquisition, development and maintenance; • information security incident management; • business continuity management; • compliance.
BS 25999	This is the 2006 standard on business continuity management and Part 2 sets out the steps that can lead to certification under this standard. The requirements are embraced in Chapter 7 of this book. Part 2 (2007) established the requirement for independent certification. See comments in various chapters.
BS ISO/IEC 27001:2005 Information technology — Security techniques — Information security management systems — Requirements	This is a standard to cover all types of organizations from commercial enterprises and government agencies to non-profit organizations. This International Standard will provide a specification for ISMS within the context of the organization's overall business risks and the foundation for third-party audit and certification.
DD ISO/PAS 28000:2005 Specification for security management systems for the supply chain	This Publicly Available Specification has an objective to improve the security of supply chains. It supports an organization's work to establish an overall supply chain security management system. It requires the organization to assess the security environment in which it operates and to determine if adequate security measures are in place.

ISO 28001:2007 Security Management Systems for the Supply Chain	See Chapter 9.
BS 33100	This is a new risk standard to be published by BSI in 2008.

Appendix 2

Selection of corporate governance and trade compliance requirements

Code of Corporate Governance (Germany)	The aim, again, is transparency and, thus, strengthening confidence in the management of German corporations.
	The Code addressed criticisms levelled against German corporate governance, namely:
	1. inadequate focus on shareholder interests;
	2. the two-tier system of executive board and supervisory board;
	3. inadequate transparency of German corporate governance;
	4. inadequate independence of German supervisory boards;
	5. inadequate independence of financial statement auditors.
	Each of these five points is addressed in the provisions and stipulations of the Code, and provides a framework for behaviour, transparency and reporting.
Cadbury Report 1992	The report made a series of recommendations on the financial aspects of corporate governance but there was no statutory power to enforce them.
	One recommendation was that the board should make a collective decision on risk management policies and should report on the effectiveness of the company's system of internal control.

	Directors' responsibilities include 'protecting the assets of the company'.
Hampel Report 1995	The Hampel Committee succeeded Cadbury. It set out to promote high standards of corporate governance in the interests of investor protection and in order to preserve and enhance the standing of companies listed on the stock exchange. Hampel requires that directors should, at least annually, conduct a review of the effectiveness of the group's system of internal control and should report to shareholders that they have done so. The review should cover all controls, including financial, operational and compliance controls and risk management.
Turnbull Report	The Institute of Chartered Accountants in England and Wales (ICAEW) established the Turnbull working party to provide guidance to listed companies in implementing these new requirements. The working party set out to produce robust and practical guidance that will help companies to ensure that they have effective risk management and control systems. The committee was absolutely clear that responsibility for risk was not something that could be delegated elsewhere.
Combined Code 2003	The UK's Financial Reporting Council's Combined Code became a requirement for the reporting years after 1 November 2003 to enhance board effectiveness and improve investor confidence. It strengthens the role of the audit committee in monitoring the integrity of the company's financial reporting, and also reinforces the independence of the external auditor.

The Sarbanes-Oxley Act (USA) July 2002	The Act amends the 1934 Securities and Exchange Act and strengthens controls to protect the public and investors, not least in the areas of accountability and transparency.
	It created the Public Company Accounting Oversight Board (PCAOB) whose role includes the registration of external auditing firms and to establish standards of auditing, ethics and independence of such firms.
International Financial Reporting Standards (IFRS)	IFRS are becoming the generally accepted accounting standards for capital market reporting outside the USA.
Basel II	The Basel Committee on Banking Supervision is a committee of banking supervisory authorities that was established by the central bank governors of the 'Group of Ten' countries in 1975.
	It consists of senior representatives of bank supervisory authorities and central banks from Belgium, Canada, France, Germany, Italy, Japan, Luxembourg, the Netherlands, Spain, Sweden, Switzerland, the UK and the USA.
	The Basel II Framework sets out the details for adopting more risk-sensitive minimum capital requirements for banking organizations. The new framework lays out principles for banks to assess the adequacy of their capital. Supervisors can now review such assessments in a consistent way to ensure banks have adequate capital to support their risks.
	The Basel II committee published a 'High level Principles for business Continuity' document in 2006.
Companies Act 2006 (UK)	The Act strengthened the rights of auditors to demand information from directors and employees. It widened the power to regulate auditors and to obtain information from them.
	There is now a statutory duty on those responsible for a company's books and accounting records to respond to enquiries from auditors, and that includes information relating to an overseas subsidiary.

Office of the Superintendent of Financial Institutions Canada (OSFI)	'Corporate governance includes oversight mechanisms, and information used for directing and overseeing the management of a company. It encompasses the means by which members of the board of directors and senior management are held accountable for their actions and for the establishment and implementation of oversight functions and processes.' Further, the Canadian regulatory body accepts that individual institutions may adopt different approaches to corporate governance taking into account the '... nature, scope, complexity and risk profile of their institution'. http://www.osfi.gc.ca
General Administration of Quality Supervision, Inspection and Quarantine (China)	Responding to major reputational issues over the quality of some goods exported from China, the Administration has developed initiatives around a national database of technical safety standards and also a national recall system should there be concern about quality.
NFPA 1600 2007	This requirement includes the 13 programme elements identified by the Federal Emergency Management Agency in its Capability Assessment for Readiness (CAR). CAR is a self-evaluation tool that assesses state emergency management programmes. It is therefore strongly biased towards emergency management.
	Chapter 4, programme management, establishes that a programme co-ordinator be appointed and also a suitable experienced advisory committee. http://www.nfpa.org
Prudential Standards on Outsourcing. 2006 (Australia)	See Chapter 9.

Appendix 3

Examples of other standards

Institute of Internal Auditors	The approach of the Institute of Internal Auditors in the UK, Ireland and US is through the production of specific guidance that promotes the following ten principles to provide a sound model for effective governance:
	• Interaction: between the board, management, the external auditor and the internal auditor
	• Board purpose: as well as understanding its own purpose to protect the shareholders, the board should consider the interests of other stakeholders
	• Board responsibilities: main areas of responsibility of the board should be monitored
	• Independence: the majority of directors should be 'independent'
	• Expertise: directors should have relevant and up to date expertise to perform their role with a balance of expertise across the board, i.e. finance, industry, governance
	• Meetings and information: board should meet as often as needed and have access to information required to deliver their responsibilities
	• Leadership: the roles of the board chairman and chief executive should be separate
	• Disclosure: proxy statements and other board communications should be reflective of reality and issued in a transparent and timely way

	• Committees: nominations, remuneration and audit committees of the board should be composed only of independent directors • Internal audit: all public companies should retain an effective, full-time internal audit function that reports directly to the audit committee. (www.theiia.org) *A Risk Management Approach to Business Continuity*, David Kaye and Julia Graham, Rothstein, 2006.
AS/NZS 4360:2004 Risk Management standard (Australia)	The Australian Risk Management Standard details a seven-step process for managing risk. The standard provides great emphasis on the importance of embedding a risk management culture into an organization and on the management of potential gains as well as losses. It provides a generic guide for managing risk and is designed to be applicable to a wide range of activities, decisions or operations of any public, private or community enterprise, group or individual.
American National Standards Institute (ANSI)	The ANSI approved a National Preparedness Standard that was worked on by the National Fire Protection Association. This standard deals with: • laws and authorities; • hazard identification and risk assessment; • hazard mitigation; • resource management; • mutual aid; • planning.
Disaster Recovery Institute International (DRII) (USA)	See Chapter 9.

Standards, Productivity and Innovation Board, Singapore, 2005	It sets out what is needed for a company to become resilient so that it can recover and continue operations in the face of a major disruption. The Business Continuity Management Technical Reference includes risk-preventive measures and methodologies to implement: <ul><li>disaster recovery planning;</li><li>business continuity planning;</li><li>emergency response and management;</li><li>crisis communications management;</li><li>supply chain co-ordination;</li><li>co-operation with industry and public authorities.</li></ul>
The Supply-Chain Operations Reference-model	This is a process reference model that has been developed and endorsed by the Supply-Chain Council as the cross-industry standard diagnostic tool for supply chain management. It is a management tool and process reference model for supply chain management, dealing through the supplier's supplier to the customer's customer. http://www.supply-chain.org.
A Risk Management Standard	This standard was developed by the Institute of Risk Management (IRM), the Association of Insurance and Risk Managers (AIRMIC) and the National Forum for Risk Management in the Public Sector (ALARM). The standard sets out to ensure that there is an agreed: <ul><li>terminology related to the words used;</li><li>process by which risk management can be carried out;</li><li>organizational structure for risk management;</li><li>objective for risk management.</li></ul> Importantly, the standard recognizes that risk has both an upside opportunity and a downside threat. (http://www.theirm.org)

Further reading

Legislation

Banking Act 1987. London: The Stationery Office Ltd.
Civil Contingencies Act 2004. London: The Stationery Office Ltd.
Companies Act 2006. London: The Stationery Office Ltd.
The Company Directors Disqualification Act 1986. London: The Stationery Office Ltd.
Consumer Protection (Distance Selling) Regulations 2000. London: The Stationery Office Ltd.
Data Protection Act 1998. London: The Stationery Office Ltd.
The Electronic Commerce (EC Directive) Regulations 2002. London: The Stationery Office Ltd.
The Financial Services Act 1986. London: The Stationery Office Ltd.
The Financial Services and Markets Act 2000 (FSMA). London: The Stationery Office Ltd.
The General Product Safety Regulations 2005 (GPS). London: The Stationery Office Ltd.
The Health and Safety at Work etc. Act 1974. London: The Stationery Office Ltd.
The Insolvency Act 1986. London: The Stationery Office Ltd.
The Money Laundering Regulations 2007. London: The Stationery Office Ltd.
The Privacy and Electronic Communications (EC Directive) Regulations 2003. London: The Stationery Office Ltd.
Regulation of Investigatory Powers Act 2000. London: The Stationery Office Ltd.
Third Parties (Rights Against Insurers) Act 1930. London: The Stationery Office Ltd.
Unfair Contract Terms Act 1977. London: The Stationery Office Ltd.
Unfair Terms in Consumer Contract Regulations 1994. London: The Stationery Office Ltd.
Regulation (EC) No 1907/2006 concerning the Registration, Evaluation, Authorisation and Restriction of Chemicals (REACH) and establishing a European Chemicals Agency (OJ L 396, 30.12.2006).

Other publications

Global logistics & Supply Chain Strategies. Great Neck, NY, USA: Keller International Publishing.
Reputational Risk; A Question of Trust, by Derek Atkins, Ian Bates and Lynn Drennan. London: Fifty Lessons Professional Publishing, 2006.
A Risk Management Approach to Business Continuity: Aligning Business Continuity with Corporate Governance, by Julia Graham and David Kaye, edited by Phil J. Rothstein. Brookfield, CT: Rothstein Associates Inc, 2006.

Managing Risk and Resilience in the Supply Chain

The Resilient Enterprise: Overcoming Vulnerability for Competitive Advantage, by Yossi Sheffi. Cambridge, MA: MIT Press, 2005.

655: Risk Management, by David Kaye. London: Chartered Insurance Institute, 2007.

Index